Object-Oriented Programming Using C++

Ira Pohl

The Benjamin/Cummings Publishing Company, Inc.
Redwood City, California ● Menlo Park, California
Reading, Massachusetts ● New York ● Don Mills, Ontario ● Wokingham, U.K.
Amsterdam ● Bonn ● Sydney ● Singapore ● Tokyo ● Madrid ● San Juan

Sponsoring Editor: J. Carter Shanklin
Editorial Assistant: Vivian McDougal
Production Editor: Gail Carrigan
Text Designer: John Edeen
Cover Designer: Yvo Riezebos
Copyeditor: Barbara Conway
Proofreader: Angela Santos
Compositor: Publication Services, Inc.

Cover image: *Faux Pas* by Daniel Langlois, Char Davies, and
Georges Mauro (SOFTIMAGE, Canada).

UNIX is a registered trademark of Bell Laboratories

Library of Congress Cataloging-in-Publication Data
Pohl, Ira
   Object-oriented programming using C++/ Ira Pohl.
      p.   cm.
   Includes bibliographical references and index.
   ISBN 0-8053-5382-8
   1. Object-oriented programming (Computer science)   2. C++
(Computer program language)   I. Title.
QA76.64.P64   1993
005.13'3—dc20   92-44961
                                                                      CIP
ISBN 0-8053-5382-8
1 2 3 4 5 6 7 8 9 10-MA-96 95 94 93

The Benjamin/Cummings Publishing Company, Inc.
390 Bridge Parkway
Redwood City, California 94065

TO MY FRIENDS: HANDBALLERS, HACKERS, & WOOD
PUSHERS, ALL. OBJECTIVELY YOURS.

PREFACE

This book is intended as an introduction to object-oriented programming (OOP) using C++ for the reader or student who already has programming experience. It explains C++ features in the context of OOP.

C++ is a powerful modern successor language to C. C++ was invented at Bell Labs by Bjarne Stroustrup in the mid 1980s. C++ adds to the concept of class a mechanism for providing user defined types also called abstract data types. It supports object-oriented programming by these means and by providing inheritance and run-time type binding.

By carefully developing working C++ programs, using the method of *dissection*, this book presents a simple and thorough introduction to OOP using C++. Dissection is a technique for explaining new elements in a program that the student is seeing for the first time. It highlights key points in the many examples of working code that are used to teach by example.

This book is intended for use in a first course in programming in C++ using the object-oriented methodology. It can be used as a supplementary text in an advanced programming course, data structures course, software methodology course, comparative language course, or other courses where the instructor wants C++ to be the language of choice. Each chapter presents a number of carefully explained programs. Many programs and functions are dissected.

All major pieces of code were tested. A consistent and proper coding style is adopted from the beginning. The style standard used is one chosen by professionals in the C++ community.

...tion with *A Book on C, Second Edition* by Al Kelley and
...edwood City, California: Benjamin/Cummings, 1990), an in-
...eatment of the C and C++ programming languages and their
...sented that is unavailable elsewhere. For the beginner a simpler
...tion to the C language is *C by Dissection: The Essentials of C
...mming, Second Edition* by Al Kelley and Ira Pohl (Redwood City,
...rnia : Benjamin/Cummings, 1992).

Chapters typically have:

)O Concept
Explains how an object-oriented programming concept is supported by a
language feature.

Working Code
Small examples of working code to illustrate concepts. Code illustrates a
language feature or an OOP concept.

Dissections
A dissection analyzes a program particularly illustrative of the themes of
that chapter. A dissection is similar to a structured walk-through of the
code. Its intention is to explain newly encountered programming elements
and idioms to the reader.

Summary
A succinct list of points covered in the chapter are reiterated as helpful
review.

Exercises
The exercises test the student's knowledge of the language. Many exercises
are intended to be done interactively while reading the text. This encourages
self-paced instruction by the reader. The exercises also frequently extend
the reader's knowledge to an advanced area of use.

The book incorporates:

Object-Oriented Programming
Object-Orientation is stressed throughout. Chapter 1 discusses how the programmer can benefit in important ways from a switch to C++ and object-
oriented programming. The terminology of object-oriented concepts are
defined and the way in which these concepts are supported by C++ is introduced. Each further chapter explains why a language construct supports
OOP. This motivates the reader to use the language in a methodologically
consistent way. This book develops and transforms the programmer to an
appreciation of the OOP point of view.

Teaching by Example

The book is a tutorial that stresses examples of working code. Right from the start the student is introduced to full working programs. Exercises are integrated with the examples to encourage experimentation. Excessive detail is avoided in explaining the larger elements of writing working code. Each chapter has several important example programs. Major elements of these programs are explained by the method of dissection.

Data Structures in C++

The text emphasizes many of the standard data structures from computer science. Stacks, safe arrays, dynamically allocated multidimensional arrays, lists, trees, and strings are all implemented. Exercises extend the student's understanding of how to implement and use these structures. Implementation is consistent with an abstract data type approach to software.

Proposed ANSI Standard and `iostream.h`

C++ continues to change at a rapid pace for an existing widely used language. This book is based on the most recent standard in draft form from the ANSI standards committee. It is expected that this standard will be adopted and be stable for many years to come. The standard includes templates and exceptions; this text treats both completely. Standard libraries include `iostream.h` and `stream.h`. Examples use the most recent standard I/O libraries.

Reference Value in Appendices

There is an easily accessible informal language reference appendix. This is not official, but specifies in a terse manner the language definition. There is also an appendix on the key I/O libraries, `iostream.h` and `stream.h`.

Pragmatic and Mainstream

The book attempts to stay with mainstream aspects of the language that are most likely to remain standard in future releases. It avoids arcane features of the language that are error-prone or confusing.

ACKNOWLEDGMENTS

My special thanks go to my wife, Debra Dolsberry, who encouraged me throughout this project. She acted as technical editor and implemented and tested all major pieces of code. Her careful implementations of the code and exercises often led to important improvements. Steve Clamage of Taumetric Corporation provided many useful insights. His careful reading of the text and suggestions strongly influenced C++ language explanations where he is an acknowledged and insightful expert. Others who provided helpful suggestions and encouragement include:

Peter Apers, University of Twente, The Netherlands; Henri Bal, Vrije University, The Netherlands; Michael Beeson, San Jose University; Nan Borreson, Borland International; Douglas Campbell, Brigham Young University; Cathy Collins, USC; Steven Demurjian, University of Connecticut; Robert Doran, University of Auckland, New Zealand; Robert Durling, UCSC; Daniel Edelson, UCSC; Anton Eliens, Vrije University, New Zealand; Ray Fujioka, USC; Thomas Judson, University of Portland; Al Kelley, UCSC; Jim Kempf, Sun Microsystems, Incorporated; Darrell Long, UCSC; Charlie McDowell, UCSC; Laura Pohl, Cottage Consultants; Reind van de Riet, Vrije University, The Netherlands; Anthony Wasserman, IDE; Salih Yurttas, Texas A&M University.

The usual disclaimer holds that these individuals are not responsible for errors or attitudes expressed in the book. In addition, my editors John Carter Shanklin and Dan Joraanstad were very supportive.

Ira Pohl
University of California, Santa Cruz

CONTENTS

4

IMPLEMENTING ADTs IN THE BASE LANGUAGE   104

5

DATA HIDING AND MEMBER FUNCTIONS   136

8

VISITATION: ITERATORS AND CONTAINERS   242

9

INHERITANCE: SUBTYPING AND CODE REUSE   274

10

PARAMETRIC POLYMORPHISM   316

11

EXCEPTIONS   348

12

OOP USING C++   374

1

WHY OBJECT-ORIENTED PROGRAMMING IN C++?

Object-oriented programming (OOP) is the programming methodology of choice in the 1990s. It is the product of 25 years of programming practice and experience that goes back to Simula 67 and continues with experience in Smalltalk, Lisp, Clu, and more recently Actor, Eiffel, Objective C, and C++ (Booch 1991; Budd 1991). It is a programming style that captures the behavior of the real world in a way that hides detailed implementation. When successful it allows the problem solver to think in terms of the problem domain.

C++ was created by Bjarne Stroustrup in the early 1980s. Stroustrup had two main goals: (1) to make C++ compatible with ordinary C, and (2) to extend C with OOP constructs based on the class construct of Simula 67. The language, in its current form, is described in Stroustrup (1991).

C was developed by Dennis Ritchie in the early 1970s as a system implementation language (SIL). It was used to build UNIX. Gradually it gained popularity not only as a SIL but also as a general-purpose language. It is a small, terse language.

The ultimate goal of C++ is to provide a language for the professional programmer that can be used to develop OOP software without sacrificing C's efficiency or portability. The steps along this path started with

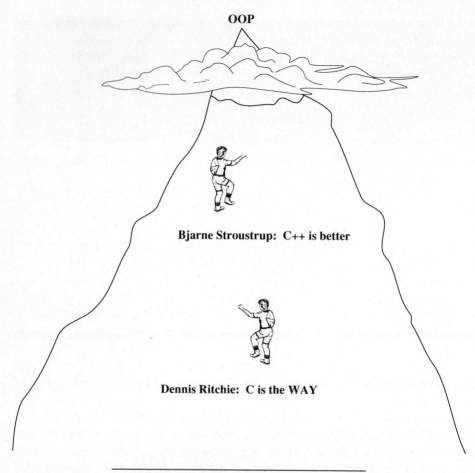

FIGURE 1.1   The Way up the Mountain

Dennis Ritchie in 1972 and continue with Bjarne Stroustrup and a growing community of practitioners today (Figure 1.1).

1.1   OBJECT-ORIENTED PROGRAMMING

Object-oriented programming (OOP) is a data-centered view of programming in which data and behavior are strongly linked. Data and behavior are conceived of as *classes* whose instances are objects. For example, a polynomial can have a range of legal values, and these values can be affected by such operations as addition and multiplication.

OOP also views computation as simulating behavior. What is simulated are objects represented by a computational abstraction. Suppose we wish to improve our poker play, and to do so we must better understand the odds of obtaining different poker hands. We need to simulate shuffling and must have appropriate ways to speak about cards and suits. Publicly we use the suit names: spades, hearts, diamonds, and clubs. Privately these suits are internally represented as integers. This internal choice is hidden and consequently should not affect our computation. Just as decks of cards can have many different physical compositions and still properly behave as cards, so can computational card decks.

We will be using the terms *abstract data type (ADT)* to mean a user-defined extension to the native types available in the language. It consists of a set of values and a collection of operations that can act on those values. For example, C does not have a complex number type, but C++ allows you to add such a type and integrate it with existing types.

Objects are class variables. Object-oriented programming allows ADTs to be easily created and used. OOP uses the mechanism of *inheritance* to conveniently derive a new type from an existing user-defined type. Biological taxonomies are akin to this mechanism: Rodents and cats are both mammals; if the category mammal is an encoding of the information and behavior that is true for all objects in this class, then creating both the category cat and the category rodent from the category mammal is an enormous saving.

In OOP, objects are responsible for their behavior. For example, polynomial objects, complex number objects, integer objects, and floating point number objects all understand addition. Each type has code for executing addition. The compiler provides the right code for integers and floating point numbers. The polynomial ADT has a function defining addition, specific to its implementation. The ADT provider should include code for any behavior the object can be commonly expected to understand. Having an object be responsible for its behavior eases the coding task for the user of that object.

Consider a class of objects called shapes. If we want to draw shapes on a screen, we need to know where the shape is to be centered and how to draw the shape. Some shapes, such as polygons, are relatively easy to draw. A general shape-drawing routine can be very expensive, requiring storage of a large number of individual boundary points. Avoiding this in the polygon case is clearly beneficial. If the individual shape object knows best how to draw itself, the programmer using such shapes needs only to give the object the message "draw."

The new class construct in C++ provides the *encapsulation* mechanism to implement ADTs. Encapsulation includes both the internal implementation details of a specific type and the externally available operations and functions that can act on objects of that type. The implementation details can be made inaccessible to client code that uses the type. For example, stack might be implemented as a fixed-length array, while the publicly available operations would include push and pop. Changing the internal implementation to a linked list should not affect how push and pop are used externally. The implementation of stack is hidden from its clients.

The term OOP refers to a collection of concepts, including the following:

- Simulating activity in the world
- Having user-defined types
- Hiding implementation detail
- Reusing code through inheritance
- Allowing run-time interpretation of function call

Some of these concepts are vague, some abstract, and some general. OOP also implies a point of view of the programming process that is frequently ideological. To mitigate frustration and confusion, we will try to illustrate OOP by examples that have concrete advantages in the programming context.

1.2   WHY C++ IS A BETTER C

Because C++ is based on C, it retains much of that language, including a rich operator set, nearly orthogonal design, terseness, and extensibility. C++ is a highly portable language, and translators for it are available on many different machines and systems. C++ was designed to be highly compatible with existing C programs. Unlike other object-oriented languages, such as Smalltalk, C++ is an extension of a programming language in wide use on many machines.

If C++ is viewed as an object-oriented language alternative to Smalltalk, it is a relatively inexpensive one. Programming in C++ does not require a graphics environment, and C++ programs do not incur run-time expense from type checking or garbage collection.

C++ improves on C in significant ways, especially in supporting strong typing. The function prototype syntax, as now supported by ANSI C (Kelley and Pohl 1990; Harbison and Steele 1991), is a C++ innovation. In general, C++ has stronger type rules than C, which makes it a safer language.

C++ is a marriage of the low level with the high level. The user can write code at the level appropriate to the problem while maintaining contact with machine-level implementation details. Unlike Smalltalk, which is a pure OOP, C++ is a *hybrid* language. This creates a range of choices for the often daunting task of designing and coding a problem. Our approach will be very pragmatic and will demonstrate techniques that work, rather than insisting on paradigmatic dogma.

Operators can be given new definitions based on the types of their arguments. This operator overloading supports the implementation of new types that may be operated upon transparently. Normal functions, like operators, can be overloaded.

C++ programs are less reliant on the preprocessor than C programs, which often use the preprocessor to implement constants and useful macros. In C usage, parameterized `#define` macros introduce insecurities. However, in C++ the `inline` keyword requests the compiler to compile a function as a macro. This preserves type checking while increasing run-time performance as compared with normal functions. Reliance on the preprocessor is further diminished by the `const` type modifier, which can specify named constants.

Among C++'s many improvements, a favorite of programmers is the addition of the // symbol for one-line comments. Also, a convenient new I/O library—the *iostream.h* library—provides a very useful alternative to *stdio.h*. And `new` and `delete` operators provide convenient access to free store.

Abstract data types are implemented in C++ through the `class` mechanism. Classes allow a programmer to control the visibility of the underlying implementation. What is public is visible, and what is private is hidden. Data hiding is one component of object-oriented programming. Classes have member functions, including those that overload operators, that allow the programmer to code the appropriate functionality for the ADT. Classes can be defined through an inheritance mechanism that allows for improved code sharing and library development. Inheritance is another hallmark of object-oriented programming.

C is often criticized as a weakly typed, unsafe language (Pohl and Edelson 1988). C++ is strongly typed. Conversions between types are allowed, provided they are well defined. In fact, the language allows the programmer to create conversion functions between arbitrary types.

The C array model is pointer-based and one-dimensional, without bounds checking. This lack of multidimensional arrays means the programmer must spend more time and effort implementing them using the one-dimensional storage mapping function that is C's paradigm. Development and use of dynamic arrays also require significant work and are not supported in the language. C++ retains the array handling of C; however, classes provide a satisfactory means of transparently implementing general arrays. Multi-dimensional, dynamic, and bounds-checked arrays can be implemented in libraries.

By and large, the semantics of C++ are much more stringently defined than those of C. For example, type conversion and typing are more carefully implemented. The C need for preprocessor extensibility is curtailed. Function overloading and `inline` can be used to replace macros with arguments, and the `const` type modifier is sufficient for most named constants. The preprocessor's primary uses are file inclusion and conditional compilation.

We will use the term *kernel language* to mean the subset of C++ that is equivalent to ANSI C, with minor extensions. It will include the non-OOP extensions to the language and will be described in Chapters 2 through 4. Our intention is to provide an explanation suitable for experienced programmers who have practice in other normal imperative languages, such as Pascal or Fortran. A detailed account of ANSI C is given by Kelley and Pohl (1990).

1.3   ENCAPSULATION AND TYPE EXTENSIBILITY

OOP is a balanced approach to writing software. Data and behavior are packaged together. This encapsulation creates user-defined types, extending and interacting with the native types of the kernel language.

An abstract data type such as a stack is a description of the ideal public behavior of the type. The user of this type understands that operations, such as push or pop, result in certain public behavior. Operations push and pop are called *methods*. A concrete implementation of the ADT also has implementation limits; for example, after a large number of pushes the stack space is exhausted. These limits affect public behavior. Also, internal or private details of the implementation do not directly affect the user's understanding. For example, a stack is frequently implemented as a large array accessed through a special index named *top*. The internal base address of this array and its name should be of no direct consequence to the user.

Encapsulation is the ability to hide internal detail while providing a public interface to a user-defined type. C++ uses `class` and `struct` declarations in conjunction with the access keywords `private`, `protected`, and `public` to provide encapsulation, as shown in the following example:

```
class stack {           //a user-defined type
private:                //hide this detail of implementation
    int   top;
    char  d[1000];
public:
    void push(char c);  //public interface approximating abstraction
    char pop();         //member function or "method"
    . . .
};

main()
{
    stack c_stk;        //c_stk is an object of type stack

    c_stk.push('A');    //c_stk understands the push "method"
    . . .
}
```

OOP terminology is strongly influenced by Smalltalk programming. The Smalltalk designers wanted programmers to break with their past habits and embrace a new programming methodology. They invented terms such as **message** and **method** to replace the traditional terms **function invocation** and **member function**. Thus in OOP terminology one would say the stack object `c_stk` was given the message `push('A')`.

1.4   CONSTRUCTION OF OBJECTS

OOP in some respects requires a more sophisticated understanding of the programming process. In the kernel language objects are implicitly created and destroyed for you by the system. For example, most compilers allocate simple local variables from a system stack. The following program reads a line of text and counts the number of left braces it finds until execution is terminated by an end-of-file condition. (We use some constructs in advance of their explanation: *iostream.h*, which provides C++-style

I/O, is described in detail in Appendix D.) The input stream object cin gets input from standard input, usually the keyed data from the terminal or workstation. The output stream object cout writes output, usually to the screen.

```
//Count the number of left brace symbols.
#include <iostream.h>

int cnt_lbrace(const char* line)
{
    int   count = 0, i;

    for (i = 0; line[i] != '\0'; ++i)
        if (line[i] == '{')
            ++count;
    return (count);
}

main()
{
    char line[256];    //array allocation
    int   count = 0;    //variable allocation and initialization

    while (cin.getline(line, 256) && cin.good())
        count += cnt_lbrace(line);    //function invocation

    cout << endl << "Left braces found = " << count << endl;
}
```

This program uses built-in allocation of the character array line. The simple variable count in main() is allocated and initialized to zero. Also, storage is automatically allocated for the local variables and parameters of cnt_lbrace(). On exit of the function cnt_lbrace(), local variables are deallocated implicitly. The programmer relies on the fact that these allocations and deallocations are done automatically and efficiently.

The *iostream* method getline() places a subsequent line of characters from standard input into the array line. The *iostream* method good() tests that input is still readable. It will detect an end-of-file condition. The operator << is overloaded to put values to the standard output.

This example of processing a character array as a line of text could be thought of as acting on an ADT string. Converting this code to one that uses a string type requires an implementation capable of allocating storage for strings. C++ has the built-in free store operators new and delete, which allocate and deallocate memory from the system free store, respectively. Typically classes provide special functions called *constructors* to construct and initialize objects dynamically. These often use new. Special functions called *destructors* are provided to deallocate memory. The following example illustrates this concept:

```
//An implementation of dynamically allocated strings.
#include <string.h>
#include <iostream.h>

class string {
private:
   char* s;        //hidden implementation
   int   len;
public:
   //constructors
   string() { s = new char[81]; len = 80; } //default constructor
   string(int n) { s = new char[n + 1]; len = n; }
   //destructor
   ~string() { delete []s; }  //array deallocation-destructor
   //methods - publicly available behavior
   void print() const { cout << s << endl; }
   . . .
};
```

The hidden representation is a pointer to char and has a variable len in which to store the maximum string length. The constructors all allocate dynamically from free store. The new operator in this example allocates an array of char. The size of the array is specified inside the brackets. A user of these objects can declare them as follows:

```
string x, y, z;      //string() allocates 81 character array
string t(60), u(n);  //string(int n) allocates given length
```

When these variable declarations go out of scope, the destructor is invoked to retrieve store for reuse. The destructor calls the `delete` operator with an empty bracket symbol. The empty bracket symbol is required because the corresponding allocation was of an array.

1.5   CONVERSIONS, OPERATORS, AND SEAMLESS TYPES

One principle of OOP is that user-defined types must enjoy the same privileges as native types. The client expects the convenience of using these types without regard to a native/nonnative distinction. For example, native arithmetic types in the kernel language can be mixed together in expressions because it is convenient and would otherwise be burdensome to designate conventionally expected conversions. A user-defined arithmetic type, such as a complex number, should be able to mix with the already available arithmetic types, such as integers and floats. This is made possible in C++ by giving operators new meanings and by specifying both implicit and explicit conversion behavior. A user-defined type that is constructed to behave as and have the privileges of a native type is called *seamless*. The implication is that user-defined types cannot in trivial ways be distinguished from native types.

An arithmetic expression such as x + y has both a value and a type. For example, if x and y are both variables of the same type, say `int`, then x + y is also an `int`. If x and y are of different types, however, then x + y is a *mixed expression*. Suppose x is a `double` and y is an `int`. Then the value of y is converted to a `double`, and the expression x + y has type `double`.

It is possible to establish such conversions for user-defined types. It is also possible to overload the meaning of operators so as to give them appropriate meanings for user-defined types. For example, the expression a + b can have different meanings, depending on the types of the variables a and b. The expression could mean string concatenation, complex number addition, or integer addition, depending, respectively, on whether the variables were the ADT `string`, the ADT `complex`, or the built-in type `int`.

```
//Overloading + for complex numbers.
class complex {
private:
   double re, im;     //hidden implementation
public:
   complex (double r = 0.0, double i = 0.0) : re(r), im(i) {}
   complex operator+ (complex a);   //overload +
   . . .
};

main()
{
   complex x(3, 5.5), y(4.2), z;
   double  t = 6.5;

   z = x + y;     //overloaded operator+ called
   z = z + t;     //t is converted to a complex first
   . . .
}
```

In this example `main` uses complex numbers mixed with doubles. Notationally the complex type has been seamlessly added to the native arithmetic types. When the variable `t` is added, it first must be converted to a `complex` value. This is done by calling the constructor that uses the default zero value for the imaginary part of the complex conversion.

1.6 INHERITANCE

Inheritance is a means of deriving a new class from existing classes, called *base* classes. As such it reuses existing code. The derived class is developed from the base by adding or altering code. Through inheritance, a hierarchy of related types can be created that share code and interface. Single inheritance occurs when there is a single base class, and multiple inheritance occurs when there is more than one base class.

Many types are variants of one another, and it is frequently tedious and error prone to develop new code for each. A derived class inherits the description of the base class. Inheritance is a method for coping with complexity. It imposes a hierarchical classification on objects. For example, the periodic table of elements includes gases, which have properties that are shared by all elements in that classification. Inert gases are another important special case. The hierarchy in this case is an inert gas, such as argon, is a gas, which in turn is an element. This hierarchy provides a convenient way to understand the behavior of inert gases. We know they are composed of protons and electrons, as this is a shared description of all elements. We know they are in a gaseous state at room temperature, as this behavior is shared with all gases. We also know they do not combine in ordinary chemical reactions with other elements as this is a shared behavior of all inert gases.

The OOP design methodology thus consists of two steps:

1   Decide on an appropriate set of types.
2   Design in their relatedness, and use inheritance to share code among classes.

The following is an example of deriving a class:

```
enum support {ta, ra, fellowship, other};
enum year {fresh, soph, junior, senior, grad};

class student {
protected:
   int        student_id;
   double     gpa;
   year       y;
   char       name[30];
public:
   student(char* nm, int id, double g, year x);
   void  print();
};


class grad_student: public student {
protected:
   support    s;
   char       dept[10];
   char       thesis[80];
public:
   grad_student (char* nm, int id, double g,
               year x, support t, char* d, char* th);
   void print();
};
```

In this example, `grad_student` is the derived class, and `student` is the base class. The use of the keyword `public` following the colon in the derived class header means that the protected and public members of `student` are to be inherited as protected and public members of `grad_student`, respectively. Private members of the base class cannot be accessed in the derived class. Public inheritance also means that the derived class `grad_student` is a subtype of `student`.

A derived class is a modification of the base class that inherits the public members and protected members of the base class. Thus, in the example of `grad_student`, the `student` members—`student_id`, `gpa`, `name`, `year`, and `print`—are inherited. Frequently a derived class adds new members to the existing class members. This is the case with `grad_student`, which has three new data members and a redefined member function `print`.

An inheritance structure provides a design for the overall system. For example, a data base that contained all the people at a college could be derived from the base class `person`. The `student`—`grad_student` relation could be extended to extension students, as a further significant category of objects. Similarly, `person` could be the base class for a variety of employee categories. This hierarchical inheritance structure is illustrated in Figure 1.2.

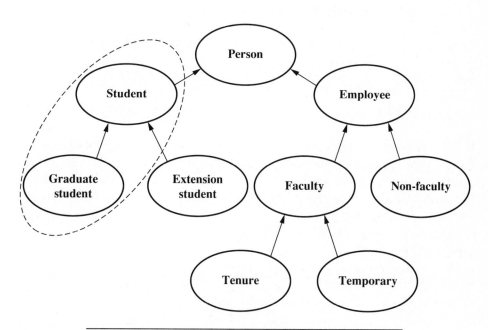

FIGURE 1.2   Diagram of Inheritance Relationship

1.7   POLYMORPHISM

Polymorphism is the genie in OOP who takes instruction from clients and properly interprets their wishes. A polymorphic function has many forms. An example in ANSI C is the division operator. If the arguments to the division operator are integral, then integer division is used. However, if one or both arguments are floating point, then floating point division is used.

In C++ a function name or operator is overloadable. A function is called based on its *signature,* which is the list of argument types in the function's parameter list. Also, using `virtual` member functions in an inheritance hierarchy allows run-time selection of the appropriate member function. Such a function can have different implementations that are invoked by a run-time determination of the subtype.

C++ also has parametric polymorphism, where type is left unspecified and is later instantiated. Manipulation of generic pointers and templates provide parametric polymorphism in C++. This will be explained in detail in Chapter 10.

The following are examples of polymorphism:

```
a / b         //divide behavior determined by native coercions

cout << a     //ad-hoc polymorphism through function overloading

p -> draw()   //pure polymorphism through virtual function call

stack <window*> win  //parametric polymorphism using templates
```

In the division expression the result depends on the arguments being automatically coerced to the widest type: If both arguments are integer, the result is an integer division, but if one or both arguments are floating point, the result is floating point. In the output statement, the shift operator $<<$ is invoking a function that is able to output an object of type a. The third statement has pointer p invoking the `draw()` function by using run-time dependent invocation of a routine appropriate to the type of object p is pointing at. The last statement is a declaration of a stack that stores "pointer to window" values. In each case, type information is used automatically to select an appropriate computation.

Polymorphism localizes responsibility for behavior. The client code frequently requires no revision when additional functionality is added to the system through ADT-provided code improvements. For example, classic coding techniques for implementing a package of routines to provide an ADT shape would rely on a comprehensive structural description of any shape. The declaration

```
struct shape{ enum{CIRCLE, ...} e_val; double center, radius; ...}
```

would have all the members necessary for any shape currently drawable in the system and an enumerator value, so that it can be identified. The area routine would then be written as

```
double area(shape* s)
{
   switch(s -> e_val) {
   case CIRCLE:  return (PI * s -> radius * s -> radius);
   case RECTANGLE: return (s -> height * s -> width);
   . . .
}
```

Question: What is involved in revising this code to include a new shape? Answer: An additional case in the code body and additional members in the structure. Unfortunately these would have ripple effects throughout our entire code body. Each routine so structured has to have an additional case, even when that case is just adding a label to a preexisting case. Thus what is conceptually a local improvement requires global changes.

The OOP coding technique for the same problem uses a shape hierarchy. The hierarchy is the obvious one, where `circle` and `rectangle` are derived from `shape`. In the revision process, code improvements are provided in a new derived class, so additional description is localized. The programmer overrides the meaning of any changed routines—in this case the new area calculation. Client code that does not use the new type is unaffected. Client code that is improved by the new type is typically minimally changed.

C++ code following this design uses `shape` as an abstract base class. Such a class cannot be used to declare concrete instances but are shared specifications for the entire hierarchy. They can be used to declare pointer types that can invoke their pure virtual function definitions at run-time polymorphically.

```
//Shape hierarchy and virtual area() calculation.
class shape {
public:
   virtual double area() = 0;
   virtual char* get_name() = 0;
};

class rectangle: public shape {
private:
   double height, width;
public:
   rectangle(double h, double w): height(h), width(w) {}
   double area() { return (height * width); }
   char* get_name() { return (" RECTANGLE "); }
};

class circle: public shape {
private:
   double radius;
public:
   circle(double r): radius(r) {}
   double area() { return ( 3.14159 * radius * radius); }
   char* get_name() { return (" CIRCLE "); }
};
```

Client code for computing an arbitrary area is polymorphic.

```
shape*   ptr_shape;

   . . .
   cout << ptr_shape -> get_name();
   cout << " area = " << ptr_shape -> area();
   . . .
```

Now imagine improving our hierarchy of types by developing a square class. The client code remains unchanged. This was not the case with the non-OOP code. Code modifications would have to be systematically included in all affected functions.

```
class square: public rectangle {
public:
    square(double h): rectangle(h,h) {}
    double area() { return (rectangle::area()); }
    char* get_name() { return (" SQUARE "); }
};
```

Furthermore, hierarchical design should minimize interface parameter passing. Each layer tends to absorb, within its implementation, state detail that is affected by function invocation. In a conventional scheme this sometimes can be accomplished by making such changes in globally defined data. This practice is almost universally condemned, because it leads to opaque side-effect-style coding that is difficult to debug, revise, and maintain.

OOP is many things to many people. Attempts at defining it are reminiscent of the blind sages' attempts at describing the elephant. We offer this simple equation:

$$OOP \ = \ type\text{-}extensibility \ + \ polymorphism$$

1.8 BENEFITS OF OBJECT-ORIENTED PROGRAMMING

The central element of OOP is the encapsulation of an appropriate set of data types and their operations. The class construct with its member functions and data members provides an appropriate coding tool. Class variables are the objects to be manipulated.

Classes also provide data hiding. Access privileges can be managed and limited to whatever group of functions needs access to implementation details. This promotes modularity and robustness.

Another important concept in OOP is the promotion of code reuse through the inheritance mechanism. This is the mechanism of deriving a new class from an existing one, called the base class. The base class can be added to or altered to create the derived class. In this way a hierarchy of related data types can be created that share code.

Many useful data structures are variants of one another, and it is frequently tedious to produce the same code for each. A derived class inherits the description of the base class. It can then be altered by adding additional members, overloading existing member functions, and modifying access privileges. Without this reuse mechanism, each minor variation would require code replication.

The OOP programming task is frequently more difficult than the normal procedural programming found in C. There is at least one extra design step before the coding of algorithms. This involves the hierarchy of types that is useful for the problem at hand. Frequently one is solving the problem more generally than is strictly necessary. This pays dividends in several ways: The solution is more encapsulated and thus more robust and easier to maintain and change. Also, the solution is more reusable. For example, where the code needs a stack, that stack is easily borrowed from existing code. In an ordinary procedural language, such a data structure is frequently wired into the algorithm and cannot be exported.

All these benefits are especially important for large coding projects that require coordination among many programmers. Here the ability to have header files specify general interfaces for different classes allows each programmer to work on individual code segments with a high degree of independence and integrity.

1.9   REFERENCES

1.   Booch, G. 1991. *Object Oriented Design with Applications*. Menlo Park, CA: Benjamin/Cummings. An excellent discussion of OOP methodology using several languages and case studies.

2.   Budd, T. 1991. *An Introduction to Object Oriented Programming*. Reading, MA: Addison-Wesley. Another excellent discussion of OOP methodology using several languages and small examples.

3.   Harbison, S. P., and G. L. Steele. 1991. *C: A Reference Manual*. 3d ed. Englewood Cliffs, NJ: Prentice-Hall. The authoritative reference book on the syntax and semantics of the C programming language.

4.   Kelley, A., and I. Pohl. 1990. *A Book on C*. 2d ed. Menlo Park, CA: Benjamin/Cummings. A comprehensive text on the C programming language. It is written in the style of this book.

5.   Pohl, I., and D. Edelson. 1988. A-Z: C Language Shortcomings. *Computer Languages*. 13, no. 2: 51–64. A brief paper criticizing 26 defects in the original C language.

6.   Stroustrup, B. 1991 *The C++ Programming Language*. 2d ed. Reading, MA: Addison-Wesley. The de facto language reference manual. This book is very difficult reading.

2

NATIVE TYPES
AND STATEMENTS

This chapter, together with Chapters 3 and 4, provide an introduction to programming in C++ using its native types and its non-OOP features. A *native type* is a type provided by the language directly. In C++ these include the simple types, such as character, integer, and floating point types. Also there are derived types—such as array, pointer, and structure types—that are aggregates of the simple types. This chapter focuses on the native simple data types and statements.

Chapters 2 through 4 give the experienced programmer the ability to program in that subset of C++ that corresponds to C. We call this subset the kernel language. As such, programmers with C experience, especially ANSI C, will find much that is common to both languages. The kernel language, however, has important extensions not found in ANSI C that affect programming methodology and style. Also, these chapters contain examples that will be in use throughout this text.

An important feature of OOP is *type extensibility*—the ability within the programming language to develop new types suitable to a problem domain. For type extensibility to work properly, the new types must work like the native types of the language. Thus native types provide part of the model for what an appropriate object-oriented design would be.

2.1   PROGRAM ELEMENTS

A program is composed of elements called *tokens*, which are collections of characters that are the basic vocabulary recognized by the compiler. The character set in use includes the following:

```
a b c d e f g h i j k l m n o p q r s t u v w x y z
A B C D E F G H I J K L M N O P Q R S T U V W X Y Z
0 1 2 3 4 5 6 7 8 9
+ = _ - ( ) * & % # ! | < > . , ; : " ' / ? { } ~ \ [ ] ^
```
white-space and nonprinting characters, such as newline, tab, and blank

See Appendix A for the ASCII table of characters. Tokens can be interspersed with white space and comment text inserted for readability and documentation. There are five kinds of tokens: keywords, identifiers, literals, operators, and punctuators.

COMMENTS

In C a comment is written as /* *possibly multiline* */. C++ adds a rest-of-line comment written as // *rest of line*. Some newer C compilers recognize this convention as well.

```
/*  Multi-Line Comments are Frequently Introductory
    Programmer:   Laura Pohl
    Date:         January 1, 1989
    Version:      DJD v4.2
*/

#include <stdio.h>    //standard I/O library ANSI C
#include <iostream.h> //usual I/O library this book
#include <stream.h>   //older I/O library C++ release 1.0
```

KEYWORDS

Keywords are explicitly reserved words that have a strict meaning in C++. They include words used for type declarations, such as `int`, `char`, and `float`; words used for statement syntax, such as `do`, `for`, and `if`; and words used for access control, such as `public`, `protected`, and `private`. See Appendix C for a complete list.

IDENTIFIERS

An identifier is a sequence of letters, digits, and underscores. An identifier cannot begin with a digit. Uppercase and lowercase letters are treated as distinct. In principle, identifiers can be arbitrarily long, but many systems can distinguish only up to the first 31 characters.

The following are some examples of identifiers:

```
n             //typically an integer variable
count         //meaningful as documentation
buff_size     //stylistically the underscore separates words
buffSize      //pascal style
_             //legal but a poor choice
q2345         //obscure
cout          //used in the standard library iostream.h
_foo          //avoid: underscore frequently starts system identifiers
```

The following are not legal identifiers:

```
for           //keyword
3q            //cannot start with digit
-count        //do not mistake - for _
```

A reserved-for-system-use status is given to identifiers containing a double underscore, as in the following:

```
_sysfoo       //reserved for system use - two leading underscores
foo_bar       //reserved for system use - two internal underscores
```

LITERALS

Literals are constant values, such as 1 or 3.14159. All C++ native data types have literals, including characters, integers, floating point numbers, and pointers. String literals are also allowed. Some examples are:

```
5        //an integer literal
5u       //u or U specifies unsigned
5L       //l or L specifies long
05       //an integer literal written as octal
0x5      //an integer literal written as hexadecimal
5.0      //a floating point literal treated as double
5.0F     //f or F specifies float - typically single precision
5.0L     //l or L specifies long double
'5'      //a character literal in ASCII 53
'A'      //letter capital A in ASCII 65
'a'      //letter small a in ASCII 97
'\0'     //the null character terminates strings
'\t'     //the character printing a tab space
'\n'     //the character printing a new line
"5"      //the string consisting of the character '5'
"a string with newline\n"
5555555555555555   //an integer that is too large for most machines
```

A string literal is stored as a series of characters terminated with the null character whose value is 0. Caveat: In principle, string literals are non-modifiable. C++ uses pointers to manipulate strings, and many compilers cannot enforce this restriction. Special characters can be represented inside strings by escaping them with the backslash character \.

```
"a"          //two bytes storing 'a' '\0'
"a\tb\n"     //five bytes 'a' '\t' 'b' '\n' '\0'
"1 \\"       //four bytes '1' ' ' '\\' '\0'
"\""         //two bytes '"' '\0'
```

   When printed these strings would produce effects required by the special characters. Thus the second string would print an a followed by the number of white-space characters determined by the tab setting, then a b followed by a new line.

OPERATORS AND PUNCTUATORS

C++ gives special meaning to many characters and character sequences, including the following:

```
+ - * / %          //arithmetic operators
-> ->*             //pointer and pointer-to-member operators
&&   ||            //logical operators
=  += *=           //assignment operators
```

Operators are used in expressions and are meaningful when given appropriate arguments. They have fixed precedence and associativity. Certain symbols stand for different operators, depending on context; for example, - can be either unary or binary minus. See Appendix B for a complete list of C++ operators.

Punctuators include parentheses, braces, commas, and colons and are used to structure elements of a program.

```
foo(a, 7, b + 8)   // ( introduces a comma separated argument list
{ a = b; c = d; } // { introduces a statement list or block
```

Operators, punctuators, and white space serve to separate language elements.

2.2 INPUT/OUTPUT

Input/output is not directly part of a language. It is added as a set of types and routines found in a standard library. Several standard libraries are in use with C++. The ANSI C standard library, *stdio.h*, is in widespread use. The early C++ stream library, *stream.h*, remains in use, but the newer *iostream.h* library is displacing it. We use *iostream.h* because we are illustrating current practice. Appendix D provides a more complete description of this and other I/O issues. This section is introductory and intended to give the bare minimum of detail—just enough to get you up and running.

The *iostream.h* library overloads the two bit-shift operators.

```
<<   // "put to" output stream normally left shift
>>   // "get from" input stream normally right shift
```

It also declares three standard streams.

```
cout  //standard out
cin   //standard in
cerr  //standard error
```

Their use in conjunction with values and variables is analogous to assignment.

```
cout << "\nEnter a double: ";
cin >> x;
cout << "\nEnter a positive integer: ";
cin >> i;
if (i < 1)
    cerr << "error i = " << i << endl;
cout << "i * x = " << i * x;
```

The first output statement places a string on the screen. The second statement expects the double variable x to get a value converted from string input typed at the keyboard. The string represents a value that must be a double or assignment convertible to double; other typed input will fail. Notice how the last two statements allow multiple assignments to their output streams. The statements are executed left to right. For example, if i had gotten a value of −1, then the following error message would be on the screen:

```
error i = -1
```

The endl is a specially recognized identifier, called a *manipulator*, that flushes the cerr output stream and adds a newline. The last statement prints the string "i * x = ", followed by the double value of the expression i * x.

2.3   PROGRAM STRUCTURE

A program in C++ is a collection of functions and declarations. The language is block-structured, and variables declared within blocks are allocated automatically upon block entry. Parameters, unless otherwise specified, are call-by-value. The following program computes the greatest common divisor of two integers:

```
//Greatest common divisor program.
#include <iostream.h>           //import I/O library

int gcd(int m, int n)          //function definition
{                              //block
   int r;                      //declaration of remainder

   while (n != 0) {            //not equal
      r = m % n;               //modulos operator
      m = n;                   //assignment
      n = r;
   }                           //end while loop
   return (m);                 //exit gcd with value m
}


main()                         //program start
{
   int x, y;                   //local variables

   cout << "\nGcdProgram";
   do {                        //enter do loop
      cout << "\nEnter two integers: ";
      cin >> x >> y;           //get data from standard input
      cout << "\nGCD(" << x << ", " << y << ") = "
           << gcd(x, y) << endl;
                               //put answers to standard output
   } while (x);                //exit condition x == 0
}
```

As you can see, C++ is very terse. Other major points are as follows:

- C++ relies on an external standard library to provide input/output. The information the program needs to use this library resides in the file *iostream.h*.

- C++ uses a preprocessor to handle a set of directives, such as the include directive, to convert the program from its preprocessing form to pure C++ syntax. These directives are introduced by the symbol #.

- A C++ program consists of declarations in possibly different files. Each function is on the external or global level and may not be declared in a nested manner. The files act as modules and may be compiled separately.
- The function main() is used as the starting point for execution of the program. It obeys the C++ rules for function declaration.

C++ compilers can compile multifile programs. Large C++ programs are prepared as separate files. Each file is conceptually a module that contains related program declarations and definitions. On many systems C++ source files have the suffix .c. The AT&T C++ translator command is *CC*. So,

```
CC module1.c module2.c my_main.c
```

is the UNIX C++ compile command *CC*, acting on the three files *module1.c*, *module2.c*, and *my_main.c*. If compilation shows no errors, then an executable *a.out* is produced.

2.4 SIMPLE TYPES

The simple native types in C++ are double, int, and char. These types have a set of values and representation that is tied to the underlying machine architecture on which the compiler is running. C++ has no native boolean type; it uses the value zero to mean *false* and any nonzero value to mean *true*. This usage is important in understanding the semantics of iterative and conditional statements.

C++ simple types can be modified by the keywords short, long, signed, and unsigned to yield further simple types. The following is a list of these types—shortest to longest:

Simple data types

char	signed char	unsigned char
short	int	long
unsigned short	unsigned	unsigned long
float	double	long double

This list runs from the conceptually shortest type, char, to the conceptually longest type, long double. There is a requirement that each longer type be at least as long as its predecessor type. Length here refers to the number of bytes used to store the type. On most machines a char is stored in a single byte. On many PCs an int is stored in two bytes, while a long and a float are stored in four bytes.

C++ also has the sizeof operator, which is used to determine the number of bytes a particular object or type requires for storage.

```
//just checking
cout << sizeof(int) << " <= " << sizeof(long) << endl;
```

The range of integral values representable on your system is defined in the standard header file *limits.h*. Some examples from our system are

```
#define CHAR_BIT 8              //bits per char
#define SCHAR_MIN (-128)        //signed character minimum
#define SCHAR_MAX 127           //signed character maximum
#define UCHAR_MAX 255U          //unsigned character maximum
#define INT_MAX 2147483647      //int maximum
#define INT_MIN (-2147483648)//int minimum
#define UINT_MAX 4294967295U //unsigned int maximum
```

The range of floating point values representable on your system is defined in the standard header file *float.h*. Some examples from our system are

```
#define FLT_EPSILON ((float)1.19209290e-07)    //single precision
#define FLT_MIN ((float)1.17549435e-38)        //float smallest
#define FLT_MAX ((float)3.40282347e+38)        //float largest
#define DBL_EPSILON 2.2204460492503131e-16     //double precision
#define DBL_MIN 2.2250738585072014e-308        //double smallest
#define DBL_MAX 1.7976931348623157e+308        //double largest
```

The term *smallest* refers to the number closest to zero. The floating point numbers are capable of representing the range (+largest, −largest).

INITIALIZATION

A variable *declaration* associates a type with the variable name. Most variable declarations also are *definitions*. A variable definition allocates memory for a variable, which may be initialized, as in the following example:

```
extern const double PI;  //declared but not defined here
main()
{
   double radius = 5.5;  //declared and defined and initialized
   double area;          //declared and defined but uninitialized

   cout << "Circle's Area is "  << (PI * radius * radius);
}
```

The variables `radius` and `area` are declared and defined inside `main()`. They are allocated storage, typically from a system stack. A declaration of a variable constitutes a *definition*, if storage is allocated for it. Informally, you can think of the definition as creating the object.

A definition can also *initialize* the value of the variable. Syntactically initialization is expressed by following the identifier name with an *initializer*. For simple variables, this is usually in the following form:

type id = expression

Here are some examples:

```
{
   int    i = 5;                  //i is initialized to 5
   char   c1, c2 = 'B';           //c1 is uninitialized; c2 is 'B'
   double x = 0.777, y = x + 1;   //y is initialized using x

   cout << c2;                    //print 'B'
   cout << c1;                    //system dependent
   . . .
}
```

Initialization can involve an arbitrary expression, provided all the variables and functions used in the expression are defined. In the above example, `y` is initialized in terms of the just-defined `x`. The uninitialized variable `c1` cannot be relied on to have any particular value associated with it. Using it in the computation before a well-defined value is assigned to it is a mistake. As a rule of thumb, when you have a choice, you should initialize a variable rather than first define it as uninitialized and subsequently assign it a value. Initialization makes the code more readable, and the compiler can be more efficient about initialization.

2.5 TRADITIONAL CONVERSIONS

An expression such as x + y has both a value and a type. For example, if x and y are both variables of the same type, say int, then x + y is also an int. If x and y are of different types, however, then x + y is a *mixed expression*. Suppose x is a short and y is an int. Then the value of x is converted to an int, and the expression x + y has type int. Note carefully that the value of x as stored in memory is unchanged. Only a temporary copy of x is converted during the computation of the value of the expression. Now suppose that both x and y are of type short. Even though x + y is not a mixed expression, automatic conversions again take place; both x and y are promoted to int, and the expression is of type int.

The general rules of conversion are straightforward.

Automatic conversion in an arithmetic expression *x op y*

First:
    Any char, short, or enum is promoted to int.
    Integral values unrepresentable as int are promoted to unsigned.
Second:
    If, after the first step, the expression is of mixed type,
    then, according to the hierarchy of types,

        int < unsigned < long < unsigned long
          < float < double < long double

    the operand of lower type is promoted to that of the higher type,
    and the value of the expression has that type.

To illustrate automatic conversion, we first make the following declarations:

```
char c;    double d;    float f;       int i;
long lg;   short s;     unsigned u;
```

Now we can list a variety of mixed expressions along with their corresponding types:

Expression	Type	Expression	Type
c - s/i	int	u * 3-i	unsigned
u * 3.0-i	double	f * 3-i	float
c + 1	int	3 * s * lg	long
c + 1.0	double	d + s	double

In addition to automatic conversions in mixed expressions, an automatic conversion also can occur across an assignment. For example,

```
d = i
```

causes the value of i, which is an int, to be converted to a double and then to be assigned to d; double is the type of the expression as a whole. A promotion, or widening, such as d = i usually is well behaved, but a demotion, or narrowing, such as i = d can lose information. Here the fractional part of d is discarded. Precisely what happens in each case is machine dependent.

In addition to automatic conversions, which are implicit and can occur across assignments and in mixed expressions, there are explicit conversions called *casts*. If i is an int, then

```
(double) i
```

casts the value of i so that the expression has type double. The variable i itself remains unchanged. Casts can be applied to expressions, as in these examples:

```
(char) ('A' + 1.0)
x = (float) ((int) y + 1)
(double) (x = 77)
```

The cast operator (*type*) is a unary operator having the same precedence and right-to-left associativity as other unary operators. Thus the expression

```
(float) i + 3 is equivalent to ((float) i) + 3
```

Conversion is synonymous with *coercion*.

The next program converts miles to kilometers. Miles are kept as an integer value and kilometers are computed in floating point.

```
//Miles are converted to kilometers.

#include <iostream.h>
inline double mi_to_km(int miles)
{
    const double m_to_k = 1.609;      //conversion constant

    return (miles * m_to_k);
}

main()
{
    int miles;

    do {
        cout << "\nEnter distance in miles: ";
        cin >> miles;
        cout << "\nThis distance is " << mi_to_km(miles) << "   km.\n";
    } while (miles > 0);
}
```

This program consists of two functions. Each function has its own local scope in which variables are declared. Each variable has a type and, in the case of m_to_k, the modifier const. Furthermore, the variable is initialized to the value 1.609, and the const modifier ensures that this value is non-modifiable. This is good programming practice because the identifier is mneumonic and provides useful documentation. Notice that such a const variable must be initialized upon definition.

Where the inline keyword modifies a function definition, it suggests to the compiler that, when invoked, the code defining it avoid a function call by being placed inline. In C code, define directives are used to produce macros that avoid function call overhead. The use of const and inline is preferred to the use of "equivalent" `define` macros. They are far safer and lead to code that is more easily maintained.

The expression `miles * m_to_k` is widened to a `double`. Conceptually the integer valued `miles` is a narrower type than a `double`. The input statement `cin >> miles` expects keyboard input in the form of a string convertible to an integer. Input such as `5.45` is converted and assigned to `miles` as the integer value 5.

Both assignment and initialization allow narrowing conversions. Narrowing conversions that are not explicit are generally bad programming practice because they lead to subtle run-time bugs that are hard to detect. Many compilers warn the programmer of such implicit conversions.

2.6 ENUMERATION TYPES

The keyword `enum` declares a distinct integer type with a set of named integer constants called *enumerators*. Consider the declaration

```
enum suit {clubs, diamonds, hearts, spades};
```

This creates an integer type with the four suit names as named integer constants. The enumerators are the identifiers `clubs`, `diamonds`, `hearts`, and `spades` whose values are 0, 1, 2, and 3, respectively. These values are assigned by default, with the first enumerator being given the constant integer value 0. Each subsequent member of the list is one more than its left neighbor. The identifier `suit` is now its own unique type, distinct from other integer types. This identifier is called a *tag-name*.

Enumerators can be defined and initialized to arbitrary integer constants.

```
enum ages { milton = 47, ira, harold = 56, philip = harold + 7};
```

The enumerators can be initialized to constant expressions. Note that the default rule applies when there is no explicit initializer, as in `ira = 48`.

The tag-name and the enumerators must be distinct identifiers within scope. The values of enumerators need not be distinct. Enumerations can be implicitly converted to ordinary integer types, but not vice-versa.

```
enum boolean {false, true} q;
enum signal {off, on} a = on;     //a initialized to on
enum answer {no, yes, maybe = -1} b;
enum negative {no, false} c;      //illegal "no" and "false" redeclared
int   i, j = true;                //legal true is converted to 1
a = off;                          //legal
i = a;                            //legal i becomes 1
q = a;                            //illegal two distinct types
q = (boolean)a;                   //legal explicit conversion by cast
b = (q ? no : yes);               //legal enumerators are of type answer
```

Enumerators can be declared *anonymously*, meaning without a tag-name.

```
enum {FALSE, TRUE};
enum {lazy, hazy, crazy} why;
```

The first declaration is a common means of declaring mneumonic integer
constants. The second declaration declares a variable why of enumerated
type, with lazy, hazy, and crazy the allowable values of this variable.

2.7   EXPRESSIONS

C++ has a great variety of operators (see Appendix B) and expression
forms. For example, assignment is an expression. The following is legal
C++ code:

```
a = b + (c = d + 3);
```

The equivalent multistatement code would be

```
c = d + 3;
a = b + c;
```

Arithmetic expressions in C++ are consistent with expected practice.
One important difference is that the results of the division operator, /,
depend on its argument types.

```
a = 3 / 2;    // a is assigned 1
a = 3 / 2.0;  // a is assigned 1.5
```

A second important difference is that C++ has a tolerant attitude about mixing types and automatic conversions. C++ allows widening conversions, so an `int` may be widened when assigned to a double. But C++ also allows assignment conversions that narrow type, so a `double` may be assigned to an `int` or even a `char`.

```
int   i;
char  ch;
double b = 1.9;

i = b / 2.0;      //i is assigned 0
ch = 'A' + 1.0;  //ch is 'B'
```

The liberal attitude taken in C++ toward implicit conversions invites bad programming practice and should not be encouraged. Narrowing conversions and mixing types can affect program correctness and should be used carefully.

In C++ the values zero and nonzero are thought of as *false* and *true*, respectively, and are used to affect flow of control in various statement types. The following table contains the C++ operators that are most often used to affect flow of control:

Relational, Equality, and Logical Operators

Relational operators:	less than:	`<`
	greater than:	`>`
	less than or equal:	`<=`
	greater than or equal:	`>=`
Equality operators:	equal:	`==`
	not equal:	`!=`
Logical operators:	(unary) negation:	`!`
	logical and:	`&&`
	logical or:	`||`

Just as with other operators, the relational, equality, and logical operators have rules of precedence and associativity that determine precisely how expressions involving these operators are evaluated (see Appendix B). The negation operator `!` is unary. All the other relational, equality, and logical operators are binary. They operate on expressions and yield either the `int` value 0 or the `int` value 1. The value for *false* can be either 0 or 0.0, and the value for *true* can be any value other than 0 or 0.0.

One pitfall in C++ is that the equality operator and the assignment operator,

```
a == b and a = b
```

are *visually* similar. The expression a == b is a test for equality, whereas a = b is an assignment expression. One of the more common C++ programming mistakes is to code something like

```
if (i = 1)
    . . .           // do something
```

intending

```
if (i == 1)
    . . .           // do something
```

The first if statement assigns 1 to i and evaluates to 1, so it is always *true*. This error can be very difficult to find.

The logical operators !, &&, and || when applied to expressions yield either the int value 0 or the int value 1. Logical negation can be applied to an arbitrary expression. If an expression has the value 0 or 0.0, then its negation yields the int value 1. If the expression has a nonzero value, then its negation yields the int value 0.

Logical negation is a very simple operator with just one subtlety: The operator ! in C++ is unlike the *not* operator in mathematics. If s is a mathematical statement, then

$$not\ (not\ s)\ =\ s,$$

whereas in C++ the value of !!5, for example, is 1.

The precedence of && is higher than ||, but both operators are of lower precedence than all unary, arithmetic, and relational operators. Their associativity is left to right.

In the evaluation of expressions that are the operands of && and ||, the evaluation process stops as soon as the outcome *true* or *false* is known.

This is called *short-circuit* evaluation. Suppose that *expr1* and *expr2* are expressions. If *expr1* has zero value, then in

   expr1 && *expr2*

expr2 is not evaluated because the value of the logical expression is already determined to be 0. Similarly, if *expr1* has a nonzero value, then in

   expr1 || *expr2*

expr2 is not evaluated because the value of the logical expression is already determined to be 1.

Here are some examples in C++:

```
a + 5 && b        parenthesized equivalent is        ((a + 5) && b)
!(a < b) && c     parenthesized equivalent is        (((!(a < b)) && c)
1 || ( a != 7)    parenthesized equivalent is        ( 1 || (a != 7))
```

Note that the last expression always short-circuits to value 1.

Of all the operators in C++, the comma operator has the lowest precedence. It is a binary operator with expressions as operands. In a comma expression of the form

   expr1 , *expr2*

expr1 is evaluated first, and then *expr2*. The comma expression as a whole has the value and type of its right operand. An example would be

```
sum = 0, i = 1
```

If i has been declared an int, then this comma expression has value 1 and type int. The comma operator typically is used in the control expression part of an iterative statement, when more than one action is required. The comma operator associates left to right.

The conditional operator ?: is unusual in that it is a ternary operator. It takes as operands three expressions. In a construct such as

   expr1 ? *expr2* : *expr3*

expr1 is evaluated first. If it is nonzero (*true*), then *expr2* is evaluated and that is the value of the conditional expression as a whole. If *expr1* is zero (*false*), then *expr3* is evaluated and that is the value of the conditional expression as a whole. The following example uses a conditional operator to assign the smaller of two values to the variable x:

```
x = (y < z) ? y : z;
```

The parentheses are not necessary because the conditional operator has precedence greater than the assignment operator. Parentheses are good style, however, because they clarify what is being tested for.

The type of the conditional expression

expr1 ? *expr2* : *expr3*

is determined by *expr2* and *expr3*. If they are different types, then the usual conversion rules apply. The conditional expression's type cannot depend on which of the two expressions *expr2* or *expr3* is evaluated. The conditional operator ?: associates right to left.

C++ provides the following bit manipulation operators. They operate on the machine-dependent bit representation of integral operands.

Bitwise Operators	Meaning
~	unary one's complement
<<	left shift
>>	right shift
&	and
^	exclusive or
|	or

C++ uses the cast operator to perform explicit type conversion. Its forms are

(type) expression
type name (expression)

The second form looks like a functional notation and is not allowed in ANSI C. C++ has a lot to say about conversions (see Chapter 7).

C++ considers function call () and indexing [] to be operators. It also has an address & operation and an indirection * operation. The address operator is a unary operator that yields the address or location where an object is stored. The indirection operator is a unary operator that is applied to an object of type pointer. It retrieves the value from the location being pointed at. This is also known as dereferencing (see Chapter 3).

2.8 STATEMENTS

C++ has a large variety of statement types. It uses the semicolon as a statement terminator. C++ is an expression-oriented language. For example, in C++ the assignment statement and the procedure statement are each syntactically an expression followed by a semicolon. This means that they may be written any place in a program that an expression can legally appear.

ASSIGNMENT AND EXPRESSIONS

In C++ assignment occurs as part of an assignment expression. Let us consider a simple assignment expression.

```
a = b + 1;   //assign (b + 1) to a
```

The right-hand side of this assignment is evaluated and converted to a value compatible with the left-hand side variable. More generally, the left-hand side must be an *lvalue*, which is a location (in memory) where a value can be stored or retrieved. Simple variables are lvalues.

C++ compilers are flexible in the order in which they evaluate expressions; they may reorder expressions for optimization purposes. In practice the order of evaluation of C++ expressions can be guaranteed by using either the comma operator or statement termination. Both forms require that expressions be evaluated sequentially.

```
a = b() + e() * f();   //could be reordered
a = b(), t = e(), t = t * f(), a = a + t;   // fixed ordering
a = b(); t = e(); t = t * f(); a = a + t;   // fixed ordering
```

C++allows multiple assignment in a single statement.

```
y = z = 3.5;         is equivalent to      z = 3.5; y = z;
a = b + (c = 3);     is equivalent to      c = 3; a = b + c;
```

C++ provides assignment operators that combine an assignment and some other operator.

```
a += b;        is equivalent to    a = a + b;
a *= a + b;    is equivalent to    a = a * (a + b);
```

C++ also provides autoincrement (++) and autodecrement (--) operators in both prefix and postfix form. In prefix form the autoincrement operator adds 1 to the value stored at the lvalue it acts upon. Similarly, the autodecrement operator subtracts 1 from the value stored at the lvalue it acts upon.

```
++i;    is equivalent to   i = i + 1;
--x;    is equivalent to   x = x - 1;
```

The postfix form behaves differently than the prefix form by changing the affected lvalue after the rest of the expression is evaluated.

```
j = ++i;    is equivalent to   i = i + 1; j = i;
j = i++;    is equivalent to   j = i; i = i + 1;
i = ++i + i++;   // hazardous practice that is system dependent
```

Note that these are not exact equivalencies. The compound assignment operators evaluate their left-hand side expression once. Therefore, for complicated expressions with side effects, results of the two forms can be different.

The null statement is written as a single semicolon. It causes no action to take place. Usually you use a null statement when a statement is required syntactically but no action is desired. This situation sometimes occurs in statements that affect the flow of control.

THE COMPOUND STATEMENT

A compound statement in C++ is a series of statements surrounded by the braces, { and }. The chief use of the compound statement is to group statements into an executable unit. The body of a C++ function is always a compound statement. In C, when declarations come at the beginning of a compound statement, the statement is called a block. This rule is relaxed in C++, and declaration statements may occur throughout the statement list. Wherever it is possible to place a statement, it is also possible to place a compound statement.

THE *if* AND *if-else* STATEMENTS

The general form of an `if` statement is

> `if` *(expression)*
>   *statement*

If *expression* is nonzero (*true*), then *statement* is executed; otherwise *statement* is skipped. After the `if` statement has been executed, control passes to the next statement. For example,

```
if (temperature >= 32)
   cout << "Above Freezing!\n";
cout << "Fahrenheit is " << temperature << endl;
```

"Above Freezing!" prints only when `temperature` is greater than or equal to 32. The second statement is always executed. Usually the expression in an `if` statement is a relational or equality or logical expression.

Closely related to the `if` statement is the `if-else` statement. It has the general form

> `if` *(expression)*
>   *statement1*
> `else`
>   *statement2*

If *expression* is nonzero, then *statement1* is executed and *statement2* is skipped; if *expression* is zero, then *statement1* is skipped and *statement2* is executed. After the `if-else` statement has been executed, control passes to the next statement. Consider the following code:

```
if (x < y)
   min = x;
else
   min = y;
cout << "min = " << min;
```

If `x < y` is *true*, then `min` is assigned the value of `x`; if it is *false*, then `min` is assigned the value of `y`. After the `if-else` statement is executed, `min` is printed.

THE *while* STATEMENT

The general form of a `while` statement is

```
while (expression)
    statement
```

First *expression* is evaluated. If it is nonzero (*true*), then *statement* is executed and control passes back to the beginning of the `while` loop. This causes the body of the `while` loop, namely *statement*, to execute repeatedly until *expression* is zero (*false*). At that point control passes to the next statement. The effect of this is that *statement* can be executed zero or more times.

The following is an example of a `while` statement:

```
int  i = 1, sum = 0;

while (i <= 10) {
    sum += i;
    ++i;
}
```

The declaration initializes the value of i to 1 and the value of sum to 0. The `while` loop increments the value of sum by the current value of i and then increments i by 1. After the body of the loop has been executed ten times, the value of i is 11 and the value of the expression i <= 10 is 0 (*false*). Thus the body of the loop is not executed and control passes to the next statement. When the `while` loop is exited, the value of sum is 55.

THE *for* STATEMENT

The `for` statement is an iterative statement typically used with a variable that is incremented or decremented. For example, the following code uses a `for` statement to sum the integers from 1 to 10:

```
sum = 0;
for (i = 1; i <= 10; ++i)
    sum += i;
```

The construction

```
for (expression1; expression2; expression3)
    statement
next statement
```

is equivalent in C++ to

```
expression1;
while (expression2) {
    statement
    expression3;
}
next statement
```

provided that *expression2* is nonempty and a `continue` statement is not in the body of the `for` loop. From your understanding of the `while` statement, you can deduce the semantics of the `for` statement. First *expression1* is evaluated. Typically *expression1* initializes a variable used in the loop. Then *expression2* is evaluated. If it is nonzero (*true*), then *statement* is executed, *expression3* is evaluated, and control passes back to the beginning of the `for` loop again, except that evaluation of *expression1* is skipped. This iteration continues until *expression2* is zero (*false*), at which point control passes to *next statement*.

Any or all of the expressions in a `for` statement can be missing, but the two semicolons must remain. If *expression1* is missing, then no initialization step is performed as part of the `for` loop. If *expression3* is missing, then no incrementation step is performed as part of the `for` loop. If *expression2* is missing, then no testing step is performed as part of the `for` loop. The special rule for when *expression2* is missing is that the test is always *true*. Thus the `for` loop in the code

```
for (i = 1, sum = 0 ; ; sum += i++ )
    cout << sum << endl;
```

is an infinite loop.

THE *do* STATEMENT

The do statement can be considered a variant of the while statement, however, instead of making its test at the top of the loop, the do statement makes it at the bottom, as in the following example:

```
do {
   sum += i;
   cin >> i;
} while (i > 0);
```

Consider a construction of the form

```
do
    statement
while (expression);
next statement
```

First *statement* is executed, and then *expression* is evaluated. If it is nonzero (*true*), then control passes back to the beginning of the do statement and the process repeats itself. When the value of *expression* is zero (*false*), then control passes to *next statement*. For example, suppose we want to read in a positive integer, and you want to insist that the integer is positive. The following code accomplishes this:

```
do {
   cout << "\nEnter a positive integer: ";
   cin >> n;
} while (n <= 0);
```

The user is prompted for a positive integer. A negative or zero value causes the loop to be executed again, and the user must enter another value. Control exits the loop only after the user enters a positive integer.

TRANSFER STATEMENTS

C++ has several statements that transfer flow of control. C++ has the invidious goto statement, which, of course, we cannot recommend using unless it is unavoidable. The break and continue statements interrupt ordinary iterative flow of control in loops. In addition, the break statement is used within a switch statement. A switch statement can select among several different cases. The `return` statement is a transfer statement that exits a function call. It is discussed in Chapter 3, as it is contextually dependent on function call semantics.

THE *break* AND *continue* STATEMENTS

To interrupt normal flow of control within a loop, you can use two special statements:

`break;` and `continue;`

The `break` statement can be used in a `switch` statement as well as a loop. It causes an exit from the innermost enclosing loop or `switch` statement.

The following example illustrates the use of a `break` statement. A test for a negative value is made, and if the test is true, the `break` statement causes the `for` loop to be exited. Program control jumps to the statement immediately following the loop.

```
for (i = 0; i < 10; ++i {
   cin >> x;
   if (x < 0.0) {
      cout << "All done\n";
      break;      // exit loop if value is negative
   }
   cout << sqrt(x) << endl;
}
// break jumps to here
   . . .
```

This is a typical use of a `break` statement. When a special condition is met, an appropriate action is taken and the loop is exited.

The `continue` statement causes the current iteration of a loop to stop and the next iteration of the loop to begin immediately. The following code processes all characters except digits:

```
for (i = 0; i < MAX; ++i) {
   cin.get(c);
   if (isdigit(c))
      continue;
   . . .   // process other characters
// continue jumps to here
}
```

In this example, when the continue statement is executed, control jumps to just before the closing brace, causing the loop to begin execution at the top again. Notice that the continue statement ends the current iteration, whereas a break statement would end the loop.

A break statement can occur only inside the body of a for, while, do, or switch statement. A continue statement can occur only inside the body of a for, while, or do statement.

THE *switch* STATEMENT

The switch statement is a multiway conditional statement generalizing the if-else statement. Its general form is

> switch (*expression*)
>   *statement*

where *statement* is typically a compound statement containing case labels and optionally a default label. A switch usually is composed of many cases, and *expression* determines which, if any, of the cases get executed.

The following switch statement counts the number of test scores by category:

```
switch (score) {
case 9: case 10:
   ++a_grades; break;
case 8:
   ++b_grades; break;
case 7:
   ++c_grades; break;
default:
   ++fails;
}
```

A case label is of the form

case *constant integral expression* **:**

In a switch statement, all case labels must be unique. Typically the action taken after each case label ends with a break statement. If there is no break statement, then execution falls through to the next statement in the succeeding case or default.

If no case label is selected, then control passes to the default label, if there is one. A default label is not required. If no case label is selected and there is no default label, then the switch statement is exited. To detect errors, programmers frequently include a default, even when all the expected cases have been accounted for.

The keywords case and default cannot occur outside of a switch.

The effects of a switch can be summarized as follows:

The effects of a switch

1	Evaluate the integral expression in the parentheses following switch.
2	Execute the case label having a constant value that matches the value of the expression found in step 1, or, if a match is not found, execute the default label, or, if there is not default label, terminate the switch.
3	Terminate the switch when a break statement is encountered, or terminate the switch by "falling off the end."

THE *goto* STATEMENT

The goto statement is the most primitive method of interrupting ordinary control flow. It is an unconditional branch to an arbitrary, labeled statement in the function. The goto statement has the following form:

goto *label;*

The *label* is an identifier. In the following example control is unconditionally transferred to the statement labeled by error:

```
if (d == 0.0)
   goto error;
else
   ratio = n / d;
 . . .
error:  cerr << "ERROR:  division by zero\n";
```

Both the `goto` statement and its corresponding labeled statement must be in the body of the same function.

In general, the `goto` should be avoided. It is considered a harmful construct in most accounts of modern programming methodology and can undermine the useful structure provided by other flow of control mechanisms (`for`, `while`, `do`, `if`, and `switch`).

2.9 SUMMARY

1   A C++ program consists of declarations in possibly different files. Each function in the kernel language is on the external or global level and may not be declared in a nested manner. The files act as modules and may be separately compiled.

2   The function `main()` is the starting point for execution of the program. It obeys the C++ rules for function declaration.

3   C++ uses a preprocessor to handle a set of directives, such as the `include` directive, to convert the program from its preprocessing form to pure C++ syntax. These directives are introduced by the symbol #.

4   C++ relies on an external standard library to provide input/output. The information the program needs to use this library resides in the file *iostream.h*. The C community uses the standard library *stdio.h*, which is also available to the C++ programmer.

5   The required simple types in C++ are `double`, `int`, and `char`. Although C++ has no built-in `boolean` type, it uses the value zero to mean *false* and nonzero values to mean *true*. This usage is important in understanding the semantics of iterative and conditional statements.

6   C++ has expression statements, transfer statements, empty statements, compound statements, conditional statements, selection

statements, and iterative statements. C++ uses the semicolon as a statement terminator.

7   The general form of an if statement is

if (*expression*)
    statement

If *expression* is nonzero (*true*), then *statement* is executed; otherwise *statement* is skipped. After the if statement has been executed, control passes to the next statement.

8   The general form of a while statement is

while (*expression*)
    statement

First *expression* is evaluated. If it is nonzero (*true*), then *statement* is executed and control passes back to the beginning of the while loop. The effect of this is that the body of the while loop, namely *statement*, is executed repeatedly until *expression* is zero (*false*). At that point control passes to the next statement.

9   To interrupt normal flow of control within a loop, the programmer can use the two special statements

break; and continue;

The break statement can be used in a switch statement as well as in a loop. It causes an exit from the innermost enclosing loop or switch statement.

10   The goto statement is the most primitive method of interrupting ordinary control flow. It is an unconditional branch to an arbitrary labeled statement in the function. The goto statement is considered a harmful construct in most accounts of modern programming methodology and should be avoided.

2.10   EXERCISES

1   The examples in this text follow an implied "pretty printing" style, which requires one statement to a line, white space where needed to enhance readability, mneumonic identifier names for key variables, and a closing statement brace sitting under the beginning statement keyword. Use this style and add comments to create a readable version of the following *gcd* program:

```
//poorly written gcd function by anonymous
int foo (int q1, int q2){int q3; while(q2){q3=q1%q2;q1=q2;
     q2=q3;} return
  q1;}
```

2   Rewrite the *gcd* program with a `for` loop replacing the `while` loop.

3   Write a `main()` function calling `gcd()`. Ask the user to input two integers and compute and print the result. Have the program exit after computing five greatest common divisors.

4   Rewrite the *gcd program* to read a value for `how_many` greatest common divisors will be computed. The variable `how_many` will be used to exit the `for` loop.

5   On most systems, input can be redirected from a file. Assume that the *gcd* program has been compiled into an executable called *gcd*. The command

     gcd < gcd.dat

will take its input from the file *gcd.dat* and write the answers to the screen. Test this with a file containing

```
4   4 6   6 21   8 20   15 20
```

On most systems output can be redirected to a file. The command

     gcd > gcd.ans

will place its output in the file *gcd.ans*, taking its input from the keyboard. Enter the same data as above, and check the file *gcd.ans* to see that it has the four correct answers. The two redirections can be combined as follows:

gcd < gcd.dat > gcd.ans

This will take its input from the file *gcd.dat* and will place its output in the file *gcd.ans*. Test this on your system.

6   On an ASCII machine, the following `while` loop will print the letters *A* to *Z*:

```
ch = 'A';
while (ch <= 'Z') {
   cout << ch << "  is ASCII " << (int)ch << endl;
   ch++;
}
```

Write a program that will print both uppercase and lowercase. Rewrite your program using `for` loops. If you are running on a non-ASCII machine, modify the program to achieve a similar result.

7   Short-circuit evaluation is an important feature. The following code illustrates the importance of the feature in a typical situation:

```
// compute roots of a quadratic a * x * x + b * x + c
cin >> a >> b >> c;
discr = b * b - 4 * a * c;
if ((discr > 0) && (sq_disc = sqrt(discr))) {
   root1 = (-b + sq_disc) / (2 * a);
   root2 = (-b - sq_disc) / (2 * a);
}
else if (discr < 0) {
   //  complex roots
   . . .
}
else
   root1 = root2 = -b / (2 * a);
```

The sqrt() function would fail on negative values, and short-circuit evaluation protects the program from this error. Complete this program by having it compute roots and print them out for the following values:

```
a = 1.0, b = 4.0, c = 3.0
a = 1.0, b = 2.0, c = 1.0
a = 1.0, b = 1.0, c = 1.0
```

8   What will the following program print?

```cpp
#include    <iostream.h>

main()
{
    char      c = 'A';
    int       i = 3, j = 1, k = -2, m = 0;
    enum      boolean { false, true } p = false, q = true;

    cout << c << " is integer value " << (int)c
         << "   and !'A' is " << !c << endl;
    cout << "i = " << i << ", !i = " << !i << endl;
    cout << "!!i = " << !!i << ", !m = " << !m << endl;
    cout << "p = " << p << ", q = " << q << endl;
    cout << "!p = " << !p << ", !q = " << !q << endl;
    cout << "!(i + j) || m = " << (!(i + j) || m) << endl;
    cout << "q || (j / m) = " << (q || (j / m)) << endl;
    cout << "(j / m) || q = " << ((j / m) || q) << endl;
}
```

9   The following C program counts various characters found in an ASCII file. Write the program in file *count.c*. Compile the program and test it using redirection on the file *count.c*.

```
/* Count blanks, digits, letters, newlines, and others. */

#include   <stdio.h>

main()
{
   int   blank_cnt = 0, c, digit_cnt = 0,
         letter_cnt = 0, nl_cnt = 0, other_cnt = 0;

   while ((c = getchar()) != EOF)
      if (c == ' ')
         ++blank_cnt;
      else if (c >= '0' && c <= '9')
         ++digit_cnt;
      else if (c >= 'a' && c <= 'z' || c >= 'A' && c <= 'Z')
         ++letter_cnt;
      else if (c == '\n')
         ++nl_cnt;
      else
         ++other_cnt;

   printf("%10s%10s%10s%10s%10s%10s\n\n",
      "blanks", "digits", "letters", "lines", "others",
         "total");
   printf("%10d%10d%10d%10d%10d%10d\n\n",
      blank_cnt, digit_cnt, letter_cnt, nl_cnt, other_cnt,
      blank_cnt + digit_cnt + letter_cnt + nl_cnt + other_cnt);
}
```

The getchar() function reads in one character value from standard input. Note that on most systems the constant EOF has value -1. It is the system value read in when an end-of-file is encountered. In exercise 17, you will recode this to be independent of the ASCII codes.

10   Change the above code to use the *iostream.h* library. Many people prefer to continue to use *stdio.h* because it is very flexible and has many years of tested use. Its demerit is that it is not type-safe. The prototype for int printf(const char* cntrl_str, ...) uses the ellipsis variable argument list convention.

11   Change the above code to use a switch statement.

12 Use `sizeof` to determine the number of bytes each of the following requires on your local system: `char`, `short`, `int`, `long`, `float`, `double`, and `long double`. Also do this for the enumerated types:

```
enum boolean {false, true};
enum suit {clubs, diamonds, hearts, spades};
```

13 Write a program to convert from centigrade to Fahrenheit. The program should accept integer values and print integer values that are rounded. Recall 0° centigrade is 32° Fahrenheit. Also, 1° centigrade is 1.8° Fahrenheit.

14 Write a program that accepts either centigrade or Fahrenheit and produces the other value as output, for example, input: 0°C output: 32°F; input 212°F, output 100°C.

15 Simplify the following code:

```
for (sum = i = 0, j = 2, k = i + j;  i < 10 || k < 15; ++i,
     ++j, ++k)
  sum += (i < j)? k : i;
```

Remember that comma expressions are sequences of left-to-right evaluations, with each subexpression that is separated by a comma evaluated in strict order.

16 In the C world, more flexible file I/O is available using the `FILE` declaration and file operations found in *stdio.h*. The C++ community uses *fstream.h,* as discussed in Appendix D. Familiarize yourself with this library, and convert the program in exercise 6 to use *fstream.h*. The program should get its arguments from the command line, as in

gcd gcd.dat gcd.ans

17 Many of our character-based exercises and examples have assumed an ASCII encoding. Other coding schemes are in wide use, including IBM's EBCDIC codes. The standard library *ctype.h* can make character processing portable and independent of the encoding. Redo exercises 9 and 10 to use *ctype.h*. For a description

of *ctype.h*, see Appendix D. For example, the test on whether a character is a decimal digit becomes

```
    . . .
else if (isdigit(c))
   ++digit_cnt;
    . . .
```

3

FUNCTIONS AND POINTERS

This chapter continues the discussion of the kernel language, focusing on functions, pointers, and arrays. In C++ the function is a primary unit for structuring a program. Aggregate data in C++ are either arrays or structures. In both cases a pointer type is used as a mechanism for accessing such data.

3.1 FUNCTIONS

The method of *stepwise refinement* involves decomposing a problem into subproblems, each of which is either directly coded or further decomposed. *Function* constructs are used to write code for directly solvable subproblems. These functions then are combined into other functions and ultimately used in `main()` to solve the original problem. C++ provides the function mechanism to perform distinct programming tasks. Some functions, such as `strcpy()` and `rand()`, are provided by libraries. Others can be written by the programmer.

FUNCTION INVOCATION

A C++ program is made up of one or more functions, one of which is main(). Program execution always begins with main(). When program control encounters a function name, the function is called, or *invoked,* and program control passes to the function. After the function does its work, program control is passed back to the calling environment, which then continues with its work. As a simple example, consider the following program *ring,* which rings a bell:

```
// ring my bell using '\a' literal for the alarm.

#include <iostream.h>
const char BELL = '\a';

void ring()
{
   cout << BELL ;
}

main()
{
   ring();
}
```

3.2   FUNCTION DEFINITION

The C++ code that describes what a function does is called the *function definition.* Its form is

> *function header*
> {
>   *statements*
> }

Everything before the first brace comprises the *header* of the function definition, and everything between the braces comprises the *body* of the function definition. The function header has the form

> *type name(parameter declaration list)*

The *type* specification that precedes the function name is the *return type*. It determines the type of the value that the function returns, if any. The `return` mechanism is explained in the next section.

In the function definition for `ring()` above, the parameter list is empty, so there are no declarations of parameters. The body of the function consists of a single statement. Since the function does not return a value, the return type of the function is `void`.

Parameters are syntactically identifiers, and they can be used within the body of the function. Sometimes the parameters in a function definition are called *formal parameters* to emphasize their role as place holders for actual values that are passed to the function when it is called. Upon function invocation the value of the argument corresponding to a formal parameter is used within the body of the executing function. Such parameters in C++ are *call-by-value*.

To illustrate the use of parameters, let us rewrite the above program, giving `ring()` a formal parameter that specifies how many times the bell is rung.

```
// Repeated bell ringing.

#include <iostream.h>
const char BELL = '\a';

void ring(int k)
{
   int   i;

   for (i = 0; i < k; ++i)
      cout << BELL;
}

main()
{
   int   n;

   cout << "\nInput a small positive integer:   ";
   cin >> n;
   ring(n);
}
```

3.3   THE *return* STATEMENT

The `return` statement has two purposes: First, when a `return` statement is executed, program control is immediately passed back to the calling environment. Second, if an expression follows the keyword `return`, then the value of the expression is returned to the calling environment. This value must be assignment-convertible to the return type of the function definition header.

A `return` statement has one of the following two forms:

```
return;
```

```
return expression;
```

Some examples are

```
return;
return 3;
return (a + b);
```

Parenthesizing the `return` expression is an optional stylistic device that some programmers use to enhance readability.

As an example, the following program computes the minimum of two integers:

```
// minimum finding.

#include <iostream.h>

int min(int x, int y)
{
   if (x < y)
      return (x);
   else
      return (y);
}

main()
{
   int    j, k, m;

   cout << "\nInput two integers:   " ;
   cin >> j >> k;
   m = min(j, k);
   cout << m << " is the minimum of " << j << " and " << k << endl;
}
```

Here the function `min()` works with integer values. If instead we want it to work with values of type `double`, we would rewrite `min()` as follows:

```
double min(double x, double y)
{
   if (x < y)
      return (x);
   else
      return (y);
}
```

3.4   FUNCTION PROTOTYPES

A function can be declared before it is defined. It can be defined later in the file, or it can come from a library or a user-specified file. Such a declaration is called a *function prototype,* which has the following general form:

type name(*argument-declaration-list*);

The *argument-declaration-list* is typically a comma-separated list of types. This list can include argument identifiers. This information allows the compiler to enforce type compatibility. Arguments are converted to these types as if they were following rules of initialization. For example, it is possible to pass a `double` actual argument into an `int` argument. The `double` value will be truncated. Many compilers warn you when implicitly using a narrowing conversion. If a function has no arguments, then the keyword `void` may be used. In C++ the preferred style for an empty parameter list is *function_name*`()`.

In the following, we recode `main()`, from the program *ring*, to introduce the function prototype for `ring()`:

```
void    ring(int); //definition in file ring.c
main()
{
    int     n;

    cout << "\nInput a small positive integer:  ";
    cin >> n;
    ring(n);
}
```

The declaration of the function prototype informs the compiler that `ring()` must be used with a single integer argument and that it does not return a value when called.

In the last section the *minimum* program used the function `min()`. Its prototype in `main()` would be

```
int min(int, int);
```

Both the function type and the argument list types are explicitly mentioned. The definition of `min()` that occurs in the file must match this declaration. The function prototype can also include the identifier names of the arguments. In the case of `min()` this would be

```
int min(int x, int y);
```

C++ uses the ellipsis symbol to mean an argument list that is unspecified. For example, the prototype of the *stdio.h* function `printf()` is declared as

```
int printf(const char* cntrl_str, . . .);
```

Such a function can be invoked on an arbitrary list of actual parameters. This practice should be avoided because of loss of type safety.

3.5 DEFAULT ARGUMENTS

A formal parameter can be given a default argument, which usually is a constant that occurs frequently when the function is called. Use of a default argument saves writing in this default value at each invocation. The following function illustrates the point:

```
int sqr_or_power(int n, int k = 2)        //k = 2 is default
{
    if (k == 2)
        return (n * n);
    else
        return (sqr_or_power(n, k - 1) * n);
}
```

We assume that most of the time the function is used to return the value of n squared.

```
sqr_or_power(i + 5)      //computes (i + 5) * (i + 5)
sqr_or_power(i + 5, 3)   //computes (i + 5) cubed
```

Only the trailing parameters of a function can have default values, as shown in the following examples:

```
void foo(int i, int j = 7);               //legal
void goo(int i = 3, int j);               //illegal
void hoo(int i, int j = 3, int k = 7);    //legal
void moo(int i = 1, int j = 2, int k = 3); //legal
void noo(int i, int j = 2, int k);        //illegal
```

3.6 OVERLOADING FUNCTIONS

The usual reason for picking a function name is to indicate the function's chief purpose. Readable programs generally have a diverse and literate choice of identifiers. Sometimes different functions are used for the same purpose. The term *overloading* refers to using the same name for multiple meanings of an operator or a function. The meaning selected depends on the types of the arguments used by the operator or function. In this chapter we restrict our discussion to function overloading; operator overloading is discussed in Chapter 7 as it is used chiefly in the context of classes. As an example, consider a function that averages the values in an array of double versus one that averages the values in an array of int. Both functions are conveniently named avg_arr:

```
double avg_arr(const double a[], int size);
double avg_arr(const int a[], int size);

double avg_arr(const int a[], int size)
{
   int   sum = 0;

   for (int i = 0; i < size; ++i)
      sum += a[i];          //performs int arithmetic
   return ((double) sum / size);
}

double avg_arr(const double a[], int size)
{
   double   sum = 0.0;

   for (int i = 0; i < size; ++i)
      sum += a[i];          //performs double arithmetic
   return (sum / size);
}
```

The following code shows how each function is invoked:

```
main()
{
   int    w[5] = { 1, 2, 3, 4, 5};
   double x[5] = { 1.1, 2.2, 3.3, 4.4, 5.5};

   cout << avg_arr(w, 5) << "  int array average\n";
   cout << avg_arr(x, 5) << "  double array average\n";
}
```

The compiler chooses the function with matching types and arguments. The rules for performing this are called the *signature-matching algorithm* (see Chapter 7). The term *signature* refers to the list of types that are used in the function declaration.

3.7 INLINING

C++ provides the keyword `inline` to preface a function declaration when the programmer intends the code replacing the function call to be inline.

```
inline double cube(double x)
{
    return (x * x * x);
}
```

The compiler parses this function, providing semantics that are equivalent to a non-inline version. Compiler limits prevent complicated functions from being inlined.

Macro expansion is a scheme for placing code inline that would otherwise use a function call. The `#define` preprocessor directive supports general macro substitution, as in the following:

```
#define   SQR(X)    ((X) * (X))
#define   CUBE(X)   (SQR(X)*(X))
#define   ABS(X)    (((X) < 0)? -(X) : X)
    . . .
    y = SQR(t + 8) - CUBE(t - 8);
    cout << sqrt(ABS(y));
```

The preprocessor expands the macros and passes on the resulting text to the compiler. So the above is equivalent to

```
    y = ((t + 8) * (t + 8)) - ((((t - 8)) * (t - 8)) * (t - 8));
    cout << sqrt((((y) < 0)? -(y) : y));
```

One reason for all the parentheses is to avoid precedence mistakes, as would occur in the following:

```
#define  SQR(X)  X * X
    . . .
    y = SQR(t + 8); //expands to t + 8 * t + 8
```

Even so, such macro expansion provides no type safety, as is given by the C++ parameter passing mechanism. Note also that inline functions have internal linkage.

3.8 SCOPE

The kernel language has two principal forms of scope: file scope and local scope. Local scope is scoped to a block. A function body is a block that contains a set of declarations and parameters. File scope has names that are external or global. We will discuss class scope rules later on.

The basic rule of scoping is that identifiers are accessible only within the block in which they are declared. They are unknown outside the boundaries of that block. Here is a simple example:

```
{
    int a = 2;              // outer block a
    cout << a << endl;      // prints 2
    {                       // enter inner block
        int a = 7;          // inner block a
        cout << a << endl;  // prints 7
    }                       // exit inner block
    cout << ++a << endl;    // 3 is printed
}
```

Each block introduces its own nomenclature. An outer block name is valid unless an inner block redefines it. If redefined, the outer block name is hidden, or masked, from the inner block. Inner blocks may be nested to arbitrary depths determined by system limitations.

In C++, declarations can be internal to a block. In ANSI C, all block scope declarations occur at the head of the block.

```
//C++ but not C

int max(int c[], int size)
{
   cout << "array size is " << size << endl;
   int  comp = c[0];                   //declaration of comp
   for (int i = 1; i < size; ++i)   //declaration of i
      if (c[i] > comp)
         comp = c[i];
   return (comp);
}
```

In C++ the scope of an identifier begins at the end of its declaration and continues to the end of its innermost enclosing block.

Even though C++ does not require that declarations be placed at the head of blocks, it is frequently good practice to do so. Frequently blocks are small, and this provides a good documentation style where their associated use is commented on.

Declarations are placed within blocks to allow a computed or inputted value to initialize a variable and, especially for large blocks, to place declarations as close as possible to where they are used.

3.9   STORAGE CLASS

Every variable and function in C++ kernel language has two attributes: *type* and *storage class*. Native types were discussed in Chapter 2. The four storage classes are automatic, external, register, and static, with corresponding keywords

```
auto          extern          register          static
```

THE STORAGE CLASS *auto*

Variables declared within function bodies are by default automatic. Thus automatic is the most common of the four storage classes. If a compound statement contains variable declarations, then these variables can be acted on within the scope of the enclosing compound statement. A compound statement with declarations will be called a "block" to distinguish it from one that does not have declarations.

Declarations of variables within blocks are implicitly of storage class automatic. The keyword `auto` can be used to explicitly specify the automatic storage class, as in

```
auto int     a, b, c;
auto float   f = 7.78;
```

Because this storage class is automatic by default, the keyword `auto` is seldom used, however.

When a block is entered, the system allocates memory for the automatic variables. The variables with initializers are initialized. Most systems use some form of stack allocation for these variables. Within that block those variables are defined, and they are considered local to the block. When the block is exited, the system no longer reserves the memory that was set aside for the automatic variables. Thus the values of these variables are lost. This is easy to implement with a stack, where the space for these variables would be deallocated by resetting the stack top. If the block is reentered, the system once again allocates memory, but previous values are unknown. If a function definition contains a block, then each invocation of that function sets up a new environment.

THE STORAGE CLASS *register*

The storage class `register` tells the compiler that the associated variables should be stored in high-speed memory registers, provided it is physically and semantically possible to do so. Since resource limitations and semantic constraints sometimes make this impossible, this storage class defaults to automatic whenever the compiler cannot allocate an appropriate physical register. Typically the compiler has only a few such registers available. Many of these are required for system use and cannot be allocated otherwise.

When speed is of concern, the programmer may choose a few variables that are most frequently accessed and declare them to be of storage class `register`. Common candidates for such treatment include loop variables and function parameters. Here is an example:

```
{
    for (register i = 0; i < LIMIT; ++i) {
        . . .
    }
}
```

The declaration

`register i;`   is equivalent to   `register int i;`

If a storage class is specified in a declaration and the type is absent, then the type is `int` by default.

The storage class `register` is of limited usefulness. It is taken only as *advice* to the compiler. Furthermore, contemporary optimizing compilers are frequently more astute than the programmer.

THE STORAGE CLASS *extern*

One method of transmitting information across blocks and functions is to use external variables. When a variable is declared outside a function, storage is permanently assigned to it, and its storage class is `extern`. A declaration for an external variable can look just the same as a declaration for a variable that occurs inside a function or block. Such a variable is considered to be global to all functions declared after it, and upon block or function exit, the external variable remains in existence. Such variables cannot have automatic or register storage class, but they can be `static`, as explained in Section 3.9.

The keyword `extern` tells the compiler to "look for it elsewhere, either in this file or in some other file." Thus two files can be compiled separately. When `extern` appears in the second file, it tells the compiler that the variable is defined elsewhere, either in this file or in some other. The ability to compile files separately is important when writing large programs.

External variables never disappear. Since they exist throughout the execution life of the program, they can be used to transmit values across functions. They may, however, be hidden if the identifier is redefined. We can think of external variables as being declared in a block that encompasses the whole file.

Information can be passed into a function by using external variables or the parameter mechanism. Although there are exceptions, the use of the parameter mechanism is the preferred method. This tends to improve the modularity of the code, and it reduces the possibility of undesirable side effects.

Here is a simple example of external declarations used in a program that exists in two separate files:

```
//In circle.c

const double pi = 3.14159;   //local to circle.c

double circle(double radius)
{
   return (pi * radius * radius);
}

//In main.c
#include <iostream.h>

double circle(double);       //function is automatically extern

main()
{
   double x;

   . . .
   cout << circle(x) << "is area of circle of radius " << x;
}
```

On the ATT system this is compiled as *CC circle.c main.c*.

The `const` modifier causes `pi` to have local file scope. It cannot be directly imported into another file. When such a definition is required elsewhere, it must be further modified explicitly with the keyword `extern`.

THE STORAGE CLASS *static*

Static declarations have two important and distinct uses. The more elementary use is to allow a local variable to retain its previous value when the block is reentered. This is in contrast to ordinary automatic variables, which lose their value upon block exit and must be reinitialized. The second and more subtle use is in connection with external declarations.

As an example of the value-retention use of static, the following function maintains a count of the number of times it is called:

```
int f()
{
    static int called = 0;

    ++called;
    . . .
    return (called);
}
```

The first time the function is invoked, the variable called is initialized to zero. On function exit, the value of called is preserved in memory. Whenever the function is invoked again, called is *not* reinitialized. Instead, it retains its previous value from the last time the function was called.

The use of static in external declarations provides a privacy mechanism that is very important for program modularity. The term *privacy* refers to visibility or scope restrictions on otherwise accessible variables or functions. Static external declarations are visible only within the file in which they are defined. Unlike ordinary declarations, which can be accessed from other files, a static declaration is available throughout its own file but no other. Again, this facility is useful in developing private modules of function definitions, as in the following:

```
static int goo(int a)
{
    . . .
}

int foo(int a)
{
    . . .
    b = goo(a); //goo() is available here, but not in other files
    . . .
}
```

By external declarations, the author means those made at file scope (~~but it~~ as against those made inside blocks)

In C++ both external variables and static variables that are not explicitly initialized by the programmer are initialized to zero by the system. This includes arrays, strings, pointers, structures, and unions. For arrays and strings this means that each element is initialized to zero; for structures and unions this means that each member is initialized to zero. In contrast, automatic and register variables usually are not initialized by the system and can start with "garbage" values. Although some C++ systems do initialize automatic variables, we cannot rely on this.

LINKAGE MYSTERIES

Multifile programs require proper linkage. C++ requires some special rules to avoid hidden inconsistencies. As already indicated, a name declared at file scope that is explicitly `static` is local and hidden from other files. So are functions that are declared `inline` and variables declared `const`. A `const` variable that is at file scope but is not static can be given external linkage by declaring it `extern`. Finally, linkage to C code is possible using the form

```
extern "C" {    //code or included file }
```

Linkage to other languages beside C is system-dependent; for example, some systems might allow `"Pascal"` (also see Appendix C).

3.10 POINTER TYPES

C++ pointers are used to reference variables and machine addresses. They are intimately tied to array and string processing. A C++ array can be thought of as a special form of pointer associated with a contiguous piece of memory for storing a sequence of values that are indexible.

Pointers are used in programs to access memory and manipulate addresses. If v is a variable, then &v is the address, or location, in memory of its stored value. The address operator & is unary and has the same precedence and right-to-left associativity as the other unary operators. Pointer variables can be declared in programs and then used to take addresses as values. The declaration

```
int    *p;
```

declares p to be of type "pointer to int." The legal range of values for any pointer always includes the special address 0 and a set of positive integers that are interpreted as machine addresses on a particular system.

Some examples of assignment to the pointer p are

```
p = &i;                // the address of object i
p = 0;                 // a special sentinel value
p = (int *) 1507;      // an absolute address in memory
```

In the first example, we think of p as referring to i, or pointing to i, or containing the address of i. The compiler decides what address to assign the variable i. This varies from machine to machine and may even be different for different executions on the same machine. The second example is the assignment of the special value 0 to the pointer p. This value typically is used to indicate a special condition. For example, a pointer value of zero is returned by a call to the operator new when free storage is exhausted. It is also used to indicate the end of a dynamic data structure, such as a tree or list. In the third example, an actual memory address is used. The cast is necessary to avoid a type error.

ADDRESSING AND DEREFERENCING

The dereferencing or indirection operator * is unary and has the same precedence and right-to-left associativity as the other unary operators. If p is a pointer, then *p is the value of the variable that p points to. The direct value of p is a memory location, whereas *p is the indirect value of p, namely the value at the memory location stored in p. In a certain sense * is the inverse operator of &. Here is code showing some of these relationships:

```
int   i = 5, j;
int*  p = &i;         //pointer initialization to the address of i

cout << *p << " = i stored at " << p << endl;
j = p;        //illegal pointer is not convertible to integer
j = *p + 1;   //legal
p = &j;       //p points to j
```

SIMULATING CALL-BY-REFERENCE

When call-by-value is employed, variables are passed as arguments to a function, their values are copied to the corresponding function parameters, and the variables themselves are not changed in the calling environment. This call-by-value mechanism is strictly adhered to in C. In this section we describe how the *addresses* of variables can be used as arguments to functions so the stored values of the variables can be modified in the calling environment.

In C, for a function to simulate call-by-reference, pointers must be used in the parameter list in the function definition. Then, when the function is called, addresses of variables must be passed as arguments. As an example of this, let us write a simple program that orders the values of two variables:

```
#include <iostream.h>

main()
{
   int   i = 7, j = 3;
   void  order(int*, int*);

   cout << i << '\t' << j << endl;   // 7  3 is printed
   order(&i, &j);
   cout << i << '\t' << j << endl;   // 3  7 is printed
}
```

Most of the work of this program is carried out by the function call to order(). Notice that the addresses of i and j are passed as arguments. As we shall see, this allows the function call order(&i, &j) to change the values of i and j in the calling environment.

```
void order(int *p, int *q)
{
   int   temp;

   if (*p > *q) {
      temp = *p;
      *p = *q;
      *q = temp;
   }
}
```

DISSECTION OF THE *order ()* FUNCTION

■ `void order(int *p, int *q)`
```
{
   int    temp;
}
```

The parameters p and q are both of type pointer to `int`. The variable `temp` is local to this function and is of type `int`.

■ `if (*p > *q) {`
```
   temp = *p;
   *p = *q;
   *q = temp;
}
```

If the value of what is pointed to by p is greater than the value of what is pointed to by q, then the following is done: First, `temp` is assigned the value of what is pointed to by p; second, what is pointed to by p is assigned the value of what is pointed to by q; and third, what is pointed to by q is assigned the value of `temp`. This has the effect of interchanging in the calling environment the stored values of whatever p and q are pointing to.

Call-by-reference using pointers

1   Declare a function parameter to be a pointer
2   Use the dereferenced pointer in the function body
3   Pass an address as an argument when the function is called

3.11 REFERENCE DECLARATIONS AND CALL-BY-REFERENCE

Reference declarations are a new feature of C++. They allow a simpler form of call-by-reference parameters. Reference declarations such as the following declare the identifier to be an alternative name, or *alias,* for an object specified in an initialization of the reference:

```
int     n;
int&    nn = n;                    //nn is an alternative name for n

double  a[10];
double& last = a[9];               //last is an alias for a[9]

const char& new_line = '\n';       //anonymous initializer expression
```

Declarations of references that are definitions must be initialized. They usually are initialized to simple variables. The initializer is an lvalue expression, which is the object's (or the variable's) location in memory. In the above examples, the names n and nn are aliases for each other; that is, they refer to the same object. Modifying nn is equivalent to modifying n and vice versa. The name last is an alternative to the single array element a[9]. These names, once initialized, cannot be changed. Also, it is possible to initialize a reference to a literal. In the examples new_line is initialized to the char constant \n, which creates a reference to the otherwise unknown location where the literal is stored.

In the following examples, when the variable i, is declared it has an address and memory associated with it. When the pointer variable p is declared and initialized to &i, it has an identity separate from i. When the reference variable r is declared and initialized to i, it is identical to i; it does not have a separate identity from the other names for the same object, as seen in Figure 3.1.

```
int   i = 5;    //i is located in memory with rvalue 5
int*  p = &i;   //p is located in memory with rvalue &i
int&  r = i;    //r and i are the same object
int&* s = p;    //s and p are the same object
```

Notice that any change to the value of i is equivalent to changing r. Such a change affects the dereferenced value of p. The pointer p can be

memory cell	variable	value	alias
2000	i	5	r
2004	p	2000	s

FIGURE 3.1   Variables, Values, Pointers, and References

assigned another address and lose its association with i. However, i and r are aliases and within scope must refer to the same object.

These declarations can be used for call-by-reference arguments. This usage allows C++ to have *call-by-reference* arguments directly. This feature is *not* available in standard C.

The function order() using this mechanism is recoded as

```
void order(int &p, int &q)
{
    int    temp;

    if (p > q) {
        temp = p;
        p = q;
        q = temp;
    }
}
```

It would be prototyped and invoked in main() as follows:

```
main()
{
    void  order(int&, int&);
    . . .
    order(i, j);
    . . .
}
```

3.12   THE USES OF *void*

The keyword void is used both as the return type of a function not returning a value and to indicate an empty argument list to a function. Two additional uses are as a cast and as part of the type pointer to void.

As the type within the cast operator, it informs the compiler that the expression's computed value is to be discarded.

```
//Simple use of void.

#include <iostream.h>

int foo(int i)
{
   cout << "i is " << i;
   return (i);
}

main()
{
   int k = 5;

   (void)foo(k);   //throw away the int return value
}
```

Most interesting, however, is the use of void* as a generic pointer type. A pointer declared as type pointer to void, as in void* gp, can be assigned a pointer value of any underlying base type. But it may not be dereferenced. Dereferencing is the operation * acting on a pointer value to obtain what is pointed at. It would not make sense to dereference a pointer to a void value, as the following examples illustrate:

```
void* gp;      //generic pointer
int*  ip;      //int pointer
char* cp;      //char pointer

gp = ip;       //legal conversion
ip = (int*)gp; //legal conversion
cp = ip;       //illegal conversion
*ip = 15;      //legal dereferencing of a pointer to int
*ip = *gp;     //illegal dereferencing of a generic pointer
```

A key use for the void* type is as a formal parameter. For example, the library function memcpy is declared in string.h as

```
void* memcpy(void* s1, const void* s2, size_t n);
```

This function copies n characters from the object based at s2 into the object based at s1. It works with any two pointer types as actual arguments. The type `size_t` is defined in *stddef.h* and often is a synonym for `unsigned int`.

Note that there are two differences in the C++ use of `void` and the ANSI C use. First, in C++

`int foo();` is equivalent in C++ to `int foo(void);`

In ANSI C leaving a function declaration empty is backward-compatible to the traditional C function definition that did not require a list of argument types for a function prototype. In C++ the variable argument list signature must be specified by an ellipsis, as in

```
int scanf(const char*, . . .);
```

The second difference is that ANSI C allows the narrowing conversion from `void *` to an arbitrary pointer type. Looking back at the pointer assignments in the above example,

```
ip = gp; /* legal ANSI C without a cast */
```

3.13 ARRAYS AND POINTERS

Arrays are a data type used to represent a large number of homogeneous values. The elements of an array are accessed by the use of subscripts. Arrays of all types are possible, including arrays of arrays. Strings are just arrays of characters. A typical array declaration allocates memory starting from a base address. In C++ an array name is in effect a pointer constant to the base address.

To illustrate some of these ideas, let us write a small program that fills an array, prints out values, and sums the elements of the array:

```
#include <iostream.h>
const int SIZE = 5;

main()
{
   int   a[SIZE];       // space for a[0], . . ., a[4] is allocated
   int   i, sum = 0;

   for (i = 0; i < SIZE; ++i) {
      a[i] = i * i;
      cout << "a[" << i << "] =  " << a[i] << '\t';
      sum += a[i];
   }
   cout << "\nsum = " << sum << endl;
}
```

The output of this program is

```
a[0] = 0      a[1] = 1      a[2] = 4      a[3] = 9      a[4] = 16
sum = 30
```

This array required memory to store five integer values. Element zero is always the first element of a C++ array. Thus, if a[0] is stored at location 1000, on a system needing four bytes for an int, then the remaining array elements are successively stored at locations 1004, 1008, 1012, and 1016. It is considered good programming practice to define the size of an array as a symbolic constant. Since much of the code may depend on this value, it is convenient to be able to change a single initialization to process different size arrays. Notice how the various parts of the for statement are neatly tailored to provide a terse notation for dealing with array computations.

SUBSCRIPTING

Assume that a declaration of the form

```
int     i, a[size];
```

has been made. Then we can write a[i] to access an element of the array. More generally we can write a[*expr*], where *expr* is an integral expression, to access an element of the array. The expression *expr* is a subscript, or index, of **a**. The value of a C++ subscript should lie in the range 0 to *size* − 1. An array subscript value outside this range often causes a run-time error. This common programming error is called overrunning the bounds of the array or subscript out of bounds. The effect of the error in a C++ program is system-dependent and can be quite confusing. One frequent result is that the value of some unrelated variable is returned or modified. Thus the programmer must ensure that all subscripts stay within bounds.

INITIALIZATION

Arrays can be initialized by a comma-separated list of expressions enclosed in braces.

```
int array[4] = { 9, 8, 7}; //a[0] = 9, a[1] = 8, a[2] = 7
```

When the list of initializers is shorter than the size of the array, the remaining elements are initialized to zero. If uninitialized, external and static arrays are automatically initialized to zero. Not so for automatic arrays, which start with undefined values.

An array declared with an explicit initializer list and no size expression is given the size of the number of initializers. Therefore,

```
char laura[] = { 'l', 'm', 'p'};
```

is equivalent to

```
char laura[3] = { 'l', 'm', 'p'};
```

3.14 THE RELATIONSHIP BETWEEN ARRAYS AND POINTERS

An array name by itself is an address, or pointer value, and pointers and arrays are almost identical in terms of how they are used to access memory. There are differences, however, and these differences are subtle and important. A pointer is a variable that takes addresses as values. An array name is a particular fixed address that can be thought of as a constant pointer. When an array is declared, the compiler must allocate a base address and a sufficient amount of storage to contain all the elements of the array. The base address of the array is the initial location in memory where the array is stored; it is the address of the first element (index 0) of the array. Suppose we write the declaration

```
const int N = 100;

int    a[N], *p;
```

and our system causes memory bytes numbered 300, 304, 308, . . . , 696 to be the addresses of a[0], a[1], a[2], . . . , a[99], respectively, with location 300 being the base address of a. Assuming that each byte is addressable and that four bytes are used to store a int, the two statements

```
p = a; and p = &a[0];
```

are equivalent and assign 300 to p. Pointer arithmetic provides an alternative to array indexing. The two statements

```
p = a + 1; and p = &a[1];
```

are equivalent and assign 304 to p. Assuming that the elements of a have been assigned values, we can use the following code to sum the array:

```
sum = 0;
for (p = a; p < &a[N]; ++p)
    sum += *p;
```

is equivalent to

```
sum = 0;
for (i = 0; i < N; ++i)
    sum += a[i];
```

In this loop the pointer variable p is initialized to the base address of the array a. Then the successive values of p are equivalent to &a[0], &a[1], . . . , &a[N-1]. In general, if i is a variable of type int, then p + i is the ith offset from the address p. In a similar manner, a + i is the *i*th offset from the base address of the array **a**. Here is another way of summing the array:

```
sum = 0;
for (i = 0; i < N; ++i)
   sum += *(a + i);
```

Just as the expression *(a + i) is equivalent to a[i], so the expression *(p + i) is equivalent to p[i].

In many ways arrays and pointers can be treated alike, but there is one essential difference. Because the array **a** is a constant pointer and not a variable, expressions such as

```
a = p          ++a          a += 2
```

are illegal. We cannot change the address of **a**.

The basic rule of pointer arithmetic is that an address calculation depends on the size of the objects being referred to.

pointer value + sizeof(*type of pointer*) * i

On a system where long double is 8 bytes, and long double *p = &x, then the expression p + 1 is an address in memory 8 bytes after the address of x.

3.15 PASSING ARRAYS TO FUNCTIONS

In a function definition a formal parameter that is declared as an array is actually a pointer. When an array is being passed, its base address is passed call-by-value. The array elements themselves are not copied. As a notational convenience, the compiler allows array bracket notation to be used in declaring pointers as parameters. This notation reminds the programmer and other readers of the code that the function should be called with an array. To illustrate this, we write a function that sums the elements of an array of type int:

```
int sum(int a[], int n)      // n is the size of a[]
{
   int   i, s = 0;

   for (i = 0; i < n; ++i)
      s  += a[i];
   return (s);
}
```

As part of the header of a function definition the declaration

   `int a[];` is equivalent to `int *a;`

In other contexts they are *not* equivalent.

Suppose that v has been declared to be an array with 100 elements of type `int`. After the elements have been assigned values, we can use the above function `sum()` to add various elements of v. The following table illustrates some of the possibilities:

Various ways that sum() might be called

Invocation	What gets computed and returned
`sum(v, 100)`	`v[0] + v[1] + ⋯ + v[99]`
`sum(v, 88)`	`v[0] + v[1] + ⋯ + v[87]`
`sum(v + 7, k)`	`v[7] + v[8] + ⋯ + v[k+6]`

The last function call illustrates again the use of pointer arithmetic. The base address of v is offset by 7, and `sum()` initializes the local pointer variable a to this address. This causes all address calculations inside the function call to be similarly offset.

In C++ a function with a formal array parameter can be called with an actual array argument of any size, provided the array has the right base type.

3.16 STRINGS: A KERNEL LANGUAGE ADT

The C community has agreed to treat the type `char*` as a form of string type. The understanding is that strings will be terminated by the `char` value zero and that the *string.h* package of functions will be called on this abstraction. The language partly supports this abstraction by defining string literals as being null-terminated. A `char*` or `char[]` can be initialized with a literal string. Note that the terminating zero is part of the initializer list.

```
char* s = "c++"; // s[0] = 'c', s[1] = '+', s[2] = '+', s[3] = '\0';
```

The *string.h* package contains over 20 functions including the following:

- ■ `size_t strlen(const char* s);`
  Computes the string length. The number of characters before `0` is returned.
- ■ `char* strcpy(char* s1, const char* s2);`
  Copies the string s2 into s1. The value of s1 is returned.
- ■ `in strcmp(const char* s1, const char* s2);`
  Returns an integer that reflects the lexicographic comparison of s1 and s2. When the strings are the same, zero is returned. When s1 is less than s2, a negative integer is returned. When s2 is less than s1, a positive integer is returned.

   Most C programmers, when asked if C has a string type, answer yes. By adhering to the above conventions, the programmer benefits by being able to reuse lots of C string code. The library routines ensure that portable, readily understood code is available.

```
//string function implementations

size_t strlen(const char* s)
{
   for (int i = 0; s[i]; ++i)
      ;
   return (i);
}

int strcmp(const char* s1, const char* s2)
{
   for (int i = 0; s1[i] && s2[i] && (s1[i] == s2[i]); ++i)
      ;
   return (s1[i] - s2[i]);
}

char* strcpy(char* s1, const char* s2)
{
   for (int i = 0; s1[i] = s2[i]; ++i)
      ;
   return (s1);
}
```

Notice how two of these functions use the convention that a string is null-terminated to end major loops. The more subtle is strcpy(), which leaves its for loop when s2[i] == 0. Thus s1[i] is assigned each character from s2 in turn.

It is also good practice to place the const keyword in front of those strings whose contents will not be modified.

3.17 MULTIDIMENSIONAL ARRAYS

The C++ language allows arrays of any type, including arrays of arrays. Two bracket pairs indicate a two-dimensional array. This idea can be iterated to obtain arrays of higher dimension. Each bracket pair adds another array dimension.

Examples of declarations of arrays	Remarks
`int a[100];`	one-dimensional array
`int b[3][5];`	two-dimensional array
`int c[7][9][2];`	three-dimensional array

A k-dimensional array has a size for each of its k dimensions. If s_i represents the size of its ith dimension, then the declaration of the array allocates space for $s_1 \times s_2 \times \cdots \times s_k$ elements. In the above table, b has 3×5 elements and c has $7 \times 9 \times 2$ elements. Starting at the base address of the array, all the array elements are stored contiguously in memory.

Initialization of multidimensional arrays can be a brace enclosed list of initializers, where each row is initialized from a brace enclosed list.

```
int a[2][3] = {{1, 2, 3,}, {4, 5, 6}} ; //same as {1, 2, 3, 4, 5, 6}
char name[3][9] = { "laura", "michelle", "pohl"}; //pad with '\0'
```

3.18   FREE STORE OPERATORS *new* AND *delete*

The unary operators `new` and `delete` are available to manipulate *free store*—the system-provided memory pool for objects whose lifetime is directly managed by the programmer. The `new` and `delete` operators are more convenient than and can replace the standard library functions `malloc`, `calloc`, and `free` in most applications. The programmer creates the object by using `new` and destroys the object by using `delete`. This is important for dynamic data structures, such as lists and trees.

The operator `new` is used in the following forms:

> `new` *type-name*
> `new` *type-name initializer*
> `new` (*type-name*)

In each case there are minimally two effects. First, an appropriate amount of store is allocated from free store to contain the named type. Second, the base address of the object is returned as the value of the `new` expression. The expression is a pointer value of type *type-name*`*`. The operator `new` returns the value 0 when memory is unavailable.

The following example uses `new`:

```
int* ptr_i;
ptr_i = new int(5);    //allocation and initialization
```

In this code the pointer to `int` variable `ptr_i` is assigned the address of the store obtained in allocating an object of type `int`. The location pointed at by `ptr_i` is initialized to the value 5. This use is not usual for a simple type such as `int`; it is far more convenient and natural to automatically allocate an integer variable on the stack or globally.

The operator `delete` destroys an object created by `new`, in effect returning its allocated storage to free store for reuse. The operator `delete` is used in the following forms:

> `delete` *expression*
> `delete [] ` *expression*

The first form is used when the corresponding `new` expression does not allocate an array. The empty brackets in the second form indicate the original allocation was an array of objects. The operator `delete` does not return a value. Equivalently, one can say its return type is `void`.

The following example uses these constructs to dynamically allocate an array:

```
//Use of new operator to dynamically allocate an array.

#include <iostream.h>

main()
{
    int*  data;
    int   size;

    cout << "\nEnter array size: ";
    cin >> size;

    data = new int[size]; //allocate an array of ints
    for (int j = 0; j < size; ++j)
        cout << (data[j] = j) << "\t";
    cout << "\n\n";
    delete []data;          //deallocate an array

    data = new int[size];
    for (j = 0; j < size; ++j)
        cout << data[j] << "\t";
}
```

DISSECTION OF THE *dynamic* PROGRAM

■
```
int*  data;
int   size;

cout << "\nEnter array size: ";
cin >> size;

data = new int[size]; //allocate an array of ints
```

The pointer variable `data` is the base address of a dynamically allocated array whose number of elements is the value of `size`. The user is prompted for the integer-valued `size`. The `new` operator allocates storage from free store capable of storing an object of type `int[size]`. On a system where integers take 2 bytes, this would allocate 2 * `size` bytes. At this point `data` is assigned the base address of this store.

■
```
for (int j = 0; j < size; ++j)
    cout << (data[j] = j) << "\t";
```

This statement initializes the values of the `data` array and prints them.

■
```
delete []data;          //deallocate an array
```

The operator `delete` returns the storage associated with the pointer variable `data` to free store. This can be done only with objects allocated by `new`. The brackets form is used because the corresponding allocation was of an array.

■
```
data = new int[size];
for (j = 0; j < size; ++j)
    cout << data[j] << "\t";
```

This code accesses free store again, but this time it does not initialize the `data` array. On a typical system the same memory just returned to free store is used, with the old values reappearing. However, there are no guarantees on what values will appear in objects allocated from free store. Test this on your system. The programmer is responsible for properly initializing such objects.

This introductory discussion of the free store operators only treats the basic cases (see Section 6.10 for a more complete discussion).

3.19 SUMMARY

1   The C++ code that describes what a function does is called the function definition. Its form is

function header
{
     statements
}

Whenever variables are passed as arguments to a function, their values are copied to the corresponding function parameters, and the variables themselves are not changed in the calling environment. This is call-by-value. For a function to effect call-by-reference, pointers must be used in the parameter list in the function definition. Then, when the function is called, addresses of variables must be passed as arguments. In C++, reference declarations are available, allowing directly a call-by-reference mechanism.

2   In C++, a function cannot be used before it is declared. It can be defined later in the file, or it can come from a library or a user-specified file. A function prototype provides the type and number of arguments explicitly. It has the following general form:

     type   name(argument-declaration-list);

The *argument-declaration-list* is typically a comma-separated list of types. This list can include the argument identifiers. The information allows the compiler to enforce type compatibility.

3   A `return` statement is used to exit a function. If the form `return` *expression* is used, it must have an expression that is assignment-convertible to the function's return type.

4   Arrays are a data type used to represent a large number of homogeneous values. Array allocation starts with element zero. The elements of an array are accessed by the use of subscripts. Therefore, an array of *size* number of elements is indexed or subscripted

from 0 to *size* − 1. Arrays of all types are possible, including arrays of arrays. Strings are just arrays of characters. Conventionally, strings are terminated with the character value `'\0'`. A typical array declaration allocates memory starting from a base address. In C, an array name is in effect a pointer constant to this base address.

5   Every variable and function in C++ kernel language has two attributes: *type* and *storage class*. The four storage classes are automatic, external, register, and static, with corresponding keywords

```
auto        extern        register        static
```

Variables declared within function bodies are by default automatic.

6   C++ pointers are used to reference variables and machine addresses. C++ arrays can be thought of as a special form of pointer associated with a contiguous piece of memory for storing a sequence of values that are indexible. Pointers are used in programs to access memory and manipulate addresses. If v is a variable, then &v is the address, or location, in memory of its stored value. The declaration

```
int    *p;
```

declares p to be of type "pointer to `int`." The legal range of values for any pointer always includes the special address 0.

7   Reference declarations are a new feature in C++. They allow for the same object to be given an alias or alternate name. These declarations can be used for *call-by-reference* arguments. This usage allows C++ to have *call-by-reference* arguments directly. The function order() using this mechanism is declared as:

```
void order(int &p, int &q);
```

8   The declaration void* is a generic pointer type. A pointer declared as type pointer to void, as in void* gp, can be assigned a pointer value of any underlying base type. But it may not be dereferenced.

9   In a function definition, a formal parameter that is declared as an array is actually a pointer. When an array is being passed, its base address is passed call-by-value. The array elements themselves are not copied. As a notational convenience, the compiler allows the use of array bracket notation in declaring pointers as parameters.

This notation reminds the programmer and other readers of the code that the function should be called with an array.

10   The unary operators new and delete are available to manipulate *free store*. Free store is a system-provided memory pool for objects whose lifetime is directly managed by the programmer. The programmer creates the object by using new and destroys the object by using delete. This is important for dynamic data structures, such as lists and trees.

3.20   EXERCISES

1   C strings are by convention terminated with the value 0. The following function implements a string equality test. Note its use of pointer arithmetic. The construct *s1++ means dereference the pointer s1, and after using this value in the expression, add 1 to its pointer value.

```
int streq(const char* s1, const char* s2)
{
    while ( *s1 != 0 && *s2 != 0)
        if ( *s1++ != *s2++)
            return (0);
    return (*s1 == *s2);
}
```

Write and test a function

```
int strneq(const char* s1, const char* s2, int n);
```

that returns 1 if the first n characters of the two strings are the same and otherwise returns 0.

2   Reimplement the above functions using array notation.

```
int streq(char s1[], char s2[])
{
    int    i = 0;
    while ( s1[i] != 0 && s2[i] != 0)
        if ( s1[i++] != s2[i])
            . . .
}
```

3   The standard header file *string.h* contains the prototypes for a number of useful string functions found in the standard library. Among them is

```
size_t strlen(const char* s);
```

which returns the length of a string. The text gave a terse definition of this function; here is another way to code this function:

```
// iterative string length
size_t strlen(const char *s)
{
    size_t len = 0;

    while (*s != '\0') { // string terminator
        ++len;      // increment length
        ++s;        // advance pointer
    }
    return (len);
}
```

This algorithm marches the pointer s down the string looking for the termination character. External to the function, the pointer value has not been changed because it is called-by-value. Write a recursive version of this function.

4   The greatest common divisor of two integers is recursively defined as follows:

```
GCD(m,n) is:
    if m mod n equals 0 then n;
    else GCD(n, m mod n);
```

Recall that the modulo operator in C++ is %. Code this routine in C++.

5   The following code counts the number of recursive function calls by gcd(). It is generally bad practice to use globals inside functions. In C++, we can use a local **static** variable instead of a global.

```
int gcd(int m, int n)
{
    static int fcn_calls = 1;   //happens once
    int r;                       //remainder

    fcn_calls++;
    r = m % n;
    . . .
}
```

Complete and test this C++ version.

6   The following C program uses traditional C function syntax:

```
/* Compute a table of cubes. */

#include <stdio.h>        /* traditional IO */
#define  N     15
#define  MAX   3.5

main()
{
    int      i;
    double   x, cube();

    printf("\n\nINTEGERS\n");
    for (i = 1; i <= N; ++i)
        printf("cube(%d) = %f\n", i, cube(i));
    printf("\n\nREALS\n");
    for (x = 1; x <= MAX; x += 0.3)
        printf("cube(%f) = %f\n", x, cube(x));
}

double cube(x)
double  x;
{
    return (x * x * x);
}
```

It gives the wrong answers for the integer arguments, and it does
so because integer arguments are passed as if their bit represen-

tation were double. This is unacceptable as C++ code. Recode
as a proper function prototype and run using a C++ or ANSI C
compiler. These compilers enforce type compatibility on function
argument values. Therefore the integer values are properly promoted to double values.

7   Predict what the following program prints:

```
#include <iostream.h>

int foo(int n)
{
    static  int  count = 0;

    ++count;
    if ( n <= 1) {
        cout << " count = " << count << endl;
        return (n);
    }
    else
        foo(n / 3);
}

main()
{
    foo(21);
    foo(27);
    foo(243);
}
```

8   The `static` storage class is useful in multifile compilation. Predict what the following program prints:

```
// file A.c

static int foo(int i)
{
    return (i * 3);
}

int  goo(int i)
{
    return (i * foo(i));
}



// file B.c
#include <iostream.h>

int foo(int i)
{
    return (i * 5);
}

int  goo(int i);  // imported from file A.c

main()
{
    cout << "foo(5) = " << foo(5) <<endl;
    cout << "goo(5) = " << goo(5) <<endl;
}
```

The program is compiled as follows: *CC A.c B.c.*
File scope functions are by default `extern`. The `foo()` in file *A.c* is private to that file, but `goo()` is not. Thus redefining `foo()` in file *B.c* does not cause an error. Try this again, this time dropping `static`, to see what error message your compiler gives. Try this again, this time making `goo()` `inline` in *A.c*, to see what error message your compiler gives.

9   C++ provides a method to pass command-line arguments into the function `main()`. The following code prints its command-line arguments:

```
// Print command-line arguments rightmost first.
#include <iostream.h>

main(int argc, char **argv)
{
    for (--argc; argc >= 0; --argc)
        cout << argv[argc] << endl;
}
```

Compile this into an executable file called *echo*. Run it with the following command-line arguments:

echo A man a plan a canal panama

The argument `argc` is passed the number of command-line arguments. Each argument is a string placed in the two-dimensional array `argv`.

10   Modify the previous program to print the command-line arguments from left to right and to number each of them.

11   Although it is obscure and poor practice, the expression `i[a]` is legal and is equivalent to `a[i]` in ANSI C. Test whether this is the case in C++.

```
/* Works in ANSI C */
int a[10] = { 1, 2, 3, 4, 5, 6, 7, 8, 9, 10};

for (i = 0; i < 10; ++i)
    if (a[i] != i[a])
        printf("Not the same at index %d  : %d != %d\n",
        i, a[i], i[a]);
```

12   One advantage of C++ over traditional languages is type extensibility. You can import a complex number type with `#include <complex.h>` that can be mixed and matched with the native arithmetic types. Overload `complex avg_arr(const complex a[], int size)` and test its behavior.

13   The problem with using `void*` is that it cannot be dereferenced. Thus to perform useful work on a generic pointer you must cast it to a standard working type, such as a `char*`. Write and test the following program:

```
void* memcpy(void* s1, const void* s2, unsigned int n)
{
    char* to = s1;
    const char* from = s2;
    //copy uses char type
    . . .
}
```

14   Write a program that performs string reversal.

```
char* strrev(char* s1, const char* s2);
//s1 ends up with the reverse of the string s2
//s1 must point at enough store for reversal to work
```

15   Write a program that performs string reversal using storage allocated with `new`.

```
char* strrev(char*& s1, const char* s2);
//s1 ends up with the reverse of the string s2
//use new to allocate s1 adequate store strlen(s2) + 1
```

16   Write a program that allocates a single dimensional array from free store using a user provided lower bound and upper bound. The program should check that the upper bound exceeds the lower bound. If not, perform an error exit using the *assert.h* package as follows:

```
#include <assert.h>
. . .  //input lower bound and upper bound
assert(ub - lb > 0);
. . .
```

The size of this array will be (upper bound − lower bound + 1) elements. Given a standard C++ array of this many elements, write a function that uses the standard array to initialize the dynamic array. Test this by writing out both arrays before and after initialization in a nicely formatted style.

17   **Project**: Use *string.h* to produce a lexicographically ordered list of all the identifiers contained in an input file that is a C++ program. Each identifier will be read into a `char buffer[MAXLEN]`. After its length is ascertained store it permanently in array storage taken from free store pointed at by `char* id_list[i]`. Try as much as possible to have each function do one job. The design should be by *step-wise refinement*. Write a `get_id()` function that gets the next identifier from the file. You can use redirection so that `get_id()` can read from `cin`. Use standard library functions as much as possible. Also use *ctype.h* to avoid reliance on system dependencies in character encodings. Tokens that are not identifiers should be ignored, including keywords. Give consideration to eliminating redundant occurrences. In this context you should also add a frequency count for each identifier. Try to use a fast sorting routine. Finally, you may wish to write the package for use with command-line arguments. In this case you will want to use *fstream.h* for file processing (see Appendix D). A sophisticated package could take a series of input files and print out a list that names the file and line number in which each identifier occurs.

4

IMPLEMENTING ADT'S IN THE BASE LANGUAGE

This chapter introduces the reader to struct as used in the kernel language. User-defined data types, such as stacks, complex numbers, and card decks, are examples of ADT implementations. Each of these types is coded in C++ and used in a major example in this chapter.

A large part of the OOP design process involves thinking up the appropriate ADTs for a problem. Good ADTs not only model key features of the problem but also are frequently reusable in other code.

4.1 THE AGGREGATE TYPE *struct*

The structure type allows the programmer to aggregate components into a single named variable. A structure has components, called *members*, that are individually named. Since the members of a structure can be of various types, the programmer can create aggregates suitable for describing complicated data.

The following simple example defines a structure that describes a playing card. The spots on a card that represent its numeric value are called *pips*. A playing card, such as the three of spades, has a pip value, 3, and a suit value, spades. An enumeration type declares suit variables.

```
enum suit {clubs, diamonds, hearts, spades};

struct card {
   suit   s;
   int    pips;  // 1 <= pips <= 13 means A, 2, ..., J, Q, K
};
```

Like an enum declaration, a struct declaration can have a tagname. The tagnames are types. In the example declaration, struct is a keyword, card is the structure tagname, and the variables pips and s are members of the structure. The variable pips is restricted to integer values from 1 to 13, representing ace to king. This declaration creates the type card.

The declaration

```
card    c1, c2;
```

allocates storage for the identifiers c1 and c2, which are of type card. The structure member operator "." accesses the members of c1 and c2. To assign to c1 the values representing the five of diamonds and to c2 the values representing the queen of spades, we can write

```
c1.pips = 5;
c1.s = diamonds;
c2.pips = 12;
c2.s = spades;
```

A construct of the form

structure_ variable.member_ name

is used as a variable in the same way a simple variable or an element of an array is used. The member name must be a unique identifier within the specified structure. Since the member name must always be prefaced or accessed through a unique structure variable identifier, there is no confusion between two members from different structures having the same identifier. Structure variables have an initializer syntax similar to array initializers. The initializer values are in order of member declaration in the structure. Here is an example:

```
struct fruit {
    char    name[15];
    int     calories;
};

struct vegetable {
    char    name[15];
    int     calories;
};

fruit       a = {"banana", 150}; //aggregate initializer
vegetable   b = {"lettuce", 70};
```

Having made these declarations, we can access **a.calories** and
b.calories without ambiguity.

In general, a structure is declared with the keyword **struct** followed
by an identifier (tagname) followed by a brace-enclosed list of member
declarations. The tagname is optional but should be expressive of the ADT
concept being modeled. When the tagname is not present, the structure
declaration is anonymous and can be used only to declare variables of that
type immediately, as in

```
struct {
    int a, b, c
} triples[2] = {{3, 3, 6}, {4, 5, 5}};
//triple[0].a = 3, . . . . triple[1].a = 4, . . . triple[1].c = 5
```

4.2   STRUCTURE POINTER OPERATOR

We have already seen the use of the member operator "**.**" in accessing
members. C provides the structure pointer operator **->** to access the members of a structure via a pointer. This operator is typed on the keyboard as
a minus sign followed by a greater-than sign.

If a pointer variable is assigned the address of a structure, then a member
of the structure can be accessed by a construct of the form

   pointer_ to_ structure -> member_ name

An equivalent construct is given by

   (*pointer_ to_ structure).member_ name

The operators `->` and ".", along with `()` and `[]`, have the second highest precedence, and they associate left to right. In complicated situations the two accessing modes can be combined. The following table illustrates their use in a straightforward manner:

Declarations and assignments		
`card cd, *p = &cd;` `card deck[52];` `cd.pips = 5;` `cd.s = spades;` `deck[0] = cd;`		
Expression	**Equivalent Expression**	**Value**
`cd.pips`	`p -> pips`	5
`cd.s`	`p -> s`	spades
`deck[0].pips`	`deck -> pips`	5
`(*p).s`	`p -> s`	spades

typedef AND CASTING

As has already been mentioned, in C++ tagnames are types. In ANSI C this is not the case. This led to the practice in ANSI C of using `typedef` declarations to provide synonyms for such declarations.

```
typedef int   miles;     //miles is a synonym for int
typedef char*  string;    //string is a pointer to char
typedef void*  gen_ptr;  //generic pointer type
typedef enum boolean  boolean;  //usually unneeded in C++

typedef struct stack  stack;    //usually unneeded in C++
```

Besides providing a form of documentation, `typedef` declarations reduce complicated declarations to simple identifiers.

In the kernel language the operator *(type)* is called a *cast*. It explicitly orders the conversion of an expression to a value of the named *type*.

```
(boolean)i;          //converts i to false or true
(int)i/3.33333;      //the double expression is truncated
(int*)p;             //convert p to a pointer to integer
(char*)p;            //convert p to a pointer to char
(double*) i/3.3;     //makes no sense
```

It is the programmer's responsibility to make these conversions sensible.

C++ allows casts using functional notation, provided the type is expressed as a single identifier.

```
boolean(i);          //converts i to false or true
int(i/3.33333);      //the double expression is truncated
int* (p + 5);        //not a legal cast

typedef int* int_ptr;
int_ptr(p + 5);      //legal cast;
```

4.3   AN EXAMPLE: STACK

The stack is one of the most useful standard data structures. A stack is a data structure that allows insertion and deletion of data to occur only at a single restricted element, the top of the stack. This is the last-in-first-out discipline (LIFO). Conceptually it behaves like a pile of trays that pops up or is pushed down when trays are removed or added. Typically a stack allows as operations push, pop, top, empty, and full. The push operator places a value on the stack. The pop operator retrieves and deletes a value off the stack. The top operator returns the top value from the stack. The empty operator tests if the stack is empty. The full operator tests if the stack is full. The stack is a typical ADT.

To implement a stack as a C++ data type using `struct` in its kernel language form, one implementation choice is to use a fixed-length `char` array to store the contents of the stack. The top of the stack is an integer-valued member named `top`. The various stack operations are implemented as functions, each with an argument list that includes a pointer to `stack` parameter. This allows the stack to be modified and avoids call-by-value copying of the stack.

```
//A kernel language implementation of type stack.

const int max_len = 1000;
enum boolean {false, true};
enum {EMPTY = -1, FULL = max_len - 1};

struct stack {
   char s[max_len];
   int  top;
};
```

We now code a set of functions to implement standard operations on the stack:

```
//A standard set of stack operations.

void reset(stack* stk)
{
    stk -> top = EMPTY;
}

void push(char c, stack* stk)
{
    stk -> s[++stk -> top] = c;
}

char pop(stack* stk)
{
    return (stk -> s[stk -> top--]);
}

char top(stack* stk)
{
    return (stk -> s[stk -> top]);
}

boolean empty(const stack* stk)
{
    return (boolean)(stk -> top == EMPTY);
}

boolean full(const stack* stk)
{
    return (boolean)(stk -> top == FULL);
}
```

DISSECTION OF THE *stack* FUNCTIONS

```
const int max_len = 1000;
enum boolean {false, true};
enum {EMPTY = -1, FULL = max_len - 1};

struct stack {
   char s[max_len];
    int  top;
};
```

A new type `boolean` is declared. In C++ the tagname of an `enum` type is a new type. The const `false` is initialized to 0, and the constant `true` is initialized to 1. The `struct` declaration creates the new type `stack`. It has two members, the array member `s` and the `int` member `top`.

```
void reset(stack* stk)
{
   stk -> top = EMPTY;
}
```

This function is used for initialization. The member `top` is assigned the value `EMPTY`. The particular stack that this works on is an argument passed in as an address.

```
void push(char c, stack* stk)
{
   stk -> s[++stk -> top] = c;
}

char pop(stack* stk)
{
   return (stk -> s[stk -> top--]);
}
```

The operation *push* is implemented as a function of two arguments. The member `top` is incremented. The value of `c` is shoved onto the top of the stack. This function assumes that the stack is not full. The operation *pop* is implemented in like fashion. It assumes the stack is not empty. The value of the top of the stack is returned, and the member `top` is decremented.

```
■ boolean empty(const stack* stk)
  {
      return (boolean)(stk -> top == EMPTY);
  }

  boolean full(const stack* stk)
  {
      return (boolean)(stk -> top == FULL);
  }
```

These functions return an enumerated type boolean value. Each tests the stack member top for an appropriate condition. For example, before calling push() you can test that the stack is not full to ensure that push() will work correctly. These functions do not modify the stack being pointed at. Therefore you can declare the pointer arguments to be const. In all functions the stack argument is passed in as an address, and the structure pointer operator -> is used to access members. A cast is required here because an integer value cannot be assigned to an enumerated type; this is an instance of strong typing in C++. The cast could be avoided by using

```
■ return ((stk -> top == EMPTY)? true : false);
```

Given that these declarations reside in the file stack.h, we can test these operations with the following program, which enters the characters of a string onto a stack and pops them, printing each character out in reverse order:

```
//Test of stack implementation by reversing a string.

#include <iostream.h>
#include "stack.h"              //stack implementation

main()
{
    stack   s;
    char    str[40] = {"My name is Betty Dolsberry!"};
    int     i = 0;

    cout << str << endl;        //print the string
    reset(&s);
    while (str[i])              //push onto stack
        if (!full(&s))
            push(str[i++], &s);
    while (!empty(&s))          //print the reverse
        cout << pop(&s);
    cout << endl;
}
```

The output from this test program is

```
My name is Betty Dolsberry!
!yrrebsloD ytteB si eman yM
```

Note that one of the actual arguments to each function is &s, the address of the stack variable declared in main. This argument is given because each function expects an address of a stack variable.

4.4   UNIONS

A union is a derived type whose syntax is the same as for structures, except that the keyword union replaces struct. The member declarations share storage, and their values are overlaid. Therefore a union allows its value to be interpreted as a set of types that correspond to the member declarations. A union initializer is a brace-enclosed value for its first member. Consider the declaration

```
union int_dbl {
   int    i;
   double x;
} n = {0};    //i member is initialized to zero
```

The variable n can be used as either an integer type or a double type.

```
n.i  = 7;   // integer value 7 is stored in n
cout << n.i << " is integer. ";
cout << n.x << " is double -value machine dependent. ";
n.x  = 7.0; // double value 7.0 is stored in n
```

This example also illustrates why unions can be dangerous and are often system-dependent. On some systems it is possible that not all bit patterns are legal values for the overlaid types. In that case a legal value with one type but accessed as the other type could lead to an exception.

A union can be anonymous, as in

```
enum week { sun, mon, tues, weds, thurs, fri, sat };
union {
    int    i;
    week   w;
};


i  = 5;
if (w == sat || w == sun)
   cout << " Its the weekend! ";
```

allowing the individual member identifiers to be used as variables. The member names must be unique within scope and no variables of the anonymous type can be declared. Note that an anonymous union declared in file scope must be static.

Let us marry the stack example to a union of different types. The idea is that a stack is a data structure useful in storing any number of types of values. Such a stack can be used to process heterogeneous values in a LIFO manner.

```
// stack rewritten to contain many types

enum type { int_type, dbl_type, chr_type, str_type };

union rainbow {
    int    i;
    double x;
    char   c;
    char*  p;
};

struct data {
    type     t;
    rainbow d;
};

struct u_stack {
    data s[max_len];
    int  top;
};
```

The u_stack data structure is more flexible, but it extracts a price in additional storage required to keep type variable t stored for each item.

```
void reset(u_stack* stk)
{
    stk -> top = EMPTY;
}

void push(data c, u_stack* stk)
{
    stk -> s[++stk -> top] = c;
}

data pop(u_stack* stk)
{
    return (stk -> s[stk -> top--]);
}
. . .
```

The client of u_stack must keep track, using the member t, of what kind of value is stored in each stack element. In the homogeneous case where the client stays with a particular value such as an integer, we would see code such as

```
u_stack a, *pa = &a;
data x;
int  v = 49;

x.d.i = v;
push(x, pa);
   . . .
x = pop(pa);
v = x.d.i;
```

In the heterogeneous case the `type` member would be used, and switch statements would likely be needed, as in

```
x.d.i = v;
x.t = int_type;
push(x, pa);
   . . .
x = pop(pa);
switch (x.t){ //right type of value must be extracted
case int_type:
   v = x.d.i; //v an int
   break;
case dbl_type:
   y = x.d.i; //y a double
   break;
   . . .
}
```

This approach is error prone and clutzy. A mistake in the setting of t leads to hard-to-detect run-time bugs. The OOP extensions to C++ give us a range of options to do much the same thing in a safer and more convenient way.

4.5 COMPLEX NUMBERS

Many scientific computations require complex numbers. Let us write an ADT for complex numbers:

```
struct complex {
   double real, imag;
};

void assign(complex& w, double r, double i = 0.0)
{
   w.real = r;
   w.imag = i;
}

complex add(complex a, complex b)
{
   complex temp;

   temp.real = a.real + b.real;
   temp.imag = a.imag + b.imag;
   return (temp);
}

void    print(complex w)
{
   cout << "( " << w.real << " , " << w.imag << "i )";
}
```

Notice how the default argument is a convenient way to assign a `double` to a `complex`. In that case the convention is that the imaginary part is zero.

Using this package we can compute the addition of a real number and a complex number as follows:

```
double  f = 2.5;
complex w, x, z;

assign(x, 5.5, -3.2);   // x = 5.5 - 3.2i
assign(w, f);           // w = 2.5 - 0i
z = add(w, x);          // z = 8.0 - 3.2i
print(z);               // "( 8 , -3.2i )"  is printed
```

In exercises 8, 9, and 10, you will add further elements of complex arithmetic to this package. The traditional approach above is unsatisfactory in that it does not allow us to use conventional expression notation, such as

```
z = f + w;   //OOP allows + to be overloaded to act on complex
```

to specify the computation. The full OOP package allows the code to be "natural."

4.6   AN EXAMPLE: FLUSHING

We want to estimate the probability of being dealt a flush. A flush occurs when at least five cards are of the same suit. We simulate shuffling cards by using a random number generator to shuffle the deck. This is a form of Monte Carlo calculation. The program is written using structures to represent the needed data types and functionality.

```
//A poker calculation on flushing

#include   <iostream.h>
#include   <stdlib.h>        //for random number generation

enum suit {clubs, diamonds, hearts, spades};
typedef int pips;

struct card {
   suit s;
   pips p;
};

struct deck {
   card d[52];
};
```

Distinguishing deck as its own type is a design decision. We can develop the program as a set of routines purely acting on an array of cards. Conceptually a deck is more than just a collection of cards. It is 52 very specific cards, namely the full set of 13 clubs, diamonds, hearts, and spades. The choice of encapsulating 52 cards as a deck is of course a simulation of the problem domain.

```
pips assign_pips(int n)
{
    return (n % 13 + 1);
}

suit assign_suit(int n)
{
    return (suit(n / 13));
}
```

These two routines provide conversions from the domain integer into `pips` and `suit` values. Conversion functions are important in allowing new user-provided types the ability to cooperate with native and other preexisting user types. Later, in Chapters 6 and 7, we will see how to build such conversions into the behavior of a new type.

```
void assign(int n, card& c)
{
    c.s = assign_suit(n);
    c.p = assign_pips(n);
}

pips get_pip(card c)
{
    return (c.p);
}

suit get_suit(card c)
{
    return (c.s);
}
```

The function `assign()` maps an integer whose value is between 0 and 51 into a unique pair of `suit` and `pips` values. The value 0 becomes the ace of clubs, and the value 51 becomes the king of spades. The next two functions provide readable output for printing the deck.

```
void print_card(card c)
{
  cout << c.p;
  switch(c.s) {
    case clubs:
      cout << "C ";
      break;
    case diamonds:
      cout << "D ";
      break;
    case hearts:
      cout << "H ";
      break;
    case spades:
      cout << "S ";
  }
}

void print_deck(deck& dk)
{
    for (int i = 0; i < 52; ++i)
      print_card(dk.d[i]);
}
```

The remaining functions are used for shuffling and dealing the cards.

```
void   shuffle(deck& dk)
{
   card t;

   for (int i = 0; i < 52; ++i) {
      int k = rand() % 52;
      t = dk.d[i]; dk.d[i] = dk.d[k]; dk.d[k] = t; //swap two cards
   }
}

void deal(int n, int pos, card* hand, deck& dk)
{
   for (int i = pos; i < pos + n; ++i)
      hand[i - pos] = dk.d[i];
}

void   init_deck(deck& dk)
{
   for (int i = 0; i < 52; ++i)
      assign(i, dk.d[i]);
}
```

The init_deck() function calls assign() to map the integers into card values. The shuffle() function uses the library-supplied pseudo-random number generator rand() to exchange two cards for every deck position. Tests show that this gives a reasonable approximation to good shuffling. The deal function takes cards in sequence from the deck and arranges them into hands.

We now can use these functions to estimate the probability that a flush occurs when poker hands are dealt. The user can choose to deal between five and nine cards per hand.

```
main()
{
   card one_hand[9];                        //max hand is 9 cards
   deck dk;
   int  i, j, k, fcnt = 0, sval[4];
   int  ndeal, nc, nhand;

   do {
      cout << "\nEnter no. of cards in each hand (5-9): ";
      cin  >> nc;
   } while (nc < 5 || nc > 9);
   nhand = 52 / nc;

   cout << "\nEnter no. of hands to deal: ";
   cin  >> ndeal;

   init_deck(dk);
   print_deck(dk);
   for (k = 0; k < ndeal; k += nhand) {
      if ((nhand + k) > ndeal)
         nhand = ndeal - k;
      shuffle(dk);
      for (i = 0; i < nc * nhand; i += nc) {
         for (j = 0; j < 4; ++j)         //init suit counts to 0
            sval[j] = 0;
         deal(nc, i, one_hand, dk);      //deal next hand
         for (j = 0; j < nc; ++j)
            sval[one_hand[j].s] ++ ;     //increment suit count
         for (j = 0; j < 4; ++j)
            if (sval[j] >= 5)            //5 or more is flush
               fcnt++;
      }
   }
   cout << "\n\nIn " << ndeal << " ";
   cout << nc << "-card hands there were ";
   cout << fcnt << " flushes\n   ";
}
```

DISSECTION OF THE *flush* PROGRAM

- ```
  card one_hand[9];                    //max hand is 9 cards
  deck dk;
  int  i, j, k, fcnt = 0, sval[4];
  int  ndeal, nc, nhand;
  ```

These are variables allocated upon block entry when `main` is executed. The variable `one_hand` is an array of nine elements, the maximum hand size allowed. It stores dealt hands from the deck. The variable `dk` represents the deck and is automatically allocated. The number of cards dealt to each hand is stored as the variable `nc`, and the number of hands to be dealt is kept in the variable `ndeal`. The variable `fcnt` counts the number of flushes. The array `sval` stores the number of cards found in the hand of a particular suit value.

- ```
  do {
      cout << "\nEnter no. of cards in each hand (5-9): ";
      cin  >> nc;
  } while (nc < 5 || nc > 9);
  nhand = 52 / nc;

  cout << "\nEnter no. of hands to deal: ";
  cin  >> ndeal;
  ```

The program prompts for the number of cards to deal to each hand. The user must respond with a number between 5 and 9 in order to proceed. The number of hands that can be dealt with the deck is computed and put into the variable `nhand`. The program then prompts for the number of deals.

- ```
  init_deck(dk);
  print_deck(dk);
  for (k = 0; k < ndeal; k += nhand) {
      if ((nhand + k) > ndeal)
          nhand = ndeal - k;
      shuffle(dk);
  ```

The deck variable `dk` is initialized, and the deck is reshuffled each time through the main loop. The test to check whether the value of `ndeal`
  ```

has been exceeded ensures that the total number of hands dealt will not exceed the request if the total number of hands is not an even multiple of the number of hands per shuffle.

```
■ for (i = 0; i < nc * nhand; i += nc) {
    for (j = 0; j < 4; ++j)              //init suit counts to 0
      sval[j] = 0;
    deal(nc, i, one_hand, dk);           //deal next hand
    for (j = 0; j < nc; ++j)
      sval[one_hand[j].s] ++ ;           //increment suit count
    for (j = 0; j < 4; ++j)
      if (sval[j] >= 5)                  //5 or more is flush
        fcnt++;
  }
```

The array `sval` stores the number of cards of each suit and is initialized to zero for each hand. The function `deal()` deals a card hand into the array `one_hand`. The expression `one_hand[j].s` is the suit value of a particular card, for example, 0 if the card were a club. This then is the index of the array `sval` that counts suits. The variable `fcnt` counts the number of flushes dealt over all these trials. Since the number of trials equals `ndeal`, the expectation of a flush is `fcnt/ndeal`.

4.7   BIT FIELDS

A member that is an integral type can consist of a specified number of bits. Such a member is called a *bit field*, and the number of associated bits is called its *width*. The width is specified by a nonnegative constant integral expression following a colon. For example,

```
struct pcard {    //packed representation of card
   unsigned  s : 2;
   unsigned  p : 4;
};
```

The compiler attempts to pack the bit fields sequentially within memory. It is at liberty to skip to the next byte or word for purposes of alignment. Arrays of bit fields are not allowed. Also, the address operator & cannot be applied to bit fields.

Bit fields are used to address information conveniently in packed form. On many machines words are 32 bits, and bit operation can be performed in parallel. In this case bit manipulation is an implementation technique for sets that contain up to 32 elements.

```
struct word {
    unsigned w0:1, w1:1, w2:1, w3:1, w4:1, w5:1, w6:1, w7:1,
    w8:1, w9:1, w10:1, w11:1, w12:1, w13:1, w14:1, w15:1,
    w16:1, w17:1, w18:1, w19:1, w20:1, w21:1, w22:1, w23:1,
    w24:1, w25:1, w26:1, w27:1, w28:1, w29:1, w30:1, w31:1;
};
```

We can overlay word and unsigned within a union to create a data structure for manipulating bits.

```
//Simple representation of sets.

#include <iostream.h>

struct word {
    unsigned w0:1, w1:1, w2:1, w3:1, w4:1, w5:1, w6:1, w7:1,
    w8:1, w9:1, w10:1, w11:1, w12:1, w13:1, w14:1, w15:1,
    w16:1, w17:1, w18:1, w19:1, w20:1, w21:1, w22:1, w23:1,
    w24:1, w25:1, w26:1, w27:1, w28:1, w29:1, w30:1, w31:1;
};

union set {
    word      m;
    unsigned u;
};

main()
{
    set x, y;

    x.u = 0x0f100f10;
    y.u = 0x01a1a0a1;
    x.u = x.u | y.u; //set union
    cout << "element 9 = " << ((x.m.w9)? "true" : "false") << endl;

}
```

The set operation `union` is performed as a word parallel operation on most systems.

4.8   AN EXAMPLE: DYNAMIC ARRAYS

As discussed in Chapter 3, the kernel language does not allow general dynamic multidimensional arrays. Scientists, engineers, and others make heavy use of general two-dimensional arrays called *matrices*. It would be inconvenient to have always to write special routines for each possible row size declared. Such an abstraction can be implemented as follows:

```
// Dynamic arrays in two dimensions.
struct twod {
   double**  base;
   int       row_size, column_size;
};
```

The underlying data structure is very simple. The pointer `base` is a pointer to a pointer to `double`. The `base` pointer contains the starting address of an array of pointers, and each pointer is a starting address of a row of doubles (see Figure 4.1).

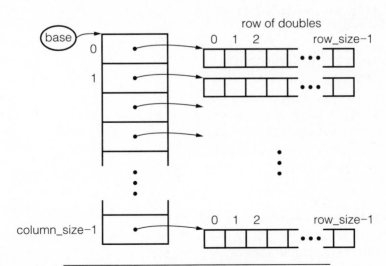

FIGURE 4.1   Dynamically Allocated `twod`

Allocation uses new to allocate first a vector of column pointers and second a row of doubles. Deallocation works in reverse order to allocation.

```
void allocate(int r, int s, twod& m)
{
   m.base = new double* [s];
   for (int i = 0; i < s; ++i)
      m.base[i] = new double[r];
   m.row_size = r;
   m.column_size = s;
}

void deallocate(twod& m)
{
   for (int i = 0; i < m.column_size; ++i)
      delete [] m.base[i];
   delete [] m.base;
   m.row_size = 0;
   m.column_size = 0;
}
```

allocate() and deallocate() are the heap or free store management routines.

```
double find_max(const twod& m)
{
   int     i, j;
   double max = m.base[0][0];

   for (i = 0; i < m.column_size; ++i)
      for (j = 0; j < m.row_size; ++j)
         if (m.base[i][j] > max)
            max = m.base[i][j];
   return (max);
}
```

find_max() is a canonical routine for processing such dynamic two-dimensional arrays. Notice in main() it is applied to different-sized dynamically allocated structures.

```
#include <iostream.h>

main()
{
  twod a, b;
  int i, j;

  allocate(2, 3, a);
  allocate(4, 6, b);
  for (i = 0; i < a.column_size; ++i)
    for (j = 0; j < a.row_size; ++j)
      a.base[i][j] = i * j ;
  for (i = 0; i < b.column_size; ++i)
    for (j = 0; j < b.row_size; ++j)
      b.base[i][j] = i * j ;

  cout << find_max(a) << " max in size 2 * 3 " << endl;
  cout << find_max(b) << " max in size 4 * 6 " << endl;
}
```

DISSECTION OF THE *dynamic_ array* PROGRAM

■ struct twod {
```
    double** base;
    int      row_size, column_size;
  };
```

The struct declaration creates the new type twod. The two-dimensional array has its base address stored in the member base. The row and column sizes also will be stored.

■ void allocate(int r, int s, twod& m)
```
  {
    m.base = new double*[s];
    for (int i = 0; i < s; ++i)
      m.base[i] = new double[r];
    m.row_size = r;
    m.column_size  = s;
  }
```

This function is used for run-time array allocation. First a column of pointer to `double` is allocated. Each of these pointers have the base address for a row of `double`s. This space is allocated off the heap iteratively using a `for` loop.

- ```
  void deallocate(twod& m)
  {
      for (int i = 0; i < m.column_size; ++i)
          delete [] m.base[i];
      delete [] m.base;
  ```

The deallocator works in reverse to the allocator. Each row is deallocated using `delete []`. It would be a mistake to deallocate `m.base` first, resulting in a system-dependent error. Only after each row of `double`s is returned to free store can the column of pointers represented by `m.base` be safely deleted.

- ```
  double find_max(const twod& m)
  ```

This function works on arbitrary two-dimensional arrays. It is not tied to a particular linear layout of memory, which would be the case for two-dimensional arrays declared automatically on the stack.

4.9   SUMMARY

1   A structure is a declaration with the keyword `struct`. It is a mechanism in kernel language for implementing ADTs, such as complex numbers and stacks.

2   The structure type allows the programmer to aggregate components into a single named variable. A structure has individually named components, called *members*. Critical to processing structures is the accessing of their members. This is done with either the member operator "`.`" or the structure pointer operator `->`. These operators, along with `()` and `[]`, have the highest precedence.

3   A union is a derived type whose syntax is the same as for structures, except that the keyword `union` replaces `struct`. The member declarations share storage, and their values are overlaid. Therefore a

union allows its value to be interpreted as a set of types that correspond to the member declarations.

4   A member that is an integral type can consist of a specified number of bits. Such a member is called a *bit field,* and the number of associated bits is called its *width.* The width is specified by a nonnegative constant integral expression following a colon.

5   The operator `new` can be used to create run-time determined two-dimensional (and higher) arrays. Functions using `new` can work regardless of row and column size.

4.10   EXERCISES

1   Design a C++ structure to store a dairy product name, portion weight, calories, protein, fat, and carbohydrates. For example, 25 grams of American cheese has 375 calories, 5 grams of protein, 8 grams of fat, and 0 grams of carbohydrates. Show how to assign values like these to the member variables of your structure. Write a function that, given a variable of type `struct dairy` and a given weight in grams (portion size), returns the number of calories for that weight.

2   Use `struct card`, defined in Section 4.1, to write a hand-sorting routine. In card games most players keep their cards sorted by pip value. Your routine will place aces first, kings next, and so forth, down to twos. A hand will be five cards.

3   The following declarations do not compile correctly. Explain what is wrong.

```
struct brother {
    char          name[20];
    int           age;
    struct sister sib;
} a;

struct sister {
    char           name[20];
    int            age;
    struct brother sib;
} a;
```

4   In this exercise use `struct stack`, defined in Section 4.3. Write
the function

```
void reverse(char s1[], char s2[]);
```

The strings `s1` and `s2` must be the same size. String `s2` should
become a reversed copy of string `s1`. Internal to `reverse`, use a
`stack` to perform the reversal.

5   Rewrite the functions `push` and `pop` from Section 4.3 to test that
`push` is not acting on a full stack and `pop` is not acting on an empty
stack. If either condition is detected, print an error message using
`cerr`, and use `exit(1)` (in *stdlib.h*) to abort the program.

6   For the `stack` type defined in Section 4.4, write

```
//push n chars from s1[1] onto the stack
void pushm(int n, const char s1[]);

//pop n chars from stack into char string
void popm(int n, char s1[]);
```

Hint: Be sure to put a terminator character into the string before
outputting it.

7   The anonymous union

```
static union {      //declared in file scope
    void* gen_ptr;
    int*  int_ptr;
    char* chr_ptr;
};
```

can be used in place of a cast. Write some code illustrating this. Is
this a good idea? What is the `sizeof` this type on your machine?

8   Add the routine `complex sub(complex& a, complex& b)` to the
complex number package from Section 4.5 and test it.

9   Add complex multiplication and division routines as well.

10   Add a routine that returns a `complex` when passed a `double`.
Use it to define `complex add(complex, double)` and `cerr`
`add(double, complex)`. Notice how this overloading of `add()`
provides a useful integration when mixing the two types `double`
and `complex`. The commutativity of addition makes it desirable to
have all these different overloadings.

11   Define the class **deque** to implement a double-ended queue. A double-ended queue allows push and pop at both ends.

```
//start with these declarations
struct deque {
    char s[max_len];
    int  bottom, top;
};

void reset(deque* deq)
{
    deq -> top = deq -> bottom = max_len / 2;
    deq -> top--;
}
```

Declare and implement push_t, pop_t, push_b, pop_b, out_stack, top_of, bottom of, empty, and full. The function push_t stands for *push on top*. The function push_b stands for *push on bottom*. The out_stack function should output the stack from its bottom to its top. The pop_t and pop_b functions correspond to *pop from top* and *pop from bottom*. An empty stack is denoted by having the top fall below the bottom. Test each function.

12   Extend the data type **deque** by adding a function **relocate**. If the **deque** is full, then **relocate** is called, and the contents of the **deque** are moved to balance empty storage around the center max_len / 2 of array s. Its function declaration header is

```
//returns true if it succeeds, false if it fails
boolean relocate(deque* deq)
```

13   Write a swap function that swaps the contents of two strings. If you pushed a string of characters onto a stack and popped them into a second string, they would come out reversed. In a swap of two strings, you want the original ordering. Use a **deque** to swap two strings. The strings will be stored in two character arrays of the same length, but the strings themselves may be of differing lengths. The function prototype is

```
void swap(char s1[], char s2[]);
```

14   Write a function **pr_hand** that prints out card hands. Add it to the *flush* program, and use it to print out each flush.

15   In Section 4.6 `main` detects flushes. Write a function

```
boolean isflush(const card hand[], int nc);
```

that returns `true` if `hand` is a flush.

16   Write a function

```
boolean isstraight(const card hand[], nc);
```

that returns `true` if `hand` is a straight. A straight is five cards that have sequential pip values. The lowest straight is ace, two, three, four, five, and the highest straight is ten, jack, queen, king, ace. Run experiments to estimate the probability that dealt cards will be a straight, and compare the results of five-card hands with results of seven-card hands.

    Hint: You may want to set up an array of 15 integers to correspond to counters for each pip value. Be sure that a pip value of 1 (corresponding to aces) is also counted as the high card corresponding to a pip value of 14.

17   Use the previous exercises to determine the probability that a poker hand will be a straight flush. This is a hand that is both a straight and a flush. It is the hardest poker hand to get and has the highest value. Note that, in a hand of more than five cards, it is not sufficient to merely check for the presence of both a straight and a flush to determine that the hand is a straight flush.

18   Write code for a three-dimensional dynamic array.

```
struct threed {
   double*** base;
   int      d1, d2, d3;
};
```

Test it by writing a `find_max(const threed&)` function.

19   Write code that works on one-dimensional arrays of arbitrary lower and upper bound.

```
struct bnd_array {
   double* base;
   int      lb, ub;
};
```

Write and test code to return an indexed element from such an array.

```
//return element of bnd_array a indexed by i
//you should assert or test that  lb <= i <= ub
double& element(bnd_array& a, int i);
```

20   Modify u_stack, defined in Section 4.4, to provide a simple encryption scheme. Read in strings as a series of four characters per word. (Note this implies that the union member c is changed to an array.) Place each four-character packet into the stack. Print out the stack as a series of integers. This scheme should work with four-byte ints. If your system has two-byte ints, then modify your declarations to appropriately perform a similar encryption algorithm.

21   *Tricky:* Use bit fields and write a deck-shuffling routine that, on your system, stores the deck in the fewest number of words. Try to make the shuffling of the deck both random and efficient. If you use six bits to store a card, then some of the bit patterns will be unused. Make sure that your routines uniquely generate 52 cards.

22   **Project:** This project is extremely open-ended. Write a poker-playing program that allows you to play against the machine. If possible use graphics to provide a reasonable display of the exposed cards.

A standard form of poker, such as five-card draw, should be implemented. The machine should be able to evaluate its hand and bet appropriately. The machine should be capable of bluffing, which involves betting that misrepresents its hand strength.

5

DATA HIDING AND MEMBER FUNCTIONS

We will use the term *client* to mean a user of an ADT. We will use the term *manufacturer* to mean the provider of the ADT. Honda is a manufacturer of a car called the Prelude. I bought and use a 1981 Prelude. I need to drive the Prelude, but am not concerned about the detailed internals of the steering mechanism. The car to me is a black box with certain capabilities. As a client, I want my car to work efficiently and provide me with all the services expected from a car, such as the ability to drive a reasonable number of miles on a tank of gas and to haul a certain amount of luggage in the trunk. The Prelude approximates an abstraction of "carness" that is satisfactory for my needs.

A client of an ADT expects an approximation to an abstraction as well. To be useful, a stack must be of reasonable size. A complex number must be of reasonable precision. A deck must be shufflable, with random outcomes in dealing hands. The internals of how these behaviors are computed is not a direct concern of the client. To be competitive with other providers, the manufacturer must, at reasonable cost and efficiency, compete in implementing a form of the ADT product. (See Figure 5.1.)

It is in the manufacturer's interest to hide details of an implementation. This simplifies what the manufacturer needs to explain to the client and it frees the manufacturer to engineer internal improvements that do not

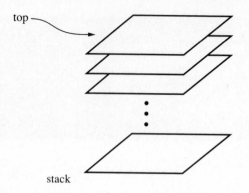

top

Client can expect
pop
push
reset

stack

Manufacturer can
choose representation
and implementation of operations

FIGURE 5.1   ADT Stack

affect the client's use. It keeps the client from dangerous and inadvertent tampering with the product.

Structures and ordinary functions allow the building of useful ADTs, but they do not support a client/manufacturer distinction. The client has ready access to internal details and may modify them in unsuitable ways. For example, a client of the last chapter's stack can extract an internal member of the array used to represent the stack. This violates the LIFO abstraction that the stack is implementing.

To avoid this tampering, OOP needs a data hiding mechanism. In C++ this is supported by the keyword `class` and associated access keywords `public`, `private`, and `protected`. In fact, the original name given by Stroustrup to his language was C with Classes. A `class` is an extension of the idea of `struct` found in C. It is a way of encapsulating a data type and associated functions.

In C++, structures may have member functions. Structures also can have parts of their descriptions `private`. Both of these extensions are described here. These extensions lead naturally to the `class` concept that, in effect, is a `struct` with a default visibility of `private`.

Allowing private and public visibility for members gives the programmer control over what parts of the data structure are modifiable. The private parts are hidden from client code, and the public parts are available. It is possible to change the hidden representation without changing the public access or functionality. The term *information hiding* is used in place of *data hiding* to emphasize that both data and function members can be hidden. If done properly, information hiding leads to more robust client code, because the client code need not change when the hidden representations of objects it depends on are modified.

5.1   MEMBER FUNCTIONS

The concept of `struct` is augmented in C++ to allow functions to be members. The function declaration is included in the structure declaration and is invoked by using access methods for structure members. The idea is that the functionality required by the `struct` data type should be directly included in the `struct` declaration. This improves the encapsulation of the ADT stack by packaging its operations together with its data representation. In OOP terminology a member function is a *method*.

Let us rewrite our stack example from Chapter 4 by declaring as member functions the various functions associated with the stack.

```
struct stack {
   //data representation

   char s[max_len];
   int   top;
   enum {EMPTY = -1, FULL = max_len - 1};

   //operations represented as member functions

   void    reset() { top = EMPTY; }
   void    push(char c) { s[++top] = c; }
   char    pop() { return (s[top--]); }
   char    top_of() { return (s[top]); }
   boolean empty() { return (boolean)(top == EMPTY); }
   boolean full() { return (boolean)(top == FULL); }
};
```

The member functions are written much as other functions. One difference is that they can use the data member names as they are. Thus the member functions in `stack` use `top` and `s` in an unqualified manner. When invoked on a particular object of type `stack`, they act on the specified member in that object. In OOP terminology an invocation is called *message passing*. In these terms a stack object receiving the message "pop" executes the pop method.

The following example illustrates these ideas. If two `stack` variables

```
stack data, operands;
```

are declared, then

```
data.reset();
operands.reset();
```

invoke the member function `reset`, which has the effect of setting both `data.top` and `operands.top` to `EMPTY`. If a pointer to `stack`

```
stack* ptr_operands = &operands;
```

is declared, then

```
ptr_operands -> push('A');
```

invokes the member function `push`, which has the effect of incrementing `operands.top` and setting `operands.s[top]` to `'A'`. One last observation: The member function `top_of` had its name changed from the previous implementation because of a naming conflict.

Member functions that are defined within the `struct` are implicitly inline. As a rule only short, heavily used member functions should be defined within the `struct`, as in the example just given. To define a member function outside the `struct`, the *scope resolution* operator `::` is used, as discussed in detail in Section 5.4. Let us illustrate this by changing the definition of `push` to its corresponding function prototype within the `struct` `stack`. We write it out fully using the scope resolution operator. In this case the function is not implicitly inline.

```
struct stack {
   //data representation

   char s[max_len];
   int  top;
   enum { EMPTY = -1, FULL = max_len - 1};

   //operations represented as member functions

   void reset() { top = EMPTY; } //implicitly inline
   void push(char c);            //function prototype
   . . .
};

   void stack::push(char c)      //definition, not inline
   {
       s[++top] = c;
   }
```

The scope resolution operator allows member functions from the different struct types to have the same names. In this case, which member function is invoked depends on the type of object it acts on. Member functions within the same struct can be overloaded. Consider adding to the data type stack a pop operation that has an integer parameter that pops the stack that many times before returning a value. It could be added as the following function prototype within the struct:

```
struct stack {
   . . .
   char pop(int n);           //declaration within stack
   . . .
};

char stack::pop(int n)         //definition at file scope
{
   while (n-- > 1)
      top--;
   return (s[top--]);
}
```

The definition that is invoked depends on the actual arguments to pop.

```
data.pop();                       //invokes standard pop
data.pop(5);                      //invokes repeated pop
```

The inline specification can be used explicitly with member functions defined at file scope. This avoids having to clutter the class definition with function bodies.

```
struct stack {
    . . .
    void reset();
    void push(char c);
    . . .
};

inline void stack::reset()
{
    top = EMPTY;
}

inline void stack::push(char c)
{
    s[++top] = c;
}

    . . .
```

The grouping of operations with data emphasizes their "objectness." Objects have a description and behavior.

5.2 VISIBILITY *private* AND *public*

The concept of struct is augmented in C++ to allow functions to have public, private and protected members. For now we should think of the protected keyword as a synonym for private. Its real use is bound up with inheritance (see Chapter 9). Inside a struct the use of the keyword private followed by a colon restricts the access of the members that follow this construct. The private members can be used by only a few categories of functions, whose privileges include access to these members. These functions include the member functions of the struct. Other categories of functions having access are discussed later.

The example of `stack` is modified to hide its data representation.

```
struct stack {
private:
   char s[max_len];
   int  top;
   enum {EMPTY = -1, FULL = max_len - 1};
public:
   void    reset() { top = EMPTY; }
   void    push(char c) { s[++top] = c; }
   char    pop() { return (s[top--]); }
   char    top_of() { return (s[top]); }
   boolean empty() { return (boolean)(top == EMPTY); }
   boolean full() { return (boolean)(top == FULL); }
};
```

The `main` function from Section 4.3 is rewritten to test the same operations.

```
main()
{
   stack  s;
   char   str[40] = {"My name is Don Knuth!"};
   int    i = 0;

   cout << str << endl;
   s.reset();                 //s.top = EMPTY; would be illegal
   while (str[i])
      if (!s.full())
         s.push(str[i++]);
   while (!s.empty())         //print the reverse
      cout << s.pop();
   cout << endl;
}
```

The output from this version of the test program is

```
My name is Don Knuth!
!htunK noD si eman yM
```

As the comment in `main` states, access to the hidden variable `top` is controlled. It can be changed by the member function `reset` but cannot be accessed directly. Also notice how the variable s is passed to each member function using the structure member operator form.

The struct stack has a private part that contains its data description and a public part that contains member functions to implement stack operations. It is useful to think of the private part as restricted to the implementor's use and the public part as an interface specification that clients may use. At a later time the implementor could change the private part without affecting the correctness of a client's use of the stack type.

Hiding data is an important component of OOP. It allows for more easily debugged and maintained code because errors and modifications are localized. Client programs need only be aware of the type's interface specification. As a rule of thumb, data members should be placed in the private part of a structure and accessed using member functions. Such an accessing discipline ensures that a client cannot tamper with or misuse the implemented ADT.

5.3 CLASSES

Classes in C++ are introduced by the keyword class. They are a form of struct whose default privacy specification is private. Thus struct and class can be used interchangeably with the appropriate privacy specification.

The following ADT for complex numbers uses struct.

```
struct complex {
    void    assign(double r, double i);
    void    print() { cout << real << "+" << imag; "i"; }
private:
    double real, imag;
};
void complex::assign(double r, double i = 0.0)
{
    real = r;
    imag = i;
}
```

Here is its equivalent class representation:

```
class complex {
   double real, imag;
public:
   void    assign(double r, double i);
   void    print() { cout << real << "+" << imag << "i"; }
};
void complex::assign(double r, double i = 0.0)
{
   real = r;
   imag = i;
}
```

Notice that the only difference is in the use of the keywords `public` and `private`. Also possible is

```
class complex {
private:            //one style is to make this explicit
   double real, imag;
public:
   void    assign(double r, double i);
   void    print() { cout << real << "+" << imag << "i"; }
};
```

It is our style to prefer `class` to `struct`, unless all members are to be treated as `public`.

5.4 CLASS SCOPE

Class adds a new set of scope rules to those of the kernel language (see Section 3.8). One point of classes is to provide an encapsulation technique. Conceptually it makes sense for all names declared within a class to be treated as within their own name space, distinct from either external names, function names, or other class names. This creates a need for the scope resolution operator.

SCOPE RESOLUTION OPERATOR ::

The scope resolution operator is new to C++ and is the highest precedence operator in the language. It comes in two forms:

```
::i          //unary operator - refer to external scope
foo_bar::i   //binary operator - refer to class scope
```

Its unary form is used to uncover or access a name that is at external scope and has been hidden by local or class scope.

```
int count = 0;   //external variable

void how_many(double w[], double x, int& count)
{
   for (int i = 0; i < N; ++i)
      count += (w[i] == x);
   ++ ::count;                    //keep track of calls
}
```

Its binary form is used to disambiguate names that are reused within classes. It will be vital to use with inheritance (see Chapter 9).

```
class widgets {public: void f();};
class gizmos  {public: void f();};

void f() { /* whatever */ }             //ordinary external f
void widgets::f() { /* whatever */ }    //f scoped to widgets
void gizmos::f() { /* whatever */ }     //f scoped to gizmos
```

One way of thinking about the scope resolution operator is to view it as providing a path to the identifier. No path is by default external. This is analogous to how structured directories work in naming files.

This qualification of name is not usually necessary within the class definition itself or when used with member selectors to call member functions, as seen in this continuation of the previous example:

```
widgets  w;
gizmos   g;

g.f();
w.f();
g.gizmos::f();     //legal and redundant
g.widgets::f();    //illegal widgets::f() cannot act on a gizmo
```

NESTED CLASSES

Classes can be nested. Nested classes, like nested blocks, have inner and outer nomenclature. The rules for nesting classes have changed from rules that existed in C. In C, nested `structs` were permitted, but the inside `structs` names were visible externally. This was conceptually illogical and has now been corrected.

The following nested classes illustrate current C++ rules:

```
char c;                 //external scope

class X {               //outer class declaration
   char c;
   class Y {            //inner class declaration
      char c;
      void foo(char e) { ::c = X::c = c = e; }
   };
};
```

In `class Y` the member function `foo`, when using `c`, references the variable `X::Y::c`. The three variables named `c` are all accessible using the scope resolution operator.

Furthermore, purely locally scoped classes can be created within blocks. These definitions are unavailable outside of their local block context.

```
void foo()
{
   class local { . . .} x;
   //  whatever
}


local y;  //illegal local is scoped within foo()
```

Notice that C++ gives you the ability to nest member functions using class nesting. This is a restricted form of function nesting. The member functions must be defined inside the local class and cannot be referred to outside this scope. As in C, ordinary nested functions are not possible.

5.5 *static* MEMBER

Data members can be declared with the storage class modifier `static`. A data member that is declared `static` is shared by all variables of that class and is stored uniquely in one place. Because of this it can be accessed in the form

> *class name* **::** *identifier*

provided it has public visibility. This is a further use of the scope resolution operator. A static member of a global class must be explicitly defined in file scope. Here is an example: *i·e, we cannot initialize it at the point of declaration.*

```
enum boolean { false, true};

class str {
   char            s[100];
public:
   static boolean  read_only;  //declared in class definition
   static int      count_strings;
   void            print();
   void            assign(const char*);
   . . .
};

int str::count_strings;        //defined
boolean str::read_only = false; //defined with explicit initializer
```

In our example str::read_only can be used to decide whether an object of type str is changed in value. The str::count_strings variable can be used to track how many str objects are in use. So,

```
str s1, s2, s3, s4;
str::count_strings = 4;
if (!str::read_only)
   s1.assign("Buzz Dolsberry");
```

is a means of conveniently maintaining a value common to the entire class.
   Note that classes defined within functions cannot have static members.

5.6   AN EXAMPLE: REVISITING FLUSHING

The flushing program of Chapter 4 can be rewritten using classes to represent the needed data types and functionality.

```
//A poker calculation on flushing

#include  <iostream.h>
#include  <stdlib.h>        //for random number generation

enum suit { clubs, diamonds, hearts, spades };
void print(suit);

class pips {
private:
   int  p;
public:
   void assign(int n) { p = n % 13 + 1; }
   int  getpip() { return (p); }
   void print() { cout << p; }
};

class card {
private:
   int  cd;                        //a cd is from 0 to 51
   suit s;
   pips p;
public:
   void assign(int n) { cd = n; s = suit(n/13); p.assign(n); }
   pips getpip() { return (p); }
   suit getsuit() { return (s); }
   void print() { p.print(); ::print(s); }
};

class deck {
private:
   card d[52];
public:
   void init_deck();
   void shuffle();
   void deal(int, int, card*);
   void print();
};
```

The clustering of member functions and the data members they act on causes improved modularity as compared to the kernel language treatment of Section 4.6. Behavior and description are logically grouped together.

```
void print(suit s)
{
    switch (s) {
    case clubs:
        cout << "C";
        break;
    case diamonds:
        cout << "D";
        break;
    case hearts:
        cout << "H";
        break;
    case spades:
        cout << "S";
    }
}

void  deck::print()
{
    cout << "DECK AS SHUFFLED";
    for (int i = 0; i < 52; ++i) {
        if ( i % 13 == 0)
            cout << endl;
        d[i].print();
    }
}
```

Each level of declaration hides the complexity of the previous level.

```
void  deck::init_deck()
{
   for (int i = 0; i < 52; ++i)
      d[i].assign(i);
}

void  deck::shuffle()
{
   for (int i = 0; i < 52; ++i) {
      int k = rand() % 52;
      card t = d[i]; d[i] = d[k]; d[k] = t; //swap two cards
   }
}

void deck::deal(int n, int pos, card* hand)
{
   for (int i = pos; i < pos + n; ++i)
      hand[i - pos] = d[i];
}
```

The parallel to the functions in Section 4.6 is obvious. The init_deck function calls card::assign to map the integers into card values. The shuffle function uses the library-supplied pseudo-random number generator rand to exchange two cards for every deck position. The deal function takes cards in sequence from the deck and arranges them into hands.

```
main()
{
   . . .

   dk.init_deck();
   dk.print();
   . . .
      dk.shuffle();
      . . .
         for (j = 0; j < nc; ++j)
            sval[one_hand[j].getsuit()]++ ;    //increment suit count
   . . .
}
```

5.7   THE *this* POINTER

The keyword `this` denotes an implicitly declared self-referential pointer. It can *only* be used in a non-static member function. Self-referentiality does not change the fact that `this` is a pointer. Therefore,

- `this -> ` *member name* points at a member object.
- `*this` is the actual total object and, depending on context, can be an lvalue or an rvalue.
- `this` is the address of the object being pointed at.

A simple illustration of its use is as follows:

```
// Use of the this pointer

#include <iostream.h>

class c_pair {
   char      c1, c2;
public:
   void init(char b) { c2 = b; c1 = 1 + b; }
   c_pair& increment() { c1++; c2++; return (*this); }
   void* where_am_I() { return (this); }
   void print() { cout << c1 << c2 << "\t"; }
};

main()
{
   c_pair   a, b, c;

   a.init('A');
   b.init('B');
   c.init('D');
   a.print();
   cout << " is at " << a.where_am_I() << endl;
   b.print();
   cout << " is at " << b.where_am_I() << endl;
   c.increment().print();
   cout << " is at " << c.where_am_I() << endl;
}
```

The member function increment uses the implicitly provided pointer this to return the newly incremented value of both c1 and c2. The member function where_am_I returns the address of the given object. The this keyword provides for a built-in self-referential pointer. It is as if c_pair implicitly declared the private member c_pair* const this.

It is poor practice to attempt to modify the this by casting or other means. Early C++ systems allowed memory management for objects to be controlled by assignment to the this pointer. Such code is obsolete because the this pointer is currently defined as non-modifiable.

5.8   *static* AND *const* MEMBER FUNCTIONS

C++ allows static and const member functions. Their implementations can be understood in terms of this pointer access. An ordinary member function invoked as

```
object.mem(i, j, k);
```

has an explicit argument list i, j, k and an implicit argument list that consists of the members of object. The implicit arguments can be thought of as a list of arguments accessible through the this pointer. In contrast, a static member function cannot access any of the members using the this pointer. A const member function cannot modify its implicit arguments. The following example illustrates these differences:

```
//Salary calculation using
//static and constant member functions.

#include <iostream.h>

class salary   {
    int        b_sal;
    int        your_bonus;
    static int all_bonus;  //declaration
public:
    init(int b) { b_sal = b; }
    void calc_bonus(double perc) { your_bonus = b_sal * perc; }
    static void reset_all(int p) { all_bonus = p; }
    int comp_tot() const
          { return (b_sal + your_bonus + all_bonus); }
};

int salary::all_bonus = 100; //definition

main()
{
    salary w1, w2;

    w1.init(1000);
    w2.init(2000);

    w1.calc_bonus(0.2);
    w2.calc_bonus(0.15);
    salary::reset_all(400);
    cout << " w1 " << w1.comp_tot() << " w2 " << w2.comp_tot() <<
          endl;
}
```

DISSECTION OF THE *salary* PROGRAM

■ class salary {
    int   b_sal;
    int   your_bonus;
    static int all_bonus; //declaration

There are three private data members. The `static` member `all_bonus` requires a file scope definition. It can exist independently of any specific variables of type `salary` being declared.

■ `static void reset_all(int p) { all_bonus = p; }`

The modifier `static` comes before the function return type. The `static` member can also be referred to as

`salary::all_bonus`

■ `int comp_tot() const`
    `{ return (b_sal + your_bonus + all_bonus); }`

The `const` modifier comes between the end of the argument list and the front of the code body. It indicates that no data member will have its value changed. As such it makes the code more robust. In effect it means that the self-referential pointer is passed as `const salary* const this`.

■ `salary::reset_all(400);`

A `static` member function can be invoked using the scope resolution operator. It could also have been invoked as

`w1.reset_all(400);`

but this is misleading, because there is nothing special about using the class variable `w1`.

5.9 CONTAINERS AND ITEM ACCESS

Container classes such as stacks and two-dimensional dynamic arrays are very useful data types. The `twod` code from Chapter 4 can be repackaged as a class, and the ability to access and modify individual elements of these objects can be added.

```
// Dynamic arrays in two dimensions.
enum boolean { false, true};

class twod {
private:
   double**  base;
   int       row_size, column_size;
public:
   boolean allocate(int r, int s);   //foreshadows constructors
   void    deallocate();             //foreshadows destructors
   double& element_lval(int i, int j) { return (base[i][j]); }
   double  element_rval(int i, int j) { return (base[i][j]); }
   int     r_size() { return (row_size); }
   int     c_size() { return (column_size); }
};

boolean twod::allocate(int r, int s)
{
   base = new double*[s];
   if (base == 0)  //allocation failed
      return (false);
   for (int i = 0; i < s; ++i) {
      base[i] = new double[r];
      if (base[i] == 0)  //allocation failed
          return (false);
   }
   row_size = r;
   column_size = s;
   return (true);
}

void twod::deallocate()
{
   for (int i = 0; i < s; ++i)
      delete [] base[i];
   delete [] base;
   row_size = 0;
   column_size = 0;
}
```

Notice how this form of twod hides internal representation. The member functions, by acting implicitly on an object, require one less parameter than the corresponding nonmember function implementation. Of course the argument is still present, but it is passed using the this pointer. The job of allocation is so crucial to manufacturing objects that a special member function category called *constructor* is available (see Chapter 6).

Two nearly identical member functions, element_lval and element_rval, are defined. The difference is in the return type. The return type double& requires that an alias to the named object be returned. The return type double requires that the value stored in the object be returned. This implies that

```
twod m;
m.allocate(5, 10);

m.element_lval(1, 1) = 5;     //okay store 5 in m.base[1][1]
m.element_rval(2, 2) = 6.5;   //illegal assignment to an rvalue
cout << (m.element_rval(1, 1) == m.element_lval(1, 1)); //okay
```

We can write a find_max() function that finds the largest element value in a two-dimensional object.

```
double find_max(const twod& m)
{
   int     i, j;
   double max = m.element_rval(0,0);

   for (i = 0; i < m.c_size(); ++i)
      for (j = 0; j < m.r_size(); ++j)
       if (m.element_rval(i, j) > max)
            max = m.element_rval(i, j);
   return (max);
}
```

Notice that element_lval() could have been used as well. Now let us write an algorithm that produces a transpose of a two-dimensional matrix.

```
void transpose(twod& m)
{
    int     i, j;
    double temp;

    for (i = 0; i < m.c_size() - 1 ; ++i)
        for (j = i + 1; j < m.r_size(); ++j) {
            temp = m.element_lval(i, j);
            m.element_lval(i, j) = m.element_lval(j, i);
            m.element_lval(j, i) = temp;
        }
}
```

Because it manipulates values stored in elements of the container object m, this algorithm makes use of *lvalues*.

5.10 SUMMARY

1   The original name given by Stroustrup to his language was C with Classes. A class is an extension of the idea of struct in traditional C. It is a way of implementing a data type and associated functions and operators. It also is the mechanism in C++ for implementing ADTs, such as complex numbers and stacks.

2   The concept of struct is augmented in C++ to allow functions to be members. In OOP terminology a member function is called a *method* and invoking it on a class object is called *message passing*. The function declaration is included in the structure declaration and is invoked by using access methods for structure members.

The idea is that the functionality required by the struct data type should be directly included in the struct declaration.

3   Member functions that are defined within the struct are implicitly inline. As a rule only short, heavily used member functions should be defined within the struct. To define a member function outside the struct, the scope resolution operator is used.

4   The scope resolution operator allows member functions from the different struct types to have the same names. Which member function is invoked depends on the type of object it acts on. Member functions within the same struct can be overloaded.

5   The concept of `struct` is augmented in C++ to allow functions to have `public` and `private` members. This provides *data hiding* or *information hiding*. Inside a `struct` the use of the keyword `private` followed by a colon restricts the scope of the members that follow this construct. The `private` members can be used by only a few categories of functions whose privileges include access to these members. These functions include the member functions of the `struct`.

6   Classes in C++ are introduced by the keyword `class`. They are a form of `struct` whose default privacy specification is `private`. Thus `struct` and `class` can be used interchangeably with the appropriate privacy specification.

7   Data members can be declared with the storage class modifier `static`. A data member that is declared `static` is shared by all variables of that class and is stored uniquely in one place. Because of this it can be accessed in the form

   class name `::` *identifier*

8   Classes can be nested. The inner class is inside the scope of the outer class. This is not consistent with C rules, where the inner declaration is equally visible globally.

5.11   EXERCISES

1   Design a class `person` that contains appropriate members for storing name, age, gender, and telephone number. Write member functions that can individually change these data members. Write a member function `person::print()` that prints a person's data nicely formatted.

2   In this exercise use the `struct stack` defined in Section 5.2. Write the function

```
void reverse(char s1[], char s2[]);
```

The strings `s1` and `s2` must be the same size. String `s2` should become a reversed copy of string `s1`. Internal to `reverse` use a `stack` to perform the reversal.

3   For the `stack` type in Section 5.2, write as member functions

```
//push n chars from s1 onto the stack
void push(int n, const char s1[]);

//pop n chars from stack into char string
void pop(int n, char s1[]);
```

Hint: Be sure to put a terminator character into the string before outputting it.

4   What is the difference in meaning between the structure

```
struct a {
   int i, j, k;
};
```

and the class

```
class a {
   int i, j, k;
};
```

Explain why the class declaration is not useful. How can you use the keyword `public` to change the class declaration into a declaration equivalent to `struct a`?

5   Define the `deque` of exercise 4.11, which is a double-ended queue that allows push and pop at both ends.

```
class deque {
   char s[max_len];
   int  bottom, top;
public:
   void reset() { top = bottom = max_len / 2; top--; }
   . . .
};
```

Declare and implement push_t, pop_t, push_b, pop_b, out_stack, top_of, bottom_of, empty, and full. The function push_t stands for *push on top*. The function push_b stands for *push on bottom*. The out_stack function should output the stack from its bottom to its top. The pop_t and push_b functions correspond to *pop from top* and *pop from bottom*. An empty stack is denoted by having the top fall below the bottom. Test each function.

6   Extend the data type deque by adding a member function relocate. If the deque is full, then relocate is called, and the contents of the deque are moved to balance empty storage around the center max_len / 2 of array s. Its function declaration header is

```
//returns true if it succeeds, false if it fails
boolean deque::relocate()
```

7   Write a swap function that swaps the contents of two strings (in other words redo exercise 4.13). If you pushed a string of characters onto a stack and popped them into a second string, they would come out reversed. In a swap of two strings, we want the original ordering. Use a deque to swap two strings. The strings will be stored in two character arrays of the same length, but the strings themselves may be of differing lengths. The function prototype is

```
void swap(char s1[], char s2[]);
```

8   Add member functions:

```
complex complex::plus(complex a, complex b);
// performs binary addition   c = plus(a, b)
complex complex::mpy(complex a, complex b);
// performs binary multiplication   c = mpy(a, b)
```

9   Write a routine that solves for the roots of a quadratic. The routine should have the prototype

```
void solve_quadratic(
        double    a,       //a*X*X term
        double    b,       //b*X   term
        double    c,       //c     term
        complex& root1,   //roots can be complex
        complex& root2
    );
```

10   Rewrite the twod class to contain values that are complex. Test it by initializing this container object to some set of complex numbers and writing it out. Then compute the transpose and write it out.

11   Use

```
typedef   int boolean;
const  boolean false = 0;
const  boolean true  = 1;
```

in place of an enumerated type. Now rewrite the stack functions empty() and full(). Discuss the advantages and disadvantages of this approach. The example in the text relies on casts that are system-dependent. Notice how the following recoding of full() avoids this cast:

```
inline boolean stack::empty()
{
    return ((top == EMPTY) ? true : false);
}
```

12   Consider c_pair::increment() modified to return c_pair.

```
inline c_pair cpair::increment()
{
    c1++;
    c2++;
    return (*this);
}
```

Discuss in what context this produces different behavior from the version in Section 5.7. Which version is more run-time efficient on your system? Test this and explain the result. If you can, you may want to generate machine code or (on AT&T and related compilers) intermediate C code for the two different functions and their invocations.

13   Rewrite the inner loop of the `transpose()` function in Section 5.9, replacing where possible calls of `twod::element_lval()` with calls of `twod::element_rval()`. Also rewrite the inner loop to replace the three assignment statements by a call to

```
inline void swap(double&, double&);
```

Test all three versions.

14   Write a matrix multiply routine using `twod` variables.

```
//  ab = a * b   -- note ab must be correctly allocated
void mmpy(const twod& a, const twod& b, twod& ab);
```

15   Write a matrix multiply member function using `twod` variables.

```
twod twod::mmpy(const twod& a, const twod& b);
```

This should be more efficient than the one written for the previous exercise. Why? Run both versions and compare timings. Use a profiler, if one is available on your system.

16   **Project:** Parameterize the data that can be stored in `twod` by using appropriate macro substitutions in place of the type `double` that is currently what is storable in this container class. Chapter 10 discusses `template` in detail. This language feature, introduced in AT&T Release 3.0, largely automates this process.

```
#define T typename
class twod {
private:
    T**   base;
    . . .
};
```

Notice that nonclass functions such as `transpose` also must be parameterized to work correctly. Add I/O to this version of `twod` by overloading `twod::print()` and `twod::read()` to perform these functions. Test the total package by defining it for integers, doubles, and complex numbers.

6

OBJECT CREATION

An object requires memory and some initial value. The kernel language provides this through declarations that are definitions. In most cases, when we discuss declarations, we mean declarations that are definitions. For example, in

```
void foo()
{
    int n = 5;
    double z[10] = { 0.0};
    struct gizmo { int i, j; } w = { 3, 4};
    . . .
}
```

all the objects are created at block entry when `foo()` is invoked. A typical implementation uses a run-time system stack. Thus the `int` object `n` on a system with four-byte integers gets this allocated off the stack and initialized to the value `5`. The `gizmo` object `w` requires eight bytes to represent its two integer members. The array of `double` object `z` requires ten times `sizeof(double)` to store its elements. In each case the system provides for the construction and initialization of these objects. Upon exit from `foo()` deallocation occurs automatically.

In creating complicated aggregates, the user can expect similar management of a class-defined object. The class needs a mechanism to specify object creation and object destruction behavior, so a client can use objects in a manner similar to native types.

A *constructor* is a member function with the same name as the class. It *constructs* values of the class type. This process involves initializing data members and, frequently, allocating free store using `new`. A destructor is a member function whose name is the class name preceded by the character ~ (tilde). Its usual purpose is to *destroy* values of the class type, typically by using `delete`. Notice the similarity of a constructor to the member function `twod::allocate()`, and the similarity of a destructor to the member function `twod:deallocate()` in the example at the end of Chapter 5.

Constructors are the more complicated of these two specially named member functions. They may be overloaded and can take arguments, neither of which is possible for destructors. A constructor is invoked when its associated type is used in a definition. It also is invoked when call-by-value is used to pass a value to a function. Constructors and destructors do not have return types and cannot use `return` (*expression*) statements. Destructors are implicitly invoked when an object of its class must be destroyed, typically upon block exit or function exit.

6.1   CLASSES WITH CONSTRUCTORS

The simplest use of a constructor is for initialization. In this and later sections, we develop some examples that use constructors to initialize the values of the data members of the class. Our first example is an implementation of a data type `mod_int` to store numbers that are computed with a modulus.

```
// Modulo numbers and constructor initialization

#include <iostream.h>

const int modulus = 60;
class mod_int {
private:
   int   v;
public:
   mod_int(int i) { v = i % modulus; }
   void assign(int i) { v = i % modulus; }
   void print() { cout << v << "\t"; }
};
```

The integer v is restricted in value to 0, 1, 2, . . . modulus − 1. It is the programmer's responsibility to enforce this restriction by having all member functions guarantee it.

The member function mod_int::mod_int() is a constructor. It does not have a return type. It is invoked when objects of type mod_int are declared. It is a function of one argument. When invoked it requires an expression that is assignment-compatible with its int parameter to be passed to it. It then creates and initializes the declared variable (object instance).

Some examples of declarations using this type are

```
mod_int   a(0);    // a.v = 0;
mod_int   b(61);   // b.v = 1;
```

but not

```
mod_int   a;       // no parameter list
```

Using this type, we can write code to convert seconds into minutes and seconds as follows.

```
main()
{
    int      seconds = 400;
    mod_int z(seconds);

    cout << seconds << " seconds equals "
         << seconds / 60 << " minutes ";
    z.print();
    cout << " seconds\n";
}
```

THE DEFAULT CONSTRUCTOR

A constructor requiring no arguments is called the *default constructor*. This can be a constructor with an empty argument list or a constructor in which all arguments have default values. It has the special purpose of initializing arrays of objects of its class.

It is often convenient to overload the constructor with several function declarations. In our example, it could be desirable to have the default value of v be 0. By adding the default constructor

```
mod_int() { v = 0; }
```

as a member function of mod_int, it is possible to have the following declarations:

```
mod_int s1, s2;  // both initialize the private member v to 0
mod_int d[5];    // arrays are properly initialized
```

In both of these declarations, the empty parameter list constructor is invoked.

If a class does not have a constructor, then arrays of objects of its type are automatically allocated by the system. If a class has constructors but does not have a default constructor, array allocation is a syntactic error.

Notice that our mod_int example could have one constructor serve as both a general initializer and a default constructor.

```
inline  mod_int::mod_int(int i = 0) { v = i % modulus; }
```

6.2   CONSTRUCTING A DYNAMICALLY SIZED STACK

A constructor can also be used to allocate space from free store. In this section we modify the `stack` type from Chapter 5 to have its maximum length be initialized by a constructor.

The design of the stack object includes hidden implementation detail, which consists of data members placed in the `private` access region of `class stack`. The public interface provides clients with the expected stack abstraction. These are all `public` member functions, such as `push()` and `pop()`. Some of these functions are accessor functions that do not change the stack object, such as `top_of()` and `empty`. It is usual to make these `const` member functions. Some of these functions are mutator functions that do change the stack object, such as `push()` and `pop()`. The constructor member functions have the job of creating and initializing stack objects.

```
//stack implementation with constructor
class stack {
private:
   enum   {EMPTY = -1};
   char* s;          //changed from s[max_len]
   int    max_len;
   int    top;
public:
   //the public interface for the ADT stack
   stack(int size) { s = new char[size];
                     max_len = size; top = EMPTY; }
   void reset() { top = EMPTY; }
   void push(char c) { s[++top] = c; }
   char pop() { return (s[top--]); }
   char top_of() const { return (s[top]); }
   boolean empty() const { return (boolean)(top == EMPTY); }
   boolean full() const { return (boolean)(top == max_len - 1); }
};
```

Now a client using `stack` can decide on the size requirement. An example of a `stack` declaration invoking this constructor is

```
stack data(1000);      // allocate 1000 elements
stack more_data(2 * n); // allocate 2 * n elements
```

Two alternate constructors would be an empty parameter constructor that would allocate a specific length stack and a two-parameter constructor whose second parameter is a string used to initialize the stack. They could be written as follows:

```
stack::stack()    //default constructor for stack
{
    s = new char[100];
    max_len = 100;
    top = EMPTY;
}

stack::stack(int size, const char str[]) //domain transfer
{
    s = new char[size];
    max_len = size;
    for ( int i = 0; i < max_len && str[i] != 0; ++i)
        s[i] = str[i];
    top = --i;
}
```

The corresponding function prototypes would be included as members of the class stack. Let us use these constructors as follows:

```
stack data;    //default constructor creating s[1000]
stack d[N];    //default constructor creates  N 1000 element stacks
stack w(4, "ABCD");  //w.s[0] = 'A' . . . w.s[3] = 'D'
```

THE COPY CONSTRUCTOR

We wish to examine our stack and count the number of occurrences of a given character. We can repeatedly pop the stack, testing each element in turn, until the stack is empty. But what if we want to preserve the contents of the stack. Call-by-value parameters accomplish this.

```
int cnt_char(char c, stack s)
{
    int count = 0;

    while (!s.empty())
        count += (c == s.pop());
    return (count);
}
```

The semantics of call-by-value require that a local copy of the argument type be created and initialized from the value of the expression passed as the actual argument. This requires a *copy constructor*. The compiler provides a default copy constructor. Its signature is

```
stack::stack(const stack&);
```

The compiler copies by memberwise initialization. This may not work in all circumstances for complicated aggregates with members who are themselves pointers. In many cases the pointer is the address of an object that is deleted when going out of scope. However, the act of duplicating the pointer value but not the object pointed at can lead to anomalous code. This deletion affects other instances that still expect the object to exist. It is appropriate for the class to explicitly define its own copy constructor.

```
//Copy constructor for stack of characters
stack::stack(const stack& str) //copy constructor
{
    s = new char[str.max_len];
    max_len = str.max_len;
    top = str.top;
    memcpy(s, str.s, max_len);
}
```

CONSTRUCTOR INITIALIZER

There is a special syntax for initializing subelements of objects with constructors. Initializers for structure and class members can be specified in a commas-separated list following the constructor parameter list and preceding the code body. We can recode the previous example as follows:

```
//Copy constructor for stack of characters
stack::stack(const stack& str)
      : max_len(str.max_len), top(str.top);
{
    s = new char[str.max_len];
    memcpy(s, str.s, max_len);
}
```

Notice how initialization replaces assignment. The individual members must be initializable as

member name (expression list)

When members are themselves classes with constructors, the expression list is matched to the appropriate constructor signature to invoke the correct overloaded constructor.

When a non-static member is either a `const` or a reference, this form of member initialization is required.

6.3   CLASSES WITH DESTRUCTORS

A destructor is a member function whose name is the same as the class name preceded by a tilde. They almost always are called implicitly, usually when exiting the block in which the object was declared (see Section 6.10). They are also invoked when a `delete` operator is called on a pointer to an object having a destructor, or when they are needed to destroy a subobject of an object being deleted.

Let us augment our stack example with a destructor.

```
//stack implementation with constructors and destructor
class stack {
private:
   enum  { EMPTY = -1};
   char* s;
   int   max_len;
   int   top;
public:
   stack();                        //default constructor
   stack(int size) { s = new char[size];
                  max_len = size; top = EMPTY; }
   stack(const stack& str)    //copy constructor
   stack(int size, const char str[]);
   ~stack() { delete [] s; }   //destructor
   . . .
};
```

The external interface of this class remains the same. In other words, all the public member functions perform in exactly the same manner as before. The difference is that the destructor is invoked implicitly upon block and function exit to clean up storage that is no longer accessible. This is good programming practice and allows programs to execute with less available memory.

6.4   AN EXAMPLE: DYNAMICALLY ALLOCATED STRINGS

A native string type is lacking in C++. Strings are represented as pointers to char and are manipulated accordingly. In this representation the end-of-string is denoted by \0. This convention has an important drawback in that many basic string manipulations are proportional to string length. When the string length is known, the efficiency of operations on strings can be significantly improved.

In this section we develop a useful string ADT that stores its length privately. We want our type to be dynamically allocated and able to represent strings of arbitrary length. A variety of constructors are coded to initialize and allocate strings, and a set of operations on strings is coded as member functions. The implementation will use the string.h library functions to manipulate the underlying pointer representation of strings.

```
//An implementation of dynamically allocated strings.
#include <string.h>
#include <iostream.h>

class string {
private:
   char* s;
   int   len;
public:
   string() { s = new char[1]; s[0] = 0; len = 0; }
   string(const string& str);              //copy constructor
   string(const char* p) { len = strlen(p);
                           s = new char[len + 1];
                           strcpy(s, p); }
   ~string() { delete [] s; }
   void assign(const string& str);
   void print() const { cout << s << endl; }
   void concat(const string& a, const string& b);
};
```

```
string::string(const string& str)
{
   len = str.len;
   s = new char[len + 1];
   strcpy(s, str.s);
}

void string::assign(const string& str)
{
   if (this == &str)
      return;
   else
      delete [] s;   //retrieve old string
   len = str.len;
   s = new char[len + 1];
   strcpy(s, str.s);
}

void string::concat(const string& a, const string& b)
{
   len = a.len + b.len;
   delete [] s;
   s = new char[len + 1];
   strcpy(s, a.s);
   strcat(s, b.s);
}
```

This type allows you to declare strings, assign by copying one string to another, print a string, and concatenate two strings. The hidden representation is pointer to char and has a variable len in which to store the current string length. The constructors all allocate dynamically from free store.

DISSECTION OF THE *string* CLASS

```
■ string() { s = new char[1]; s[0] = 0; len = 0; }
  string(const string& str);                    //copy constructor
  string(const char* p) { len = strlen(p);
                   s = new char[len + 1];
                   strcpy(s, p); }
```

Three constructors are overloaded. The first is the empty parameter default. This is used to declare an array of strings. The second is the copy constructor. The third constructor has a pointer to char argument that can be used to transform the char* representation of strings to our class type. It uses two library functions: strlen and strcpy. We allocate one additional character to store the end-of-string character \0, although this character is not counted by strlen. The copy constructor is explained below.

■ ~string() { delete [] s; }

The destructor automatically returns memory allocated to strings back to free store for reuse. The empty bracket pair form of delete is used because array allocation was used. The operator delete [] knows the amount of memory associated with the pointer s as the base address for an array.

■
```
string::string(const string& str)
{
   len = str.len;
   s = new char[len + 1];
   strcpy(s, str.s);
}
```

This is a *copy constructor,* which is used to perform copying of one string value into another when

■ A string is initialized by another string
■ A string is passed as an argument in a function
■ A string is returned as the value of a function

In C++, if this constructor is not present, then these operations are member-by-member assignment of value. This is discussed further in Section 6.10.

```
■ void string::assign(const string& str)
  {
     if (this == &str)
        return;
     else
        delete [] s;   //retrieve old string
     len = str.len;
     s = new char[len + 1];
     strcpy(s, str.s);
  }
```

The assignment semantics are based on *deep copy semantics*. The copying requires a check against copying over the same string. Each time the value of a string is copied, the value is physically recopied using strcpy(). This is in distinction to a later implementation that will show how to use shallow copy semantics (see Section 6.10).

```
■ void string::concat(const string& a, const string& b)
  {
     len = a.len + b.len;
     delete [] s;
     s = new char[len + 1];
     strcpy(s, a.s);
     strcat(s, b.s);
  }
```

This is a form of string concatenation. It assumes that the target string is not one of the two source strings. The two string arguments are not modified. The implicit argument, whose hidden member variables are s and len, is modified to represent the string a followed by the string b. Note that in this member function the use of len, a.len, and b.len is possible. Member functions have access not only to the private members of the implicit argument but also to the private representation of any of the arguments of type string.

The following code tests this `string` type by concatenating several strings:

```
main()
{
    char*   str = "The wheel that squeaks the loudest\n";
    string  a(str), b, author("Josh Billings\n"), both, quote;

    b.assign("Is the one that gets the grease\n");
    both.concat(a, b);
    quote.concat(both, author);
    quote.print();
}
```

The printout from this program is

```
The wheel that squeaks the loudest
Is the one that gets the grease
Josh Billings
```

We deliberately use a variety of declarations to show how different constructors can be called. The string variables b, `both`, and `quote` all use the default constructor. The declaration for `author` uses the constructor whose argument type is `char*`, which is the type of a literal string. The concatenation takes place in two steps. First strings a and b are concatenated into `both`. Next strings `both` and `author` are concatenated into `quote`. The quotation then is printed out.

The constructor `string::string(const char*)` is invoked to create and initialize objects a and `author`. This constructor is also called implicitly as a conversion operation when invoking `string::assign()` on the string literal `"Is the one that gets the grease\n"`.

6.5   A CLASS *vect*

The one-dimensional array in C is a very useful, efficient aggregate type. However, the traditional C array is error prone. A common mistake is to access elements that are *out of bounds*. C++ allows us to control this problem by defining an analogous array type in which bounds can be tested.

```cpp
//Implementation of a safe array type vect
#include <iostream.h>
#include <stdlib.h>      //for exit

class vect {
private:
   int* p;
   int  size;
public:
   vect() { size = 10; p = new int[size]; }
   vect(int n);
   ~vect() { delete [] p; }
   int& element(int i);
   int  ub() const { return (size - 1); }
};

vect::vect(int n)
{
   if (n <= 1) {
      cerr << "illegal vect size " << n << endl;
      exit(1);
   }
   size = n;
   p = new int[size];
}

int& vect::element(int i)
{
   if (i < 0 || i >= size) {
      cerr << "illegal vect index " << i << endl;
      exit(1);
   }
   return (p[i]);
}
```

The constructor `vect::vect(int n)` allows the user to build dynamically allocated arrays. Such arrays are much more flexible than those in languages, such as Pascal and C, that require array sizes to be constant expressions. The constructor also initializes the variable `size`, whose value is the number of elements in the array. Access to individual elements is through the safe indexing member function

```
int& vect::element(int i)
```

An index that is outside the expected array range 0 through ub causes an error message and error exit. This safe indexing member function returns a reference to int that is the address of p[i] and that can be used as the left operand of an assignment or lvalue. The technique is much used in C++ and is an efficient mechanism for operating on complicated types.

As an example, the declarations

```
vect a(10), b(5);
```

construct an array of ten integers and an array of five integers, respectively. Individual elements can be accessed by the member function element, which checks whether the index is out of range. The statements

```
a.element(1) = 5;
b.element(1) = a.element(1) + 7;
cout << a.element(1) - 2;
```

are legal. In effect we have a safe dynamic array type.

Classes with default constructors use them to initialize a derived array type. For example,

```
vect a[5];
```

is a declaration that uses the default constructor to create an array a of five objects, each of which is a size 10 vect. The ith element's address in the jth array would be given by

```
a[j].element(i)
```

6.6 MEMBERS THAT ARE CLASS TYPES

In this section we use the type vect as part of a new class. We want to store multiple values for each index. For example, we may want to store the age, weight, and height of a group of individuals. We could group three arrays together inside a new class.

```
#include "vect.h"

class multi_v {
public:
   vect a, b, c;
   multi_v(int i): a(i), b(i), c(i) {}
};
```

The class has three vect members and a constructor, which has an empty body but a list of constructor calls separated by commas. These constructors are executed with the integer argument i creating the three class objects a, b, and c. The members of a class are initialized in order of declaration.

Let us test this class by writing code to store and print a set of values for age in years, weight in pounds, and height in inches.

```
main()
{
    multi_v a_w_h(5);   //age weight and height

    for (int i = 0; i <= a_w_h.a.ub(); ++i) {
       a_w_h.a.element(i) = 21 + i;
       a_w_h.b.element(i) = 135 + i;
       a_w_h.c.element(i) = 62 + i;
    }
    for (i = 0; i <= a_w_h.a.ub(); ++i) {
       cout << a_w_h.a.element(i) << " years ";
       cout << a_w_h.b.element(i) << " pounds ";
       cout << a_w_h.c.element(i) << " inches\n";
    }
}
```

The declaration of a_w_h creates three vect members each of five elements. When the program is executed, the individual destructors for each vect member will be called upon block exit from main. The ordering of destructor calls is the reverse of the call on constructors. When executed, the above program prints

```
21 years 135 pounds 62 inches
22 years 136 pounds 63 inches
23 years 137 pounds 64 inches
24 years 138 pounds 65 inches
25 years 139 pounds 66 inches
```

6.7   AN EXAMPLE: A SINGLY LINKED LIST

In this section we develop a singly linked list data type. (See Figure 6.1.) This is the prototype of many useful dynamic data structures called *self-referential* structures. These data types have pointer members that refer to objects of their own type.

The following class declaration implements such a type.

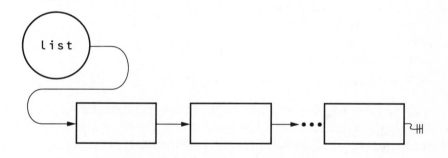

Operations

prepend	**Add to front of list**
first	**Return first element**
print	**Print list contents**
del	**Delete first element**
release	**Destroy list**

FIGURE 6.1   LIST as an ADT

```
//A singly linked list

struct listelem {
    char        data;
    listelem*   next;
};

class list {
private:
    listelem*   h;              //head of list
public:
    list() { h = 0; }           //0 denotes an empty list
    ~list() { release(); }
    void prepend(char c);       //adds to front of list
    void del() { listelem* temp = h;
                 h = h -> next;
                 delete temp; }
    listelem* first() { return (h); }
    void print();
    void release();
};
```

The link member next is self-referential. In this example the variable data
is a simple variable, but it could be replaced by a complicated type capable
of storing a range of information. The constructor initializes the head-of-
list pointer h to the value 0, which is called the *null pointer constant*. It
can be assigned to any pointer type. In linked lists it typically denotes the
empty list or end-of-list value. The member function prepend() is used
to build the list structure.

```
void list::prepend(char c)
{
    listelem* temp = new listelem;   //create new element

    temp -> next = h;                //link to list
    temp -> data = c;
    h = temp;                        //update head of list
}
```

A list element is allocated from free store, and its data member is initialized from the single argument c. Its link member next points at the old

head-of-list. The head pointer h is then updated to point at this element as the new first element of the list.

The inline member function del has the inverse role. It returns the first element of the list to free store. It does this by using the delete operator on the head-of-list pointer h. The new head-of-list is the value of the next member.

Much of list processing is repetitively chaining down the list until the null pointer value is found. The following two functions use this technique:

```
void list::print()
{
    listelem*  temp = h;

    while (temp != 0) {             //detect end of list
       cout << temp -> data << " -> ";
       temp = temp -> next;
    }
    cout << "\n###\n";
}

void list::release()  //elements are returned to free store
{
    while (h != 0)
       del();
}
```

DISSECTION OF THE *print* AND *release* FUNCTIONS

■ void list::print()

     listelem* temp = h;

We use the auxiliary pointer temp to chain down the list. It is initialized to the address of the list head h. The pointer h cannot be used because its value would be lost, in effect destroying access to the list.

```
■ while (temp != 0) {                    //detect end of list
     cout << temp -> data << " -> ";
     temp = temp -> next;
  }
```

The value 0 represents the end-of-list value. It is guaranteed to be such because the constructor `list::list` initialized it and the `list::prepend` function maintains it as the end-of-list pointer value. Notice that the internals of this loop could be changed to process the entire list in some other manner.

```
■ void list::release()    //each element is returned
to free store
```

The `release` function is used to return all list elements to free store. It marches down the list when doing so.

```
■ while (h != 0)
     del();
```

Each element of the list must be returned to free store in sequence. This is done for a single element by the member function `del`, which manipulates the hidden pointer h. Since we are destroying the list, it is unnecessary to preserve the original value of pointer h. This function's chief use is as the body of the destructor `list::~list`.
We could not use a destructor written

```
■ list::~list()
  {
     delete h;
  }
```

because it only deletes the first element in the list.

We demonstrate the use of the list type in the following code:

```
main()
{
    list*   p;
    {
        list        w;

        w.prepend('A');
        w.prepend('B');
        w.print();
        w.del();
        w.print();
        p = &w;
        p -> print();
    }
    p -> print(); //system dependent
}
```

Notice that main includes an inner block to test that the destructor is invoked upon block exit, returning storage associated with w to free store. The output of this program is

```
B -> A ->
###
A ->
###
A ->
###

###
```

The first print() call prints the two-element list storing B and A. After a del operation is performed, the list contains one element storing A. The outer block pointer to list p is assigned the address of the list variable w. When the list is accessed through p in the inner block, it prints A. After block exit, on many systems the same print command prints the empty list. This output shows that the destructor works at block exit on the variable w.

The last invocation of list::print() is system-dependent. It is a run-time error to dereference p here because the address it refers to has been possibly overwritten at block exit by the deletion routine.

6.8   POLYNOMIALS AS A LINKED LIST

A polynomial is *sparse* when it has relatively few nonzero coefficients in comparison to its degree. The degree of the polynomial is just the highest exponent of a nonzero term. For example, the degree 1000 polynomial $P(x) = x^{1000} + x^1 + 1$ has only three nonzero terms. When manipulating large sparse polynomials, it is often efficient to base the representation on a linked list. In such a representation each list cell contains a nonzero term of the polynomial.

We will write a routine that manipulates such polynomials and does polynomial addition. The list is sorted with terms in descending order of their exponents. Also, we will allow only one term per exponent.

```
//A polynomial represented as a singly linked list
struct term {
    int        exponent;
    double     coefficient;
    term*      next;
    term(int e, double c, term* n = 0)
        : exponent(e), coefficient(c), next(n) {}
    void print()
        { cout << coefficient << "x^" << exponent << " "; }
};


class polynomial {
private:
    term*    h;
    int      degree;
    void     prepend(term*  t);     //add term to front
    void     add_term(term*& a, term*& b);
    void     release();             //garbage collect polynomial
    void     rest_of(term* rest);   //add terms to polynomial
    void     reverse();             //reverse the terms
public:
    polynomial(): h(0), degree(0) {}
    polynomial(const polynomial& p);
    polynomial(int size, double coef[], int expon[]);
    ~polynomial() { release(); }
    void print() const;
    void plus(polynomial a, polynomial b);
};
```

In this representation a polynomial is coded as a list of terms. Each term is a coefficient-exponent pair. A polynomial will have its terms listed in decreasing order by exponent. This canonical form makes addition as well as other operations simpler. A polynomial will either be empty, initialized using the copy constructor, or constructed from a pair of arrays that contains a properly ordered sequence of coefficient-exponent pairs.

We have three important auxiliary member functions that manipulate the underlying list representation. We navigate through the list using advance(). The pointer parameter t is call-by-reference so it can be updated. The assertion is applied to guarantee that it does not run off the end of the list. The prepend() function links a term to the head of the list. The reverse() function reverses a list in place. (See Figure 6.2.)

```cpp
inline void advance(term*& t) { assert(t != 0); t = t -> next; }
inline void polynomial::prepend(term*  t) { t -> next = h; h = t; }

void polynomial::reverse()  //in place
{
    term*  pred, *succ, *elem;

    if (h && (succ = h -> next)) {
        pred = 0;
        elem = h;
        while (succ) {
            elem -> next = pred;
            pred = elem;
            elem = succ;
            advance(succ);
        }
        h = elem;
        h -> next = pred;
    }
}
```

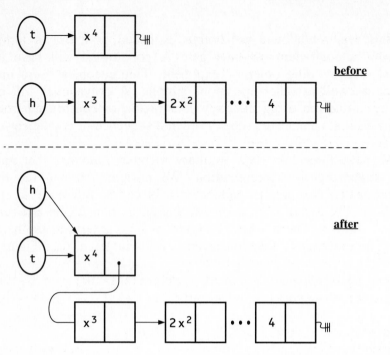

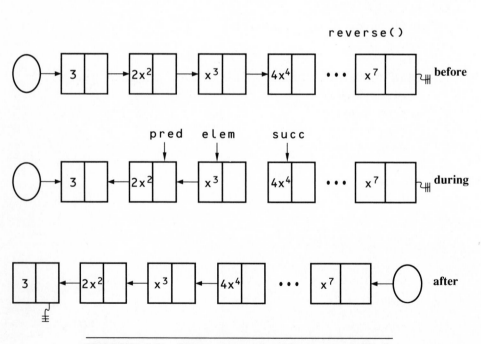

FIGURE 6.2   How reverse and prepend Work

The constructors build an explicit list for each polynomial. It would be incorrect to rely on the default copy constructor.

```
//assumes ordering is correct expon[i] < expon[i+1]
polynomial::polynomial(int size, double coef[], int expon[])
{
    term* temp = new term(expon[0], coef[0]);

    h = 0;
    prepend(temp);      //create initial term
    for (int i = 1; i < size; ++i) {
        assert(expon[i - 1] < expon[i]);
        temp = new term(expon[i], coef[i]);
        prepend(temp); //add term
    }
    degree = h -> exponent;
}


polynomial::polynomial(const polynomial& p) : degree(p.degree)
{
    term* elem = p.h, *temp;

    h = 0;
    while (elem) {    //term by term copying
        temp = new term(elem -> exponent, elem -> coefficient);
        prepend(temp);
        advance(elem);
    };
    reverse();
}
```

The next set of functions implements a merge-sort polynomial addition, using the auxiliary functions add_term() and rest_of().

```cpp
void polynomial::add_term(term*& a, term*& b)
{
    term*  c;

    if (a -> exponent != b -> exponent) {
        if (a -> exponent > b -> exponent) { //add a
            c = new term(a -> exponent, a -> coefficient) ;
            advance(a);
        }
        else { //add b
            c = new term(b -> exponent, b -> coefficient) ;
            advance(b);
        }
        prepend(c);
    }
    else { //check on cancellation
        if (a -> coefficient + b -> coefficient != 0) {
            c = new term(a -> exponent,
                         a -> coefficient + b -> coefficient) ;
            prepend(c);
        }
        advance(a); advance(b);
    }
}
```

This merges the terms at the head of the two lists. The exponents can be either of different values or the same. If the exponents are of different values, the larger term is the result, and only its list pointer is advanced. If the exponents are the same, both list pointers are advanced. Cancellation occurs when both exponents are the same and their coefficients sum to zero; no term is produced. Otherwise zero terms might proliferate and it would defeat our attempt to have an efficient representation of a sparse polynomial.

When one list of terms is exhausted by the merge, the terms from the remaining list are added to the front of the list by rest_of().

```
void polynomial::rest_of(term* rest)
{
    term* temp = h;

    while (rest) {
        temp  = new term(rest -> exponent, rest -> coefficient);
        prepend(temp);
        advance(rest);
    }
}


//c.plus(a,b) means c = a + b
void polynomial::plus(polynomial a, polynomial b)
{
    term*    aterm = a.h, *bterm = b.h;

    release();    //garbage collect c polynomial
    h = 0;
    while (aterm && bterm)  //merge step
        add_term(aterm, bterm);
    if (aterm)
        rest_of(aterm);
    else if (bterm)
        rest_of(bterm);
    reverse();
    degree = ((h) ? h -> exponent: 0);
}
```

The function polynomial::plus() uses add_term() and rest_of() to put the terms in the reverse order to the expected representation. It calls reverse() to correct this.

In exercise 20 you will write the undefined functions polynomial:: release() and polynomial::print() needed to test this code.

6.9 STRINGS USING REFERENCE SEMANTICS

Allocation at run-time of large aggregates can readily exhaust memory resources. Our list example showed one scheme for handling this: The system reclaimed memory by traversing each list and disposing of each element. This model of reclamation is a form of *garbage collection*. In languages such as LISP and Smalltalk, the system itself is responsible for this reclamation. Such systems periodically invoke a garbage collector whose business it is to identify all cells currently accessible and reclaim the remaining cells that are inaccessible. Most such schemes require traversal and marking of cells accessible from pointers—a computationally expensive procedure.

Reference counting is a disposal scheme that avoids this procedure. Each dynamically allocated object tracks its active references. When an object is created, its reference count is set to one. Each time the object is newly referenced, a reference count is incremented. Each time the object loses a reference, the count is decremented. When the reference count becomes zero, the object's memory is disposed of.

In the following example we create a string class that has reference semantics for copying. The techniques illustrated are common ones for this type of aggregate. We use the class `str_obj` to create actual object values. The type `str_obj` is required implementation detail for `string`. The detail could not be placed directly in `string` without destroying the potential many-one relationship between objects of type `string` and referenced values of type `str_obj`. The values of `string` are in the class `str_obj`, which is an auxiliary class for its use. The publicly used class `string` *handles* the `str_obj` instances and thus sometimes is called a *handler* class.

```
//Reference counted strings.
#include <string.h>
#include <iostream.h>

class str_obj {
public:
   int  len, ref_cnt;
   char* s;
   str_obj(): len(0), ref_cnt(1) { s = new char[1]; s[0] = 0; }
   str_obj(const char* p):ref_cnt(1)
      { len = strlen(p); s = new char[len + 1]; strcpy(s, p); }
   ~str_obj() { delete [] s; }
};
```

The `str_obj`s are string objects used by `string`. In Chapter 7 we will explain how these can be made `private` and accessed using the `friend` mechanism. Notice how this class is basically used for construction and destruction of objects using free store. Upon construction the `ref_cnt` variable is initialized to one.

```
class string {
private:
    str_obj* st;
public:
    string() { st = new str_obj; }
    string(const char* p) { st = new str_obj(p); }
    string(const string& str)
        { st = str.st; st -> ref_cnt++; }
    ~string();
    void assign(const string& str);
    void print() const { cout << st -> s; }
};
```

The client will use objects of type `string`. These objects are implemented as pointers `st` to values of type `str_obj`. Notice the copy constructor for this class and how it uses reference semantics to produce a copy.

```
void string::assign(const string& str)
{
    if (str.st -> s != st -> s) {
        if (--st -> ref_cnt == 0)
            delete st;
        st = str.st;
        st -> ref_cnt++;
    }
}
```

The semantics of `assign()` show some of the pitfalls of using copy semantics. The assignment occurs if the string is not being assigned to itself. The assignment causes the assigned variable to lose its previous value. This is equivalent to decrementing the reference count of that pointed-at object value. Anytime an object's reference count is decremented, it gets tested for deletion. The new object value now has an additional reference to it, and thus its reference counter is incremented.

The advantage of this over normal copying is clear. A very large aggregate is copied by reference, with a small, fixed number of operations. The reference counter uses a small amount of additional storage. Also, each possible change to a pointer adds a reference count operation. The destructor must also test the reference count before actual deletion.

```
string:: ~string()
{
   if (--st -> ref_cnt == 0)
      delete st;
}
```

6.10   NO CONSTRUCTOR, COPY CONSTRUCTOR, AND OTHER MYSTERIES

Object creation for native types is usually the task of the compiler. The writer of a class wishes to achieve the same ease of use for the defined ADT. Let us reexamine some issues in simple terms.

Does every class need an explicitly defined constructor? Of course not, as is already clear from Chapter 5. When no constructor is written by the programmer, the compiler provides a default constructor, if needed.

```
struct pers_data {
   int    age;       //in years
   int    weight;    //in kilograms
   int    height;    //in centimeters
   char   name[20];  //last name
};

void print(pers_data d)
{
   cout << s d.name << " is " << d.age << " years old " << endl;
   cout << "weight : " << d.weight << "kg,  height : "
        << d.height << "cm." << endl;
}

main()
{
   pers_data laura = { 3, 14, 88, "POHL"};  //construction off
           the stack

   print(laura);    //call by value -local copy constructed
}
```

What if we use constructors and allow the copy constructor to be default? We frequently get the wrong semantics, namely *shallow copy semantics*. In shallow copy semantics a new value is not created; instead a pointer variable is assigned the address of the existing value. In reference semantics a copy implies that the reference counter is incremented. This does not happen in shallow copy semantics. Objects copied by a default constructor are undercounted and prematurely returned to free store. As a rule of thumb, the class provider should explicitly write out the copy constructor, unless it is self-evident that memberwise copy is safe. Always be cautious if the aggregate has any members that are pointer-based.

Are there special rules for unions? Yes, unions are frequently a special case. This should not be surprising because unions are a technique for having different objects share space. Unions cannot have `static` data members. Anonymous unions can only have public data members. Also global anonymous unions must be declared `static`.

new, delete OPTIONS AND SYNTAX

Destructors usually involve the application of `delete`. The two standard forms are

> `delete` *expression*
> `delete` [] *expression*

The expression is typically a pointer variable used in assignment from a `new` expression. The brackets are used when allocation involves a bracketed expression, meaning an array of objects are allocated off of free store. A bracketed deletion ensures that destructors will be called on each object stored in the array.

Deletion of a zero-valued pointer is harmless. Multiple deletions of the same object is an error (system-dependent behavior results), as is a deletion of a pointer value not gotten from a `new` expression.

Constructors usually involve the application of `new`. The two standard forms are

> `new` *new type name optional initializer list*
> `new` *(type name) optional initializer list*

These operators return a pointer to the base address of the created object. In the case of an array of objects, this is the address of its first element.

The initializer list is a parenthesized list of expressions used by the object's constructor, or a single value used for a native type.

```
p = new int(9);   //p is pointer to int initialized to 9
p = new int[9];   //p is pointer to a 9 element array of int
```

The second form of the new expression is used when parenthesizing the type name is required to properly parse the object's type.

```
q = new (char*)[9];   //q is a char**
```

Operator new can be overloaded and given different signatures. This form requires an additional argument list matching the overloaded form (see Chapter 8).

   If new fails to allocate store, it returns with the value 0. Different strategies exist for coping with this failure (see Chapters 8 and 11).

DESTRUCTOR DETAILS

A destructor is implicitly invoked when an object goes out of scope. Common cases include block and function exit.

```
string sub_str(char c, string b)    //friend of string
{
    string  substring;
    for (int i = 0; i <= b.len; ++i)
        if (c == s[i])
            break;

    substring.assign(s + i);
    return (substring);
}
```

In sub_str() we have b, a call-by-value argument of type string. Therefore the copy constructor is invoked to create a local copy when the function is invoked. Correspondingly a destructor is called on function exit. There is a local string variable substring that is constructed upon block entry to this function and therefore must have its destructor invoked upon block exit. Finally, the return argument must be constructed and passed back into the calling environment. Whether the corresponding destructor is invoked depends on the scope of the object it is assigned to.

A destructor can be explicitly called.

```
p = new string("I dont need you long");
. . .
p -> ~string();  //also possible is p -> string::~string()
. . .
```

CONSTRUCTORS AS CONVERSIONS

Constructors of a single parameter automatically are conversion functions.
Conversions are an aspect of polymorphism (see Chapter 7) and simplify
client code. Consider the following class, whose purpose is to print non-
visible characters with their ASCII designation; for example, the code 07
(octal) is alarm or bel.

```
//ASCII printable characters
class pr_char {
private:
    int   c;
    static char* rep[128];
public:
    pr_char(int i = 0): c(i % 128) {}
    void print() { cout << rep[c]; }
};

char* pr_char::rep[128] = { "nul", "soh", "stx",
     //and so on
     . . .
     "w", "x", "y", "z", "{", "|", "}", "~", "del"};

main()
{
    int i;
    pr_char c;

    for (i = 0; i < 128; ++i) {
       c = i;  // also c = pr_char(i); or c = (pr_char)i;
       c.print();
       cout << endl;
    }
}
```

The constructor creates an automatic conversion from integers to pr_char. Notice that the statement

```
c = i;
```

in the loop implies this conversion. It is also possible to explicitly use a cast. Inordinate reliance on implicit conversions can lead to obscure type-insecure code.

Conversions are a major part of the discussion in Chapter 7. One reason OOP requires such a possibility is that user-defined types should have the look and feel of native types.

6.11   SUMMARY

1   A constructor is a member function with the same name as the class. It constructs objects of the class type. This process may involve initializing data members and allocating free store using new. A constructor is invoked when its associated type is used in a definition.

```
TYPE_foo y(3);   //invoke TYPE_foo::TYPE_foo(int)

extern TYPE_foo x;   //declaration but not definition
```

Not all declarations are definitions. When they are not definitions, constructors are not invoked.

2   A destructor is a member function whose name is the class name preceded by the character ~(tilde). Its usual purpose is to *destroy* values of the class type, typically by using delete.

3   A constructor requiring no arguments is called the *default* constructor. This can be a constructor with an empty argument list or a constructor where all arguments have default values. It has the special purpose of initializing arrays of objects of its class.

4   An example of a class with both a constructor and destructor is

```
class stack {
private:
    enum { EMPTY = -1};
    char* s;
    int   max_len;
    int   top;
public:
    stack(int size) { s = new char[size];
                      max_len = size; top = EMPTY; }
    ~stack() { delete [] s; }
    . . .
};
```

5   A copy constructor of the form

type::type (const *type*& x)

performs copying of one *type* value into another when

■ A *type* variable is initialized by a *type* value
■ A *type* value is passed as an argument in a function
■ A *type* value is returned from a function

In C++, if this constructor is not present, then these operations are member-by-member initializations of value.

6   A class having members whose type requires a constructor may have these specified after the argument list for its own constructor. The constructor has a comma-separated list of constructor calls following a colon. The constructor is invoked by using the member name followed by an argument list in parentheses. Initialization occurs in the order of declaration of the members.

7   A singly linked list is the prototype of many useful dynamic data structures called *self-referential* structures. A linked list is like a clothesline on which the data elements hang sequentially. The head of the line is the only immediate access point, and items can readily be added to or deleted from this point.

8   The value 0 is called the *null pointer constant*. It can be assigned
        to any pointer type. In linked lists, it typically denotes the empty
        list or end-of-list value.

9   *Reference counting* is an efficient disposal scheme for large ag-
        gregates. Each dynamically allocated object tracks its active ref-
        erences. When an object is created, its reference count is set to
        one. Each time the object is newly referenced, a reference count is
        incremented. Each time the object loses a reference, the count is
        decremented. When the reference count becomes zero, the object's
        memory is disposed of.

6.12   EXERCISES

1   Discuss why constructors are almost always `public` member func-
        tions. What goes wrong if they are `private`?

2   Write a member function for the class `mod_int`.

```
void add_to(int i);   //add i to v modulo 60.
```

        It should add the number of seconds in i to the current value of v
        while retaining the modulo 60 feature of v.

3   Run the following program and explain its behavior. Placing de-
        bugging information inside constructors and destructors is a very
        useful step in developing efficient and correct classes.

```
//Constructors and destructors invoked

#include <iostream.h>

class A {
private:
    int xx;
public:
    A(int n) { xx = n;
              cout << "A(int " << n << ") called\n"; }
    A(double y) { xx = y + 0.5;
                cout << "A(fl " << y << ") called\n"; }
    ~A() { cout << "~A() called A::xx = " << xx << endl; }
};

main()
{
    cout << "enter main\n";
    int x = 14;
    float y = 17.3;
    A z(11), zz(11.5), zzz(0);

    cout << "\nOBJECT ALLOCATION LAYOUT\n";
    cout << "\nx is at " << &x;
    cout << "\ny is at " << &y;
    cout << "\nz is at " << &z;
    cout << "\nzz is at " << &zz;
    cout << "\nzzz is at " << &zzz;
    cout << "\n_____\n";
    zzz = A(x);
    zzz = A(y);
    cout << "exit main\n";
}
```

4   Add a default constructor for class A.

```
A() { xx = 0; cout << "A() called\n"; }
```

Now modify the previous program by declaring an array of type A

```
A d[5];    //declares an array of 5 elements of type A
```

Assign the values 0, 1, 2, 3, and 4 to the data member xx of each
d[i]. Run the program and explain its behavior.

5   Use the **stack** type from Section 6.2 in this exercise, and include
a default constructor to allocate a stack of 100 elements. Write a
program that swaps the contents of two stacks, using an array of
stacks to accomplish the job. The two stacks will be the first two
stacks in the array. One method would be to use four stacks: st[0],
st[1], st[2], and st[3]. Push the contents of st[1] into st[2].
Push the contents of st[0] into st[3]. Push the contents of st[3]
into st[1]. Push the contents of st[2] into st[0]. Verify that the
stacks have their contents in the same order by implementing a print
function that outputs all elements in the stack. Can this be done
with only three stacks?

6   Add a constructor to the type **stack** with the following prototype:

```
stack::stack(const char* c);    //initialize from string array
```

7   Use the **string** type from Section 6.4 in this exercise, and code
the following member functions:

```
//strcmp is negative if s < s1,
//        is 0 if s == s1,
//        and is positive if s > s1
//        where s is the implicit string argument
int string::strcmp(const string& s1);

//strrev   reverses the implicit string argument
void string::strrev();

//print   is overloaded to print the first n characters
void string::print(int n);
```

8   Write a function that swaps two strings. Use it and **string::strcmp**
from the previous exercise to write a program that sorts an array
of strings.

9   Use the **vect** type from Section 6.5 in this exercise, and code the
following member functions:

```
//adds up all the element values and returns their sum
int vect::sumelem();

//prints all the elements
void vect::print();

//adds two vectors into a third  v(implicit) = v1 + v2
void vect::add(const vect& v1, const vect& v2);

//adds two vectors and returns  v(implicit) + v1
vect vect::add(const vect& v1);
```

10   Write a further constructor for vect that accepts an int array and its size and constructs a vect with these initial values:

```
vect::vect(const int* d, int sz);
```

11   Try to benchmark the speed differences between safe arrays as represented by class vect and ordinary integer arrays. Repeatedly run an ordinary element summation routine on int a[10000] and one using the vect a(10000). Time your trials.

12   Define the class multi_v as follows:

```
class multi_v {
private:
   vect a, b, c;
   int  size;
public:
   int  ub;
   multi_v(int i) : a(i), b(i), c(i) { size = i;
                                       ub = size -1; }
   void assign(int ind, int i, int j, int k);
   void retrieve(int ind, int& i, int& j, int& k);
   void print(int ind) const;
};
```

Write and test code for each member function: assign, retrieve, and print. The function assign should assign i, j, and k to a[ind], b[ind], and c[ind], respectively. The function retrieve does the inverse of assign. The function print should print the three values a[ind], b[ind], and c[ind].

13   Use the list type from Section 6.7 in this exercise, and code the following member functions:

```
//list a constructor whose initializer is a char array
list::list(const char* c);

//length returns the length of the list
int list::length();

//return the number of elements whose data value is c
int list::count_c(char c);
```

14   Write a member function append that adds a list to the rear of the implicit list argument and then clears the appended string by zeroing the head.

```
void list::append(list& e);
```

15   Write a member function copy that copies a list.

```
//the implicit argument ends up a copy of e
void list::copy(const list& e);
```

Be sure you destroy the implicit list before you do the copy.

16   Use the list type to add the equivalent five member functions that give you stack functions.

```
reset    push    pop  top_of  empty
```

17   Construct a three-dimensional safe array type called v_3_d.

```
//Implementation of a three-dimensional safe array
class v_3_d {
    int*** p;
    int     s1, s2, s3;
public:
    int     ub1, ub2, ub3;
    v_3_d(int l1, int l2, int l3);
    ~v_3_d();
    int& element(int i, int j, int k);
    void print();
};
```

Initialize and print a three-dimensional array.

18   Add a constructor to listelem and use it to simplify the coding of the member function list::prepend(char c).
As written, list::del() expects a nonempty list. What goes wrong if it is passed an empty list? See the effect on your system. Modify this routine to test for this condition. Note that this can be tested as an assertion.

19   We wish to define a C++ class that resembles sets in Pascal. The underlying representation will be a 32-bit machine word.

```
// Implementation of an ADT for type set.
const unsigned long int masks[32] = {
    0x80000000, 0x40000000, 0x20000000, 0x10000000,
    . . .
    0x80, 0x40, 0x20, 0x10, 0x8, 0x4, 0x2, 0x1};

class set {
  private:
    unsigned long int t;
  public:
    set(unsigned long int i) { t = i; }
    set() { t = 0x0; }
    void u_add(int i) { t |= masks[i]; }
    void u_sub(int i) { t &= ~masks[i]; }
    boolean in(int i)
        { return (boolean)((t  & masks[i]) == masks[i]); }
    void pr_mems() const;
    set set_union(const set& v)
        { set temp; temp.t  = v.t  | t; return (temp); }
};
```

Write the code for **pr_mems** to print out all the elements of the set. Write the code for the member function **intersection** to return the resulting set intersection.

20   Complete the polynomial package by writing code for the routines **void polynomial::release()** and **void polynomial::print()**, which are not found in the text.

21   Write code that tests the polynomial addition routine **void polynomial::plus()**.

22   Make the constructor for **polynomial** more robust. Assume that the coefficient-exponent pairs are not necessarily in sorted order. The constructor then must be written to take this into account.

23   Improve the reference-counted form of **class string** from Section 6.9 by asserting in appropriate member functions that **ref_cnt** is nonnegative. Why would you want to do this?

24   **Project:** Recode the class **twod** used in Chapter 5 using constructors and destructors, and rename it **matrix**.

```
class matrix {
private:
   double** base;
   int      row_size, column_size;
public:
   matrix(int r, int s); //replaces allocate(int r, int s);
   ~matrix ();           //replaces deallocate();
   double&  element(int i, int j) { return (base[i][j]; }
   int      r_size() { return (row_size); }
   int      c_size() { return (column_size); }
};
```

Modify the `matrix::element()` function to check that each index is within range. Use assertions for this test. Write the copy constructor `matrix::matrix(const matrix&)`. Also write a constructor that performs a transpose. It should have an enumerated type as a second argument that indicates what transformation should be made on the array.

```
enum transform {transpose, negative, upper};

matrix::matrix(const matrix& a, transform t)
{
   //transpose base[i][j] = a.base[j][i]
   //negative  base[i][j] = -a.base [i][j]
   //upper     base[i][j] = a.base[i][j] i <= j else 0
   . . .
}
```

Add I/O routines to this package. Properly overload `<<` and `>>` to work with matrix values.

7

AD HOC
POLYMORPHISM

Polymorphism is a means of giving different meanings to the same message. The meanings are dependent on the type of data being processed. *Conversion* is the explicit or implicit change of value between types. Conversions provide a form of polymorphism. Overloading of functions gives the same function name different meanings. The same name has different interpretations that depend on function selection. The selected function satisfies the signature-matching algorithm for C++. This form of polymorphism is called *ad hoc polymorphism*. This chapter discusses overloading, especially operator overloading, and conversions of data types.

Operators are overloaded and selected based on the signature-matching algorithm. Overloading operators gives them new meanings. For example, the expression a + b has different meanings depending on the types of the variables a and b. Overloading operator + for user-defined types allows them to be used in addition expressions, in much the same way as a native type. The expression a + b could mean string concatenation, complex number addition, or integer addition, depending on whether the variables were the ADT string, the ADT complex, or the native type int. Mixed type expressions are also possible by defining conversion functions. This chapter also discusses friend functions and how they are crucial to operator overloading.

One principle of OOP is that user-defined types must enjoy the same privileges as native types. The client expects the convenience of using these types without regard to a native/nonnative distinction. As far as the manufacturer can achieve this result is the test of the adequacy of the language for OOP use. Native types in the kernel language can be mixed in expressions because it is convenient and would otherwise be burdensome to designate conventionally expected conversions.

7.1   CLASS-DEFINED CONVERSIONS

Explicit type conversion of an expression is necessary when either the implicit conversion is not desired or the expression is not legal otherwise. One aim of C++ is the integration of ADTs and native types. To achieve this there is a mechanism for having a member function provide an explicit conversion.

A functional notation of the form

type-name (expression)

is equivalent to a cast. The type must be expressible as an identifier. Thus the two expressions

```
x = float(i);   //C++ functional notation
x = (float) i;
```

are equivalent. The expression

```
p = (int*) q;   //legal cast
```

cannot be directly expressed functionally as

```
p = int*(q);    //illegal
```

However, a `typedef` can be used to achieve this result.

```
typedef int* int_ptr;
p = int_ptr(q);
```

Functional notation is the preferred style.

A constructor of one argument is de facto a type conversion from the argument's type to the constructor's class type. In Section 6.4 the string type had a constructor

```
string(const char* p) { len = strlen(p);
                        s = new char[len + 1]; strcpy(s, p); }
```

This is automatically a type transfer from char* to string. It is available both explicitly and implicitly. Explicitly it is used as a conversion operation in either cast or functional form. Thus

```
string s;
char*  logo = "Geometrics Inc";

s = string(logo);     //performs conversion then assignment
```

and

```
s = logo;             //implicit invocation of conversion
```

both work.

These are conversions from an already defined type to a user-defined type. However, it is not possible for the user to add a constructor to a native type such as int or double. In the string example a conversion from string to char* also may be desired. This can be done by defining a special conversion function inside the string class, as follows:

```
operator char*() { return (s); }
```

The general form of such a member function is

```
    operator type () { ... }
```

Such a conversion function must be a non-static member function without a return type and with an empty argument list. These conversions occur implicitly in assignment expressions, in arguments to functions, and in values returned from functions.

A conversion member function of the form A::operator B() and a constructor of the form B::B(const A&) both provide conversions from type *A* objects to type *B* objects. Having both can result in ambiguity errors.

7.2   OVERLOADING AND FUNCTION SELECTION

Overloaded functions are an important feature of C++. The overloaded meaning is selected by matching the argument list of the function call to the argument list of the function declaration. When an overloaded function is invoked, the compiler must have a selection algorithm with which to pick the appropriate function. The algorithm that accomplishes this depends on what type conversions are available. A best match must be unique. It must be best on at least one argument and as good on all other arguments as any other match.

The matching algorithm for each argument is as follows:

Overloaded Function Selection Algorithm

1   Use an exact match if found.
2   Try standard type promotions.
3   Try standard type conversions.
4   Try user-defined conversions.
5   Use a match to ellipsis if found.

Let us write an overloaded function `greater` and follow our algorithm for various invocations. In this example, the user type `complex` is available.

```
//overloading functions

#include <iostream.h>
#include <math.h>            //for sqrt

class complex {
private:
   double real, imag;
public:
   complex(double r) { real = r; imag = 0; }
   void assign(double r, double i) { real = r; imag = i; }
   void print() { cout << real << " + " << imag << "i "; }
   operator double() { return (sqrt(real * real + imag * imag)); }
};

inline int    greater(int i, int j)
              { return ( i > j ? i : j); }
```

```
inline double  greater(double x, double y)
               { return ( x > y ? x : y); }
inline complex greater(complex w, complex z)
               { return ( w > z ? w : z); }

main()
{
    int     i = 10, j = 5;
    float   x = 7.0;
    double  y = 14.5;
    complex w(0), z(0), zmax(0);

    w.assign(x, y);
    z.assign(i, j);
    cout << "compare " << i << " and " << j << "  greater is "
         << greater(i, j) << endl;
    cout << "compare " << x << " and " << y << "  greater is "
         << greater(x, y) << endl;
    cout << "compare " << y << " and " ;
    z.print();
    cout << "  greater is " << greater(y, double(z)) << endl;
    zmax = greater(w, z);
    cout << "compare ";
    w.print();
    cout << "  and  ";
    z.print();
    cout << "  greater is  ";
    zmax.print();
    cout << endl;
}
```

The output from this program is

```
compare 10 and  5  greater is 10
compare 7 and 14.5  greater is 14.5
compare 14.5 and 10 + 5i  greater is 14.5
compare 7 + 14.5i   and  10 + 5i   greater is  7 + 14.5i
```

A variety of conversion rules, both implicit and explicit, are applied in this program. We explain these in the following dissection.

DISSECTION OF THE *overloading* PROGRAM

■ `complex(double r) { real = r; imag = 0; }`

This constructor provides a conversion from `double` to `complex`.

■ `operator double() { return (sqrt(real * real + imag * imag)); }`

This member function provides a conversion from `complex` to `double`.

■
```
inline int     greater(int i, int j)
               { return ( i > j ? i : j); }
inline double  greater(double x, double y)
               { return ( x > y ? x : y); }
inline complex greater(complex w, complex z)
               { return ( w > z ? w : z); }
```

Three distinct functions are overloaded. The most interesting has `complex` type for its argument list variables and its return type. The conversion member function `operator double` is required to evaluate `w > z`. The `complex` variables w and z are converted to `double`. Later in this chapter we discuss overloading operators, a construct that allows us to provide new meanings to existing C++ operators. No conversion is necessary for the return type.

■
```
w.assign(x, y);
z.assign(i, j);
```

The first invocation of the member function `assign` requires the `float` argument x to be converted to `double`. The `double` argument y needs no conversion. The second invocation has both arguments as `int`, which require conversion. Integer arguments are assignment-compatible with `double`.

■
```
cout << "compare " << i << " and " << j << "  greater is "
     << greater(i, j) << endl;
cout << "compare " << x << " and " << y << "  greater
is "
     << greater(x, y) << endl;
```

The first statement selects the first definition of `greater` because of the exact match rule. The second statement selects the second definition of `greater` because of the use of a standard widening conversion `float` to `double`. The value of variable x is widened to `double`.

■ `cout << "  greater is " << greater(y, double(z)) << endl;`

The second definition of `greater` is selected because of the exact match rule. The explicit conversion `double(z)` is necessary to avoid ambiguity. If instead the function call

```
greater(y, z);   //ERROR
```

were used, it would have two available conversions to achieve a match. The user-defined conversion of `double` to `complex` for the argument y matches the third definition. The user-defined conversion from `complex` to `double` for the argument z matches the second definition. The second function definition has a best match in argument one and the third function has a best match in argument two. This violates the requirement that "a best match must be unique. It must be best on at least one argument and as good on all other arguments."

■ `zmax = greater(w, z);`

An exact match for definition three.

7.3   *Friend* FUNCTIONS

The keyword `friend` is a function specifier. It gives a nonmember function access to the hidden members of the class. Its use is a method of escaping the strict strong-typing and data-hiding restrictions of C++. We must have a good reason for escaping these restrictions, however, as they are both important to reliable programming. The use of `friend` functions in the C++ language is controversial.

One reason for using `friend` functions is that some functions need privileged access to more than one class. A second reason is that a `friend` function passes all its arguments through the argument list, and each argument value is subject to assignment-compatible conversion. Conversions would apply to a class variable passed explicitly and would be especially useful in cases of operator overloading, as seen in the next section.

A friend function declaration must appear inside the class declaration to which it is a friend. The function is prefaced by the keyword friend and can appear in either the public or private part of the class without affecting its meaning. A member function of one class can be a friend function of another class. When this is the case, the member function is declared in the friend's class using the scope resolution operator to qualify its function name. If all member functions of one class are friend functions of a second class, this can be specified by writing friend class *class name*.

The following declarations illustrate the syntax:

```
class tweedledee {
    . . .
    friend void alice();            //friend function
    int         cheshire();         //member function
    . . .
};

class tweedledum {
    . . .
    friend int tweedledee::cheshire();
    . . .
};

class tweedledumber {
    . . .
    friend class tweedledee;     //all member functions
                                 //of tweedledee have access
    . . .
};
```

Consider a class matrix (see exercise 6.25) and a class vect (see Chapter 6). A function multiplying a vector by a matrix, as represented by these two classes, could be written efficiently if it had access to the private members of both classes. It would be a friend function of both classes. In our discussion in Chapter 6, safe access was provided to the elements of vect and matrix with their respective member functions vect::element() and matrix::element(). We could write a function using this access that would multiply without requiring friend status. However, the price in functional call overhead and array bounds checking would make such a matrix multiply unnecessarily inefficient.

```
class matrix;                    //forward reference

class vect {
private:
   int*       p;
   int        size;
   friend vect mpy(const vect& v, const matrix& m);
public:
   . . .
};

class matrix {    //stores integer elements
private:
   int**      base;
   int        row_size, column_size;
   friend vect mpy(const vect& v, const matrix& m);
public:
   . . .
};

vect mpy(const vect& v, const matrix& m)
{
   if (v.size != m.row_size) {    //incorrect sizes
      cerr << "multiply failed - sizes incorrect "
           << v.size << " and " << m.row_size << endl;
      exit(1);
   }
   //use privileged access to p in both classes
   vect ans(m.column_size);
   int  i, j;
   for (i = 0; i <= m.ub2(); ++i) {
      ans.p[i] = 0;
      for (j = 0; j <= m.ub1(); ++j)
         ans.p[i] += v.p[j] * m.base[j][i];
   }
   return (ans);
}
```

A minor point is the necessity of a forward declaration of the class `matrix`. This is necessary because the function `mpy` must appear in both classes, and it uses each class as an argument type.

We can view `friend` functions as part of the public interface of a class. There are a number of situations for which they are an appropriate alternative to member functions. The use of `friend` is controversial because they break through the encapsulating wall surrounding private members of classes. The OOP paradigm is that objects (in C++ these are class variables) should be accessed through their public members. Only member functions should have access to the hidden implementation of the ADT. This is a neat, orderly design principle. The `friend` function, however, straddles this boundary. It has access to private members but is not itself a member function. It can be used to provide quick fixes to code that needs access to the implementation details of a class. The mechanism can be abused easily. However, as in the previous example where efficiency was a concern, some coding situations benefit from its use.

7.4   OVERLOADING OPERATORS

The keyword `operator` also is used to overload the built-in C++ operators. Just as a function name, such as `print`, can be given a variety of meanings that depend on its arguments, so can an operator, such as `+`, be given additional meanings. Overloading operators allows ADTs to use C++ expression syntax. It is an important notational convenience and in many instances leads to shorter, more readable programs.

The previous section's `mpy` function could have been written as

```
vect operator* (const vect& v, const matrix& m)
   . . .
```

where `*` is the binary multiplication operator. If this had been done, and if r and s were `vect`s and t was a `matrix`, then the natural looking expression

```
r = s * t;
```

would invoke the multiply function. This replaces the functional notation

```
r = mpy(s, t);
```

It is also possible to invoke an overloaded operator using the functional notation

```
r = operator*(s, t);
```

Although meanings can be added to operators, their associativity and precedence remain the same. For example, the multiplication operator remains of higher precedence than the add operator. (The operator precedence table for C++ is included in Appendix B.) Almost all operators can be overloaded. The exceptions are the member operator `.`, the member object selector operator `.*` (see Chapter 8), the ternary conditional expression operator `? :`, the `sizeof` operator, and the scope resolution operator `::`.

Available operators include all the arithmetic, logical, comparison, equality, assignment, and bit operators. Both prefix and the postfix forms of the increment and decrement operators can be overloaded. The subscript operator `[]` and the function call `()` can also be overloaded. The class pointer operator `->` and the member pointer selector operator `->*` can be overloaded (see Chapter 8). It is also possible to overload `new` and `delete`.

7.5   UNARY OPERATOR OVERLOADING

We continue our discussion of operator overloading by demonstrating how to overload unary operators, such as `!`, `++`, `~`, and `[]`. For this purpose we develop the class `clock`, which can be used to store time as days, hours, minutes, and seconds. We will develop familiar operations on this `clock`.

```
class clock {
private:
   unsigned long int  tot_secs, secs, mins, hours, days;
public:
   clock(unsigned long int i); //constructor and conversion
   void print();                 //formatted printout
   void tick();                  //add one second
   clock operator++() { this -> tick(); return (*this); }
};
```

This class overloads the prefix increment operator. The signature for overloading the comparable postfix increment operator would be `clock` operator++(int). When this form of the increment operator is over-loaded and used, it is invoked implicitly with the integer value zero as the actual integer parameter. The overloaded operator is a member function and can be invoked on its implicit single argument. The member function tick adds one second to the implicit argument of the overloaded ++ operator.

```
inline clock::clock(unsigned long int i)
{
    tot_secs = i;
    secs = tot_secs % 60;
    mins = (tot_secs / 60) % 60;
    hours = (tot_secs / 3600) % 24;
    days = tot_secs / 86400;
}

void clock::tick()
{
    clock  temp(++tot_secs);

    secs = temp.secs;
    mins = temp.mins;
    hours = temp.hours;
    days = temp.days;
}
```

The constructor performs the usual conversions from tot_secs to days, hours, minutes, and seconds. For example, since a day is 86,400 seconds, integer division by this constant gives the whole number of days. The member function tick constructs clock temp, which adds one second to the total time. The constructor acts as a conversion function that properly updates the time.

The overloaded operator++() also updates the implicit clock variable and returns the updated value as well. It could have been coded in the same way as tick(), except that the statement

```
return (temp);
```

would have to be added.

We can test our functions, adding the following code:

```
void clock::print()
{
    cout << days << " d :" << hours << " h :"
         << mins << " m :" << secs << " s\n";
}

main()
{
    clock t1(59), t2(172799);   //min - 1 sec and 2 days - 1 sec
    cout << "initial times are\n";
    t1.print();
    t2.print();
    ++t1;   ++t2;
    cout << "after one second times are\n";
    t1.print();
    t2.print();
}
```

The output is

```
initial times are
0 d :0 h :0 m :59 s
1 d :23 h :59 m :59 s
after one second times are
0 d :0 h :1 m :0 s
2 d :0 h :0 m :0 s
```

It would have been possible to overload *prefix* ++ using a friend function as follows:

```
friend clock operator++(clock& cl)
                    { cl.tick(); return (cl); }
```

Note that since the clock variable must advance by one second, we call it by reference. The decision to choose between a friend representation and a member function representation typically depends on whether or not implicit conversion operations are available and desirable. Explicit argument passing, as in friend functions, allows the argument to be automatically coerced.

7.6   BINARY OPERATOR OVERLOADING

We continue with our clock example and show how to overload binary operators. Basically the same principles hold. When a binary operator is overloaded using a member function, it has as its first argument the implicitly passed class variable and as its second argument the lone argument list parameter. A friend function or an ordinary function has both arguments specified in the parameter list. Of course an ordinary function cannot access private members.

Let us create an adding operation for type clock that adds two values together.

```
class clock {
    . . .
    friend clock operator+(const clock& c1, const clock& c2);
};

clock operator+(const clock& c1, const clock& c2)
{
    clock temp(c1.tot_secs + c2.tot_secs);
    return (temp);
}
```

Both arguments are specified explicitly. They are both candidates for assignment conversions. The line of code

```
clock temp(c1.tot_secs + c2.tot_secs);
```

uses the constructor to convert unsigned long int expression into a clock value.

Using this definition, we have

```
int  i = 5;
clock c(900);
    . . .
c + i   //legal: i converted to a clock
i + c   //legal: i converted to a clock
```

In contrast, let us overload binary minus with a member function.

```
class clock {
   . . .
   clock operator-(const clock& c);
};

clock clock::operator-(const clock& c)
{
   clock temp( tot_secs - c.tot_secs);
   return (temp);
}
```

Remember that there is an implicit first argument. This takes some getting used to. It can also cause asymmetric behavior for binary operators.

```
int  i = 5;
clock c(900);
 . . .
c - i              //legal: i converted to a clock
c.operator-(i)   //function call notation
i - c              //illegal: i is not a clock
i.operator-(c)   //illegal: function call notation
```

As seen clearly in the use of function call notation, the variable i is not a clock and as such does not "understand" the meaning of minus.

We will define a multiplication operation as a binary operation with one argument an unsigned long int and the second argument a clock variable. The operation is implemented as a friend function.

```
clock operator*(unsigned long int m, const clock& c)
{
   clock temp(m * c.tot_secs);
   return (temp);
}
```

This implementation forces the multiplication to have a fixed ordering that is type-dependent. To avoid this, it is common practice to write a second overloaded function

```
clock operator*(const clock& c, unsigned long int m)
   . . .
```

7.7   OVERLOADING ASSIGNMENT AND SUBSCRIPTING OPERATORS

C++ has reference declarations, and such type modifiers produce lvalues. Remember, *lvalue* stands for *location value*. On the right side of an assignment expression, an lvalue is automatically dereferenced. On the left side of an assignment expression, an lvalue specifies where an appropriate value is to be stored. Both subscripting and assignment make use of these properties of lvalues. For ADTs we must define such expressions, unless satisfactory defaults are available. We will reimplement the class vect from Section 6.5, extending its functionality by applying operator overloading.

The reimplemented class has several improvements to make it both safer and more useful. A constructor that converts an ordinary integer array to a safe array is added to allow us to develop code using safe arrays and later to convert the same code to run efficiently using ordinary arrays. The public data member ub is changed to a member function. This prevents a user from inadvertently introducing a program error by modifying the member. Finally, the subscript operator [] is overloaded and replaces the member function element.

```
//A safe array type vect with [] overloaded
class vect {
private:
   int* p;                            //base pointer
   int size;                          //number of elements
public:
   //constructors and destructor
   vect();                            //create a size 10 array
   vect(int n);                       //create a size n array
   vect(const vect& v);               //initialization by vect
   vect(const int a[], int n);        //initialization by array
   ~vect() { delete [] p};
   //other member functions
   int  ub() { return (size - 1); }   //upper bound
   int& operator[](int i);            //range checked element
   vect& operator=(const vect& v);    //overload assignment
   vect operator+(const vect& v);     //overload addition
};
```

We add two further constructors.

```
vect::vect(const int a[], int n)    //convert a normal array
{
   if (n <= 0) {
      cerr << "illegal vect size: " << n << endl;
      exit(1);
   }
   size = n;
   p = new int[size];
   for (int i = 0; i < size; ++i)
      p[i] = a[i];
}


vect::vect(const vect& v)           //copy constructor
{
   size = v.size;
   p = new int[size];
   for (int i = 0; i < size; ++i)
      p[i] = v.p[i];
}
```

The overloaded subscript operator takes an integer argument and tests that this value is within range. If so, it uses it to return the lvalue of the indexed element.

```
int& vect::operator[](int i)
{
   if (i < 0 || i > (size - 1)) {
      cerr << "illegal vect index: " << i << endl;
      exit(1);
   }
   return (p[i]);
}
```

An overloaded subscript operator has a return type and a single argument. It must be a non-static member function. It is good style to maintain the consistency between a user-defined meaning of the subscripting operator [] and standard usage. Thus a most common function prototype is

class name& operator[] *(integral type)*;

A reference value is returned in such functions that can be used on either side of an assignment expression.

When assignment is *not* overloaded it is defined by default, with the semantics being memberwise assignment of value. This is sometimes called shallow copy semantics and can be incorrect (see Chapter 6). It behooves the class provider to make sure that the default semantics are correct. If not, as is the case here with `vect`, the class provider must overload the construct with the correct semantics, or alternatively overload the assignment operator with error-signalling behavior.

The following member function overloads assignment for `class vect`:

```
vect& vect::operator=(const vect& v)
{
    int s = (size < v.size) ? size : v.size;

    if (v.size != size)
        cerr << "copying different size arrays "
             << size << " and " << v.size << endl;
    for (int i = 0; i < s; ++i)
        p[i] = v.p[i];
    return (*this);
}
```

DISSECTION OF THE *vect::operator=(const vect& v)* FUNCTION

■ `vect& vect::operator=(const vect& v)`

The `operator=` function returns reference to `vect` and has one explicit argument of type reference to `vect`. The first argument of the assignment operator is the implicit argument. The function could have been written to return `void`, but then it would not have allowed multiple assignment.

■ `int s = (size < v.size) ? size : v.size;`

The smaller size is used in the element-by-element assignment. This function allows a smaller array to have its contents copied into the beginning of a larger array. When assigning from the larger array, it uses only as many elements as are in the smaller array.

■ if (v.size != size)
```
    cerr << "copying different size arrays "
         << size << " and " << v.size << endl;
```

This is a warning to the user in case this use was inadvertent.

■ for (int i = 0; i < s; ++i)
```
    p[i] = v.p[i];
return (*this);
```

The explicit argument v.p[] is the right side of the assignment; the implicit argument, as represented by p[], is the left side of the assignment. The self-referential pointer is dereferenced and passed back as the value of the expression. This allows multiple assignment with right-to-left associativity to be defined.

Expressions of type vect can be evaluated by overloading in appropriate ways the various arithmetic operators. As an example, let us overload binary + to mean element-by-element addition of two vect variables.

```
vect vect::operator+(const vect& v)
{
    int s = (size < v.size) ? size : v.size;
    vect  sum(s);

    if (v.size != size)
       cerr << "adding different size arrays "
            << size << " and " << v.size << endl;
    for (int i = 0; i < s; ++i)
       sum.p[i] = p[i] + v.p[i];
    return (sum);
}
```

Now with the class vect, as extended, all of the following expressions are meaningful:

```
a = b;                      //a, b are type vect
a = b = c;                  //a, b, c are type vect
a = vect(data, DSIZE);      //convert array data[DSIZE]
a = b + a;                  //assignment and addition
a = b + (c = a) + d;        //complicated expression
```

The class vect is a full-fledged ADT. It behaves and appears in client code much as any built-in type behaves and appears.

7.8   MORE SIGNATURE-MATCHING

The rules given in simplified form in Section 7.2 are further clarified with examples in this section.

The function argument type list is called its *signature*. The return type is not a part of the signature, but the order of the arguments is crucial.

```
int  sqr(int i);            //signature is int
double  sqr(int i);         //signature is int
void print(int i = 0);      //signature is int
void print(int i, double x); //signature is int, double
void print(double y, int i); //signature is double, int
```

In this example sqr is illegally redeclared, but print has three distinct signatures. When the print function is invoked, the compiler matches the actual arguments to the different signatures and picks the best match. In general there are three possibilities: a best match, an ambiguous match, and no match. Without a best match, the compiler issues an appropriate syntax error.

```
print(15);                  //matches int
print('A');                 //converts and matches int
print(9.90);                //converts and matches int
print(str[]);               //no match wrong type
print(15, 9);               //ambiguous
print(15.0, 9);             //matches double, int
print(15, 9.0);             //matches int, double
print(15.0, 9.0);           //ambiguous
print(i, j, k);             //no match too many arguments
print();                    //match  int by default
```

The matching algorithm has two parts: The first part determines a best match for each argument. The second part sees if there is one function that is a unique best match in each argument. The argument list `15.0, 9.0` has a best match in its first argument to `print(double, int)` and a best match in its second argument to `print(int, double)`. Thus it has no unique best match and is ambiguously overloaded.

For a given argument a best match is always an exact match. An exact match also includes *trivial conversions*. For type `T` these are as follows:

From	To
`//equally good`	
`T`	`T&`
`T&`	`T`
`T`	`const T`
`T`	`volatile T`
`T[]`	`T*`
`T(args)`	`(*T)(args)`
`//not as good`	
`T*`	`const T*`
`T*`	`volatile T*`
`T&`	`const T&`
`T&`	`volatile T&`

The first six trivial conversions cannot be used to disambiguate exact matches. The last four are considered worse than the first six. Thus

```
void print(int i);
void print(const int& i);
```

can be unambiguously overloaded.

The rule in Section 7.2 distinguishes promotions from other standard conversions. A promotion goes from a narrower type to a wider type. Thus going from `char` to `int` is a promotion. Promotions are better than other standard conversions. Among promotions, conversion from `float` to `double` and conversion from `char`, `short`, or `enum` to `int` are better than other promotions. Standard conversions also include pointer conversions. These need to be explained in the context of inheritance (see Chapter 9).

It is important to remember that user-defined conversions include constructors of a single argument. This constructor can be implicitly called to perform a conversion from the argument type to its class type. This can happen for assignment conversions, as in the argument-matching algorithm. For example,

```
//clock with a reset function.
class clock {
private:
    unsigned long int  tot_secs, secs, mins, hours, days;
public:
    clock(unsigned long int i); //constructor and conversion
    void print();               //formatted printout
    void tick();                //add one second
    clock operator++() { this -> tick(); return (*this); }
    void reset(const clock& c); //alternate to operator=()
};


    . . .


void clock::reset(const clock& c)
{
    *this = c;
}


main()
{
    clock c1(900), c2(400);
    . . .
    c1.reset(c2);
    c2.reset(100);
    . . .
}
```

The call to reset(100) involves an argument match between int and clock that is a user-defined conversion invoking the constructor clock(unsigned).

One last piece of advice: Explicitly casting arguments can be both an aid to documentation and a useful way to avoid poorly understood conversion sequences.

7.9   POLYNOMIAL: TYPE AND LANGUAGE EXPECTATIONS

A type's behavior is largely dictated by expectations found in the community that uses it. So how a polynomial behaves is determined by the mathematical community's definitions. When we come to write a polynomial type, we expect that the basic mathematical operations, such as + - * /, are available and work appropriately. Furthermore, we expect that assignment operators, equality operators, and increment and decrement operators are provided, consistent with the C community expectations. A class provides a public interface that is easy to use insofar as it meets both expectations. Where there is no normal expectation for operators, they should not be overloaded.

A more realistic polynomial class based on the representation in Chapter 6 could have the following declaration:

```
//A polynomial package with overloaded arithmetic operators
class polynomial {
private:
    term*    h;
    int      degree;
    void     prepend(term*  t);
    void     add_term(term*& a, term*& b);
    void     release();
    void     rest_of(term* rest);
    void     reverse();
public:
    polynomial();
    polynomial(const polynomial& p);
    polynomial(int size, double coef[], int expon[]);
    ~polynomial() { release(); }
    void print() const;
    double operator()(double x) const;        //evaluate P(x)
    polynomial& operator=(const polynomial& a);
    friend polynomial& operator+(const polynomial& a, const
        polynomial& b);
    friend polynomial& operator-(const polynomial& a, const
        polynomial& b);
    friend polynomial& operator*(const polynomial& a, const
        polynomial& b);
    friend polynomial& operator/(const polynomial& a, const
        polynomial& b);
    friend polynomial& operator-(const polynomial& a);  //unary -
    friend polynomial& operator+=(const polynomial& a, const
        polynomial& b);
    friend boolean operator==(const polynomial& a, const
        polynomial& b);
    friend boolean operator!=(const polynomial& a, const
        polynomial& b);
};
```

We expect both the basic mathematical operations to work and the basic relationships among C++ operators to hold. It would be very undesirable to have operator=(), operator+(), and operator+=() all defined and not have a = a + b give the same result as a += b.

The code for overloading operator= is

```
polynomial& polynomial::operator=(const polynomial& a)
{
    if (h != a.h) { //avoid a = a case
        release(); //garbage collect old value
        polynomial* temp = new polynomial(a);
        h = temp -> h;
        degree = temp -> degree;
    }
    return (*this);
}
```

The implementation of the other operators is left as an exercise.

7.10 SUMMARY

1   Overloading operators gives them new meanings for ADTs. The ADT can then be used in much the same way as a built-in type. For example, the expression a + b has different meanings depending on the types of the variables a and b. The expression could mean string concatenation, complex number addition, or integer addition, depending on whether the variables were the ADT string, the ADT complex, or the built-in type int, respectively.

2   A functional notation of the form

type-name (expression)

is equivalent to a cast. The type must be expressible as an identifier. Thus the two expressions

```
x = float(i);    //C++ functional notation
x = (float) i;
```

are equivalent.

3   A constructor of one argument is de facto a type conversion from the argument's type to the constructor's class type. A conversion from a user-specified type to a built-in type can be made by defining a special conversion function. The general form of such a member

function is

```
operator type () { . . . }
```

These conversions occur implicitly in assignment expressions, in arguments to functions, and in values returned from functions.

4   Overloaded functions are an important addition in C++. The over-loaded meaning is selected by matching the argument list of the function call to the argument list of the function declaration. The algorithm that accomplishes this depends on what type conversions are available. A best match must be unique. It must be best on at least one argument and as good on all other arguments as any other match. The matching algorithm for arguments is as follows:

1 Use an exact match if found.

2 Try standard type promotions.

3 Try standard type conversions.

4 Try user-defined conversions.

5 Use a match to ellipsis if found.

5   The keyword friend is a function specifier. It allows a nonmember function access to the hidden members of the class of which it is a friend. Its use is a method of escaping the strict strong-typing and data-hiding restrictions of C++.

6   The keyword operator is also used to overload the built-in C operators. Just as a function name, such as print, can be given a variety of meanings that depend on its arguments, so also can an operator, such as +, be given additional meanings. Overloading operators allows expressions of both user types and native types to be written. The precedence and associativity remain fixed.

7   Operator overloading typically uses either member functions or friend functions because they both have privileged access. When a unary operator is overloaded using a member function, it has an empty argument list because the single operator argument is the implicit argument. When a binary operator is overloaded using a member function, it has as its first argument the implicitly passed class variable and as its second argument the lone argument list parameter. A friend function or an ordinary function has both arguments specified in the parameter list.

8   An overloaded subscript operator must be a non-static member function. Overloaded assignment, function call, and member access must also be non-static member functions. The subscript operator can have any return type and any argument type. However, it is good style to maintain the consistency between a user-defined meaning and standard usage. Thus a most common function prototype is

class name& operator[] (*integral type*);

A reference value is returned in such functions that can be used on either side of an assignment expression.

7.11   EXERCISES

1   The following table has a variety of mixed type expressions. Fill in both the type the expression is converted to and its value when well defined.

Declarations and initializations		

`int i = 3, *p = &i;`
`char c = 'b';`
`float x = 2.14, *q = &x;`		

Expression	*Type*	*Value*
`i + c`		
`x + i`		
`p + i`		
`p == & i`		
`* p - * q`		
`(int)x + i`		

2   For the type `complex` provide a constructor that converts an `int` to a `complex`. Explain why this is redundant where a constructor

from double has been provided. Write an explicit conversion that converts complex to double, meaning that its value is its real component.

3   If the following line of code from the greater program

```
cout << "  greater is " << greater(y, double(z)) endl;
```

is replaced by

```
cout << "  greater is " << greater(y, z) endl;
```

what goes wrong?

4   Write a function that adds a vect v to a matrix m. The prototype to be added to class matrix and class vect is

```
friend vect add(const vect&v, matrix&m);
```

The vect v will be added element by element to each row of m.

5   The class complex as defined in this chapter is

```
class complex {
   double real, imag;
public:
   complex(double r) { real = r; imag = 0; }
   void assign(double r, double i) { real = r; imag = i; }
   void print() { cout << real << " + " << imag << "i "; }
   operator double()
           { return (sqrt(real * real + imag * imag)); }
};
```

We wish to augment it by overloading a variety of operators. For example, the member function print could be replaced by overloading the ~operator.

```
void operator~() { cout << real << " + " << imag << "i "; }
```

Rewrite this as a friend function. Also, code and test a unary minus operator. It should return a complex whose value in each part is negated.

6   For the type complex write the following binary operator functions: add, multiply, and subtract. Each should return complex. Write two versions, a friend version and a member function version.

7   Write two friend functions:

```
friend complex operator+(complex, double);
friend complex operator+(double, complex);
```

In the absence of a conversion from type double to type complex, both types are needed in order to allow completely mixed expressions of complex and double. Explain why writing one with an int parameter is unnecessary when these friend functions are available.

8   Overload assignment for complex. In the presence of the conversion operator for converting complex to double, what is the effect of assigning a complex to double?

9   Program a class vec_complex that is a safe array type whose element values are complex. Overload the operators + and * to mean element-by-element complex addition and dot-product of two complex vectors, respectively. For added efficiency you can make the class vec_complex a friend of class complex.

10   The following member function is a form of *iterator*:

```
int& vect::iterate()
{
    static int i = 0;
    i = i % size;
    return (p[i++]);
}
```

It is called an iterator because it returns each element value of a vect in sequence. Use it to write a print function that is not a member function and that writes out all element values of a given vect.

11   Exercise 10 has a serious limitation. By providing an iterator that is contained in the class, the element sequencing does not depend on the individual vect variable. Thus, if a and b are both vect variables, the first call of a.iterate() will get the first element of a, and a subsequent call of b.iterate() will get the

second element of b. So instead we will define a new class vect_iterator as follows:

```
class vect_iterator {
    int  i;
    int *p;
public:
    vect_iterator(vect& v) { p = v.p; i = 0; }
    int& iterate();
};
```

This class must be a friend of vect. Write the code for iterate. Then each declaration of a vect has a corresponding declaration of its iterator. For example,

```
vect a(5), b(10);
vect_iterator it_a(a), it_b(b);
```

Use this to write a function that finds the maximum element value in a vect.

12   Define a new class matrix_iterator as the iterator that sequences through all elements of a matrix (see Section 4.7). Use it to find the maximum element in a matrix.

13   Redo the string ADT of Section 4.3 by using operator overloading. The member function assign should be changed to become operator=. The member function concat should be changed to become operator+. Also, overload operator[] to return the ith character in the string. If there is no such character, the value −1 should be returned.

14   Redo the list ADT of Section 4.6 by using operator overloading. The member function add should be changed to become operator+. The member function del should be changed to become operator--. Also, overload operator[] to return the ith element in the list.

15   Modify the class set in Chapter 6, exercise 18, to have overloaded
     operators +, -, and *.

```
class set {
    . . .
    set operator+(set& v); //define union
    set operator*(set& v); //define intersection
    set operator-(set& v); //define difference
};
```

Test your complete set ADT with the following:

```
main()
{
    set   s(0x5555), t(0x10303021), w, x;
    s.pr_mems(); t.pr_mems(); w.pr_mems(); x.pr_mems();
    w = s + t;        //set union
    x = s * t;        //set intersection
    t = t - s;        //set difference
    s.pr_mems(); t.pr_mems(); w.pr_mems(); x.pr_mems();
}
```

Notice that we now have added a set type that is similar to the
built-in Pascal set type.

16   Take the polynomial::plus() member function found in Chap-
     ter 6 and convert it to code for overloading polynomial
     operator(const polynomial&, const polynomial&).   It
     should be a friend of the class polynomial.

17   **Project:** Write code to implement a polynomial multiplication oper-
     ator. The code can repeatedly call the polynomial addition routine.
     Did you make sure that intermediate results would be properly
     garbage collected? Write a "consistent with community expecta-
     tions" full blown polynomial package. You could include differen-
     tiation and integration of polynomials as well.

8

VISITATION: ITERATORS AND CONTAINERS

Container classes are used to hold a large number of individual items. The types `stack` and `vect` are two such container classes. Many of the operations on container classes involve the ability to visit individual elements conveniently. Classes also are the means to attain abstraction in C++. Abstraction is a question of ignoring detail. A class hides detail. It publicly provides a convenient way to handle a computational task. In this chapter we explore a variety of techniques to perform visitation and the extraction of elements from a class. One technique is to create a class whose function is to visit the elements of an object in a container class. This class iterates over the elements of the other class. Using visitation as the theme, we will more completely use the concepts of the previous three chapters.

8.1 VISITATION

Conventional programming uses the `for` statement as its preferred means of structuring iteration, especially when processing arrays.

```
//archetypal for-array processing
//visit each a[i] and do something
for (i = 0; i < size; ++i)
   sum += a[i];
```

The homogeneous aggregate a[] is processed element by element. The
for statement specifies a specific order of visitation and is controlled by
an index i, which is visibly modified. The order of visitation and the index
used are generally details of implementation that do not affect the computation. Here is an alternate coding that performs the same computation:

```
for (j = size - 1; j > -1; --j)
   sum += a[j];
```

Abstractly the computation is:

> *until no new elements*
> sum += *next element*

We could capture getting a *next element* with a member function. Let us
modify the class vect from Chapter 7 to add next().

```
class vect {
private:
   int* p;                              //base pointer
   int size;                            //number of elements
   int cur_ind;                         //visitation value
public:
   vect();                              //create a size 10 array
   vect(int n);                         //create a size n array
   vect(const vect& v);                 //initialization by vect
   vect(const int a[], int n);          //initialization by array
   ~vect() { delete [] p; }
   int  ub() { return (size - 1); }     //upper bound
   int& operator[](int i);              //range checked element
   vect& operator=(const vect& v);
   int& next();                         //visit next element
   int& current() { return (p[cur_ind]); }      //retrieve lvalue
   void reset_index(int n = 0) { cur_ind = n; } //reposition index
};
```

The function next() cannot go out of range of the implementation of vect::p[i]. When cur_ind reaches the last element of array p[size - 1], it is reset to zero, the first element.

```
int& vect::next()    //implements circular visitation
{
    if (cur_ind == size)        //at end
        return (p[cur_ind = 0]); //reset and return first element
    else
        return (p[cur_ind++]);   //return element and advance index
}
```

The code for the constructors must be changed to initialize cur_ind, for example vect(int n) becomes

```
vect::vect(int n): cur_ind(0)
{
    if (n <= 0) {
        cerr << "illegal vect size: " << n << endl;
        exit(1);
    }
    size = n;
    p = new int[size];
}
```

The code for summing such an aggregate would be:

```
for (i = 0; i <= a.ub(); ++i)
    sum += a.next();
```

The index i is decoupled from visitation. It is less likely that such code will accidentally modify i within the for loop, because i is not required for array indexing within the loop.

The idea of visitation as its own set of operations leads to adding other member functions.

```
int& vect::previous();  //decrement cur_ind and retrieve element
                        //exercise 1
```

8.2   ITERATORS

In the previous section visitation was coupled to an index `cur_ind` that was manipulated for each object. This means that visitation over the object was restricted to one use of this index at any one time. An extreme analogy would be restricting visitation of a large art museum, such as the Van Gogh Museum in Amsterdam, to only one art patron at a time. One way to avoid this is to duplicate the aggregate for each task that requires visitation. In the real world this is impossible for the Van Gogh Museum. (Of course each visitor could be given a book containing all the paintings in the museum.) Another possibility is to create a number of indices and pass them to the visitation function. This leads to a proliferation of possible unneeded variables and additional function call overhead for what is basically a fundamental operation. The solution is to create a separate but related class, called an *iterator class,* whose function is to visit and retrieve elements from the aggregate.

```
class vect {
private:
    friend  vect_iterator;       //confer special relationship
    int* p;                      //base pointer
    int size;                    //number of elements
public:
    . . .
};
class vect_iterator {
private:
    vect* pv;                    //associated vect object
    int    cur_ind;              //visitation index
public:
    vect_iterator(vect& v): cur_ind(0), pv(&v) {}
    int& next();
};

int& vect_iterator::next()
{
    if (cur_ind == pv -> size)         //end of vect?
        return (pv -> p[cur_ind = 0]); //reset to first element
    else
        return (pv -> p[cur_ind++]);
}
```

The two classes have a friendship relation. Iteration as a fundamental operation needs to be efficient. Generally this requires access to private implementation detail of the aggregate. Note that this complete decoupling of visitation from the aggregate object allows as many iterator objects to be declared as required by the computation. To return to our analogy, declaring an iterator is like letting yet another art patron into the Van Gogh museum. That person can enter the museum and visit its rooms independently of how many other visitors are already in the museum.

8.3   AN EXAMPLE: *quicksort()*

The *quicksort* sorting procedure, designed by Anthony Hoare, works by partitioning elements into a less-than pile and a greater-than or equal-to pile. The partitioning element divides the two piles, which now can be recursively partitioned. We wish to use iterators to keep track of the partitioning.

```
enum boolean { false, true};

class vect_iterator {
private:
   vect* pv;
   int cur_ind;
public:
   vect_iterator(vect& v): cur_ind(0), pv(&v) {}
   boolean successor();
   boolean predecessor();
   int& item() { return (pv -> p[cur_ind] ); }
   void reset(int n = 0) { cur_ind = n % pv -> size; }
   int position() { return (cur_ind); }
};

boolean vect_iterator::successor()
{
   if (cur_ind >= pv -> size - 1)
      return (false);      //no further successor
   else {
      ++cur_ind;           //advance index
      return (true);
   }
}

boolean vect_iterator::predecessor()
{
   if (cur_ind <= 0)
      return (false);      //no predecessor
   else {
      --cur_ind;           //decrement index
      return (true);
   }
}
```

In this version of the iterator class, we have decoupled moving through the aggregate from selecting the currently visited item. This allows a simple looping scheme for visiting the aggregate in general.

```
//ask user for size of aggregate
int   n;

cout << "Enter Size: ";
cin >> n;
cout << "\nEnter elements: ";

//create the aggregate and its relevant iterators
vect v(n);   vect_iterator front(v);

do {
   cin >> front.item();
   process(front.item());
} while (front.successor());
```

Similar code can be written with the `predecessor()` visiting the aggregate in the backward direction. (See Figure 8.1.)

The sorting algorithm `quicksort()` is a highly efficient internal sort. It is tricky to code because of the different indices that are tracked in a traditional implementation (see Kelley and Pohl, *A Book on C: 2nd Edition*, Benjamin/Cummings, 1990). We will replace indexing with iterators, which while still tricky, are easily reused for different types.

The `quicksort` algorithm works by recursively decomposing unordered values into two subsets separated by a mid-value. The mid-value is larger than all elements in the first set and smaller or equal to all elements in the second set. This segregation leads to smaller and smaller subsets that are in turn separated until they are trivially sorted. The use of `quicksort`

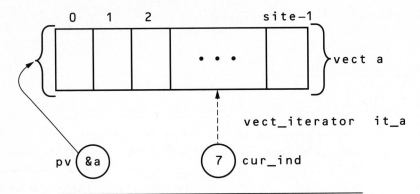

FIGURE 8.1   Iterator Declared on an Aggregate

is an illustration of the effectiveness of the divide-and-conquer method of programming.

```
//QUICKSORT using an iterator class
void quicksort(vect& v, int from, int to)
{
    int mid;

    if (from < to) {
        if (from == to - 1) { //2 elements
            if (v[from] > v[to])
                swap(v[from], v[to]);
        }
        else {
            mid = partition(v, from, to);
            quicksort(v, from, mid - 1);
            quicksort(v, mid + 1, to);
        }
    }
}
```

The swap() function interchanges out-of-order elements. By making swap() inline, we make the inner-loop code of both partition() and quicksort() efficient at no additional effort to the programmer. It is not error prone, as would be comparable code using macros.

```
inline void swap(int& i, int& j)
{
    int temp = i;

    i = j;
    j = temp;
}
```

The real work occurs in the `partition()` function. It arbitrarily uses the first element as the basis for separating all the elements into a less-than and a greater-than-or-equal-to pile. When it finds an out-of-order element that is on the less-than side, it switches to looking for an out-of-order element that is on the greater-than side. Pairwise it swaps these elements until it completes the partitioning. (See Figure 8.2.)

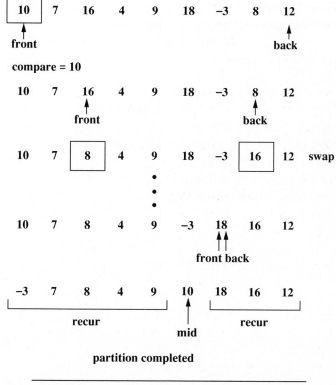

FIGURE 8.2   Quicksort Partition Described

```
int partition(vect& v, int from, int to)
{
   vect_iterator front(v), back(v);
   int  compare;

   back.reset(to);
   front.reset(from);
   compare = front.item(); //comparison element
   front.successor();      //advance to next element

   while (front.position() < back.position()) {
      //search forward for out of order element
      while ((front.position() < back.position())
                       &&(compare > front.item())))
         front.successor();

      //search backward for out of order element
      while ((front.position() < back.position())
                       &&(compare <= back.item())))
         back.predecessor();

      swap(front.item(), back.item());
   }

   //insert  mid position comparison element
   if (compare >= front.item()) {
      swap(v[from], front.item());
      return (front.position());
   }
   else {
      swap(v[from], v[front.position() - 1]);
      return (front.position() - 1);
   }
}
```

8.4   FRIENDLY CLASSES AND ITERATORS

A class can define objects that are needed as internal detail for other classes. To preserve its anonymous role, such a class needs to be private. A class that handles these private objects must be on friendly terms with them.

Recall the `string` type defined with reference-counting semantics in Chapter 6. Individual string values were ultimately referencing objects of type `str_obj`. This decoupling allowed one instance of `str_obj`, which might require many bytes of store, to be used by many instances of `string`. We can convert that example using friendship to preserve the privacy of the class `str_obj`.

```
class str_obj {
private:
    friend class string;
    friend class string_iterator;
    friend ostream& operator<<(ostream& out, const string& str);
    int   len, ref_cnt;
    char* s;
    str_obj():len(0), ref_cnt(1) { s = new char[1]; }  //initializers
    str_obj(int n):len(n), ref_cnt(1) { s = new char[n + 1]; }
    str_obj(const char* p):ref_cnt(1)
        { len = strlen(p); s = new char[len + 1]; strcpy(s, p); }
    ~str_obj() { delete [] s; }
};
```

This two-class design has the advantage of increasing flexibility by further segregating implementation detail from client code.

Iterators also typically need friendly relations to the object they are visiting. Let us add an iterator class and modify our `string` to overload assignment and the put-to operator to fill out this example.

```
class string {
private:
   friend class string_iterator;
   friend ostream& operator<<(ostream& out, const string& str);
   str_obj* st;
public:
   string() { st = new str_obj; }
   string(int n) { st = new str_obj(n); }
   string(const char* p) { st = new str_obj(p); }
   string(const string& str) { st = str.st; st -> ref_cnt++; }
   ~string();
   void assign(const string& str);
   void print() const { cout << st -> s ; }
   string& operator=(string& str) { assign(str); return (str); }
};

//A friend function of class string.
//This is a typical method for overloading << "put to".
//Since ostream_var <<  type_var  is the required syntax,
//a member function of class string is not possible.
ostream& operator<<(ostream& out, const string& str)
{
   out << str.st -> s;
   return (out);
}
```

As written, `ostream& operator<<(ostream&, const string&)` requires friendly relations to `str_obj` (see exercise 3). Because its return value is an `ostream&`, it can be used in a multiple put-to expression. This stays within the conventions of *iostream.h*.

We reuse the previously written `assign()` member function to generate the semantics of `operator=()`. We return a reference value to permit multiple assignment. It is worth pointing out that in the absence of overloading assignment, the default assignment semantics would fail. It would not properly handle the reference count.

The related iterator class follows a common design. We have a constructor associate the iterator object with the object to be visited by initializing `string* ptr_s`. We keep a private position variable `cur_ind`. Since the friendship relation between `string` and `str_obj` is not transitive, our design requires `string_iterator` to be friendly with `str_obj` as well.

```
enum boolean { false, true};

class string_iterator {
private:
   string* ptr_s;
   int cur_ind;
public:
   string_iterator(string& s): cur_ind(0), ptr_s(&s) {}
   boolean successor();
   char& item() { return ((ptr_s -> st -> s)[cur_ind]); }
   void reset(int n = 0) { cur_ind = n; }
   int position() { return (cur_ind); }
};

boolean string_iterator::successor()
{
   if (cur_ind >= ptr_s -> st -> len - 1)
      return (false);
   else {
      ++cur_ind;
      return (true);
   }
}
```

Let us use the iterator to search the string for the next word.

```
#include <ctype.h>
void word(string_iterator& it_s, char* w)
{
   while (isspace(it_s.item()) && it_s.successor())
      ;                         //find non-whitespace character
   if (!isspace(it_s.item())) {
      *w = it_s.item();         //first character of word
      while (it_s.successor() && !isspace(it_s.item()))
         *++w = it_s.item();    //successive characters
   }
   *++w = 0;                    //add '\0' terminator
}
```

This routine skips over characters for which `isspace()` is true. It then collects a word as a series of non-`isspace()` characters and terminates this with 0.

8.5   OVERLOADING OPERATOR *()* FOR INDEXING

A matrix type that provides dynamically allocated two-dimensional arrays can be designed with the function call operator overloaded to provide element selection. This is a good example of a container class useful in both scientific and nonscientific computation. The main idea for building this type is taken from Chapter 5. The matrix is allocated as a column of pointers that are base addresses for a row of elements.

In this example we make use of *assert.h*. This methodology is described in detail in Chapter 11. The package provides an assertion macro that dynamically tests a condition and reports failure if the condition is not met.

The function call operator `()` is overloadable as a non-static member function. It can be overloaded with respect to different signatures. It is frequently used to provide an iterator operation (see exercises 13–15) or an operation requiring multiple indices (see exercise 5 for a substring operation).

```
#include <assert.h>

//dynamic matrix type
class matrix {
private:
   int c_size, r_size;
   double **p;
public:
   matrix(int c, int r);
   ~matrix();
   double& operator()(int i, int j) { return (p[i][j]); }
   matrix& operator=(const matrix& m);
   matrix& operator+=(matrix& m);
};
```

```
matrix:: matrix(int c, int r):c_size(c), r_size(r)
{
   p = new double*[c];
   for (int i = 0; i < c; ++i)
      p[i] = new double[r];
}

matrix:: ~matrix()
{
   for (int i = 0; i < c_size; ++i)
      delete [] p[i];
   delete [] p;
}

matrix& matrix::operator=(const matrix& m)
{
   assert(m.c_size == c_size && m.r_size == r_size);
   int i, j;

   for (i = 0; i < c_size; ++i)
      for (j = 0; j < r_size; ++j)
         p[i][j] = m.p[i][j];
   return (*this);
}

matrix& matrix::operator+=(matrix& m)
{
   assert(m.c_size == c_size && m.r_size == r_size);
   int i, j;

   for (i = 0; i < c_size; ++i)
      for (j = 0; j < r_size; ++j)
         p[i][j] += m.p[i][j];
   return (*this);
}
```

DISSECTION OF THE CLASS *matrix*

■ `matrix:: matrix(int c, int r):c_size(c), r_size(r)`
```
matrix:: matrix(int c, int r):c_size(c), r_size(r)
{
    p = new double*[c];
    for (int i = 0; i < c; ++i)
        p[i] = new double[r];
}
```

The constructor first allocates an array of pointer-to-`double` off the heap. Then each array of `double` is allocated with its base address stored in a corresponding element `p[i]`. This scheme is necessary to provide correct addressing to individual matrix components regardless of size.

■ `double& operator() (int i, int j) { return (p[i][j]); }`

This member function gives a convenient multiple argument notation for element access. This results in client code using expressions of the form `m(i, j)` to access explicit matrix elements. Notice how through an assertion or conditional statement, matrix indices could be bounds-tested (see exercise 7).

■ `matrix& matrix::operator+=(matrix& m)`

```
    assert(m.c_size == c_size && m.r_size == r_size);
```

The assertion macro is used with a testable precondition for arguments needed by this member function. The matrix being assigned to must be the same size as the matrix expression being computed. The code replaces an `if-else` statement that would perform an error exit. Compare this to the code written for `class vect` (see Chapter 7).

■ `for (i = 0; i < c_size; ++i)`
```
for (i = 0; i < c_size; ++i)
    for (j = 0; j < r_size; ++j)
        p[i][j] += m.p[i][j];
```

This inner loop is efficient and transparent. Elementwise addition is being accomplished without overhead.

■ `return (*this);`

The return type is a *reference* to `matrix`. Dereferencing the `this` pointer causes the lvalue of the `matrix` object to be returned. This is the usual trick that allows multiple assignment to occur.

8.6   OVERLOADING *new* AND *delete*

Most container classes involve free store memory allocation and deallocation. The user of a container class wants it to be as flexible and general as possible. This can require more sophisticated use of memory than is provided by simple calls to operator `new` and `delete`.

Operator `new` has the general form

$::_{opt}$ `new` *placement*$_{opt}$ *type initializer*$_{opt}$

Some examples are

```
::new char[10];      //insist on global new
new(buff) X(a);      //call with buff using X::X(a)
```

Up to now we have been using the global `operator new()` to allocate free store. The system provides a `sizeof` (*type*) argument to this function implicitly. Its function prototype is

```
void* operator new(size_t size);
```

The operators `new` and `delete` can be overloaded. This feature provides a simple mechanism for user-defined manipulation of free store. For example, traditional C programming uses `malloc()` to access free store and return a `void*` pointer to the allocated memory. In this scheme memory is deallocated by the *stdlib.h* function `free()`. We use operator overloading of `new` and `delete` to allow an X object to utilize C traditional free store management.

```
#include <stdlib.h>    //malloc() and free() defined
class X {
  . . .
public:
  void* operator new(size_t size) { return (malloc(size)); }
  void  operator delete(void* ptr) { free(ptr); }
  X(unsigned size) { new(size); }
  ~X() { delete(this); }
  . . .
};
```

In this example, the class X has provided overloaded forms of new() and delete(). When a class overloads operator new(), the global operator is still accessible using the scope resolution operator ::.

One reason to overload these operators is to give them additional semantics, such as providing diagnostic information or being more fault tolerant. Also, the class can have a more efficient memory allocation scheme than provided by the system.

The *placement* syntax provides a comma-separated argument list used to select an overloaded operator new() with a matching signature. These additional arguments are often used to place the constructed object at a particular address. This form of operator new uses the *new.h* header file.

```
//Placement syntax and new overloaded.
#include <iostream.h>
#include <new.h>

char*  buf1 = new char[1000]; //use in place of free store
char*  buf2 = new char[1000];

class object {
private:
   . . .
public:
   . . .
};

main()
{
   object *p = new(buf1) object;   //allocate at buf1
   object *q = new(buf2) object;   //allocate at buf2
   . . .
}
```

Placement syntax allows the user to have an arbitrary signature for the overloaded **new** operator. This signature is distinct from the initializer arguments used by calls to **new** that select an appropriate constructor.

The **delete** operator comes in two flavors. It can have as signatures

```
void operator delete(void* p);
void operator delete(void* p, size_t);
```

The first signature makes no provision for the number of bytes to be returned by **delete**. In this case the programmer provides code that supplies this value. The second signature includes a **size_t** argument passed to the **delete** invocation. This is provided by the compiler as the size of the object pointed at by **p**. Only one form of **delete** can be provided as a static member function in each class.

The *new.h* file has the function pointer **_new_handler** that calls the error handler for **operator new**. If memory is exhausted, the function pointer **_new_handler** is used to call a default system routine. The user can specify an explicit *out of free store* routine, which can replace the default by using **set_new_handler()**. This will be looked at again in Chapter 11 when we discuss exceptions, error-handling, and program correctness.

```
//Simple fault tolerance using _new_handler.
#include <new.h>

void heap_exhausted()    //user defined error handling
{
   cerr << "HEAP EXHAUSTED" << endl;
   exit(1);
}

main()
{
   set_new_handler(&heap_exhausted);
   . . . //memory exhaustion is treated heap_exhausted()

};
```

These class `new()` and `delete()` member functions are always implicitly `static`. The `new()` is invoked before the object exists and therefore cannot have a `this` yet. The `delete()` is called by the destructor, so the object is already destroyed.

8.7   POINTER OPERATORS AND SMART POINTERS

The structure pointer operator `->` can be overloaded as a non-static class member function. The overloaded structure pointer operator is a unary operator on its left operand. The argument must be either a class object or a reference of this type. It can return either pointer to a class object or an object of a class for which `operator ->` is defined.

In the following example we overload the structure pointer operator inside the class t_ptr. Objects of type t_ptr act as controlled access pointers to objects of type triple.

```cpp
// Overloading the structure pointer operator.
#include <iostream.h>
enum boolean { false, true};

class triple {
private:
   int       i, j, k;
public:
   triple(int a, int b, int c) { i = a; j = b; k = c; }
   void print() { cout << "\ni = " << i
                       << ", j = " << j << ", k = " << k; }
};

triple   unauthor(0, 0, 0);

class t_ptr {
private:
   boolean   access;
   triple*   ptr;
public:
   t_ptr(boolean f, triple* p) { access = f; ptr = p; }
   triple*   operator ->() ;
};

triple* t_ptr::operator ->()
{
   if (access)
      return (ptr);
   else {
      cout << "\nunauthorized access";
      return (&unauthor);
   }
}
```

The variable t_ptr::access is tested by the overloaded operator ->, and, if true, access is granted. The following code illustrates this:

```
main()
{
    triple  a(1, 2, 3), b(4, 5, 6);
    t_ptr ta(false, &a), tb(true, &b);

    ta -> print();    //access denied
    tb -> print();    //access granted
}
```

POINTER TO CLASS MEMBER

A member is a subobject. Its type is bound to the type of the object it is a part of. Conceptually being an integer member of class *T1* is different than being an integer member of class *T2*.

A pointer to class member is distinct from a pointer to class. A pointer to class member's type is $T::*$, where T is the class name. C++ has two operators that act to dereference a pointer to class member. The pointer to member operators are:

```
.*
->*
```

Think of *obj* .* *ptr_mem* and *pointer->* ptr_mem* as first accessing the object and then accessing and dereferencing the member that is specified.

The following code shows how to use these operators:

```
//Pointer to class member.

#include <iostream.h>

class X {
private:
   int  hide;
public:
   int  visible;
   void print()
      { cout << "\nhide = " << hide
             << " visible = " << visible; }
   void reset() { visible = hide; }
   void set(int i) { hide = i; }
};

typedef void (X::*pfcn)();

main()
{
   X   a, b, *pb = &b;
   int X::*pXint = &X::visible;
   pfcn pF = &X::print;

   a.set(8); a.reset();
   b.set(4); b.reset();
   a.print();
   a.*pXint += 1;
   a.print();
   cout << "\nb.visible = " << pb ->*pXint;
   (b.*pF)();
   pF = &X::reset;
   (a.*pF)();
   a.print();
   cout << endl;
}
```

DISSECTION OF THE *ptr_mem* PROGRAM

■ `typedef void (X::*pfcn)();`

This says that `pfcn` is a pointer to class `X` member whose base type is a function with no arguments that returns `void`. Member functions `X::print` and `X::reset` match this type.

■ `int X::*pXint = &X::visible;`
  `pfcn pF = &X::print;`

This declares `pXint` to be a pointer to class `X` member whose base type is `int`. It is initialized to point at the member `X::visible`. The pointer `pF` is initialized to point at the member function `X::print`.

■ `a.*pXint += 1;`

This is equivalent to `++a.visible`.

■ `cout << "\nb.visible = " << pb ->*pXint;`
  `(b.*pF)();`

The pointer expression is equivalent to `pb -> visible`. The function call is equivalent to `b.print()`.

■ `pF = &X::reset;`
  `(a.*pF)();`

The pointer `pf` is assigned the address of `X::reset`. The function call is equivalent to `a.reset()`.

Consider the memory layout for representing an object. The object has a base address and the various non-static members are offset relative to this base address. In effect, a pointer to class member is used as an offset and is not a true pointer which has general memory addresses as values. A static member is not offset and as such a pointer to a static member is a true address.

8.8   GENERICITY WITH *void**

The pointer type void* serves as a generic or universal pointer type. Any other pointer type can be assigned it. This allows us to use it polymorphically by developing code that indirectly manipulates objects of any type. We can see this in the definition of the standard memory copying function memcpy.

```
#include <stddef.h>        //define size_t
#include <iostream.h>

void* memcpy(void* to, const void* from, size_t n_bytes)
{
    char* f = (char *)from, *t = (char *)to;
    for (int i = 0; i < n_bytes; ++i)
        t[i] = f[i];
    return (to);
}

main()
{
    char v[4];
    int   w  = 0x41424344;

    memcpy(v, &w, 4);          //polymorphic interface
    cout << w << " == " << v;
}
```

The function memcpy allows pointer arguments of any type to bytewise copy characters starting at the address specified by from. In the sample code we initialize a four-byte character array using an integer value stored in w. This technique can also work to allow a container class, such as stack, to store arbitrary values indirectly.

```
//generic pointer stack implementation
typedef void* generic_ptr;
enum boolean { FALSE, TRUE};

class stack {
private:
   enum   { EMPTY = -1};
   generic_ptr* s;
   int    max_len;
   int    top;
public:
   //the public interface for the ADT stack
   stack(): max_len(1000), top(EMPTY) { s = new generic_ptr[1000]; }
   stack(int size): max_len(size), top(EMPTY)
      { s = new generic_ptr[1000]; }
   ~stack() { delete [] s; }
   void reset() { top = EMPTY; }
   void push(generic_ptr c) { s[++top] = c; }
   generic_ptr pop() { return (s[top--]); }
   generic_ptr top_of() { return (s[top]); }
   boolean empty() { return boolean(top == EMPTY); }
   boolean full() { return boolean(top == max_len - 1); }
};
```

Of course, to do useful work with such a class, values must be properly cast. For example, assume that you have an array of words stored as a two-dimensional array of characters, and you wish to use the standard stack algorithm for printing the words in reverse order.

```
#include <iostream.h>
#include "genstack.h"

char* months[12] = { "january", "february", "march",
    "april", "may", "june", "july", "august",
    "september", "october", "november", "december"};

main()
{
    stack a;

    for (int i = 0; i < 12; ++i)
        a.push(months[i]);
    for (i = 0; i < 12; ++i)
        cout << (char*)a.pop() << endl;
}
```

We leave as an exercise writing a generic reversal routine that internally uses a stack (exercise 9).

8.9 SUMMARY

1   Visitation of the elements of an aggregate is a fundamental operation. When the aggregate is a class, an elegant solution to providing visitation operations is to create a separate but related class, called an *iterator class*, whose function is to visit and retrieve elements from the aggregate. As a fundamental operation, iteration must be efficient. Generally this requires access to private implementation detail of the aggregate. Note that this causes complete decoupling of visitation from the aggregate object, as many iterator objects can be declared as required by the computation.

2   The function call operator () is overloadable as a nonstatic member function. It can be overloaded with respect to different signatures. It is frequently used to provide an iterator operation or an operation requiring multiple indices, as in our matrix example.

3   The operators new and delete can be overloaded. This feature provides a simple mechanism for user-defined manipulation of free store. Reasons for wanting to overload these operators include giving them additional semantics, such as providing diagnostic

information or being more fault tolerant. Also important can be a case where the class can have a more efficient memory allocation scheme than that provided by the system.

4   The structure pointer operator `->` can be overloaded as a non-static class member function. The overloaded structure pointer operator is a unary operator on its left operand. The argument must be either a class object or a reference of this type. It can return either a pointer to a class object or an object of a class for which `operator ->` is defined.

5   A pointer to class member is distinct from a pointer to class. A pointer to class member's type is $T::*$, where T is the class name. C++ has two operators that act to dereference a pointer to class member. The pointer to member operators are

```
.*
->*
```

Think of *obj.*ptr_mem* and *pointer->*ptr_mem* as first accessing the object and then accessing and dereferencing the member that is specified.

6   The pointer type `void*` serves as a generic or universal pointer type. Any other pointer type can be assigned it. This allows us to use it polymorphically by developing code that indirectly manipulates objects of any type. We can see this in the definition of the standard memory copying function `memcpy`.

```
void* memcpy(void* to, const void* from, size_t n_bytes);
```

The function `memcpy` allows pointer arguments of any type to byte-wise copy characters starting at the address specified by `from`. This technique can also work to allow a container class, such as `stack`, to store arbitrary values indirectly.

8.10   EXERCISES

1   Write the visitation member function

```
int& vect::previous();
```

It should use `cur_ind` and decrement it. It should visit element `p[size - 1]` after visiting `p[0]`.

2   Discuss the difficulty of writing a bubble sort on `vect` in which visitation is with the member functions `next()`, `previous()`, and `same()`.

3   Explain why friendship to `str_obj` was required when overloading `<<` to act on objects of type `string`. Rewrite `string` by adding a member function `char* rep()`. This now can be used directly by `<<`. Discuss this solution. What access category within class `string` should `rep()` have.

4   What goes wrong with the following client code when the over-loaded definition of `operator=()` is omitted from `string`.

```
//Swapping strings that are reference counted.
#include <iostream.h>

class string {
   . . .
};

void swap(string x, string y)
{
   string temp;

   temp = x;
   x = y;
   y = z;
}

main()
{
   string  b("dont try me "), c(" try me");

   cout << b << c << endl;
   swap(b, c);
   cout << b << c << endl;
}
```

5   We can develop our `string` class with a substring operation by over-loading function call. The notation is `string(from, to)`, where `from` is the beginning point of the substring and `to` is the end point.

```
string string::operator()(int from, int to)
{
    string temp(to - from + 1);

    for (int i = from; i < to + 1; ++i)
        temp.st -> s[i - from] = st -> s[i];
    temp.st[to - from + 1] = 0;
    return (temp);
}
```

Use this substring operation to search a string for a given character sequence and return true if the subsequence is found.

6   Rewrite the substring function using a char* constructor. Is this better or worse? If you have a profiler, run this example with both forms of substring creation on the following client code:

```
main()
{
    string large("A very verbose phrase to search")

    for (i = 0; i < MANY; ++i)
        count += (large(i, i + 3) == "ver");
}
```

7   Use assertions to test indices for being within bounds when accessing a matrix element. Do this by modifying `double& matrix::operator() (int i, int j)`. Use a conditional compilation flag **NDEBUG** to signal the compiler whether or not to include insertions. This gives a simple mechanism that allows both safe and unsafe classes to be compiled from the same source code. Run an application such as a large matrix addition with both forms of code, and measure the run-time overhead required by the assertion statements.

8   Write a `matrix_iterator` class with the same interface as the `vect_iterator` class. It should have `successor()`, `predecessor()`, `reset()`, and `item()`. If you want you can extend this with member functions `int row()` and `int column()`.

9   Write the function

```
void reverse(double data[], int size);
// data[size] will be reversed
// internally declare a stack of generic pointers
// push values onto stack and pop them back into data[]
```

10   Use a stack to write out subsequences that are in increasing order by
     value. In the sequence (7, 9, 3, 2, 6, 8, 9, 2), the subsequences are
     (7, 9), (3), (2, 6, 8, 9), (2). Use a stack to store increasing values.
     Pop the stack when a next-sequence value is no longer increasing.
     Keep in mind that the stack pops values in reverse order. Redo this
     exercise using a queue, thus avoiding this reversal problem.

11   For the stack of generic pointers, add the constructor

```
stack::stack(int size, generic_ptr[]);
```

12   Write a bubble sort (or some other sort) for `vect` using iterators.
     Discuss in this context the value of using the iterator abstraction.

13   Overload `operator()` to provide the next element of `class vect`.

14   Overload `operator()(int step = 1)` to provide the next ele-
     ment of `class vect`, where `cur_ind + step` is used as the in-
     dex into the private representation. Be careful about staying within
     range of the dynamically allocated `vect`.

15   Create a version of the iterator in exercise 14 that cycles through
     all elements of a `vect`. For a particular `step` have subcycles that
     start with `cur_ind = 0, 1, 2, . . . step - 1`.

16   Rewrite `quicksort()` to sort `matrix()`. Use the iterator class
     developed in exercise 8 and model the code on Section 8.3.

17   **Project:** Code your own text editor. The model will be a page of
     text. The text will be made up of strings as a primary unit. You
     are to design an iterator class that can usefully navigate across the
     text. It can go to a next word, a next string, a next line—whatever
     you decide is useful. Minimally you should be able to enter, delete,
     and print text with or without line numbers. The text replacement
     commands should allow you to substitute one word for another.
     Also try to use file oriented I/O (see Appendix D). You want text
     to be *persistent*, which means when you are done with text, it
     should be written to an output file.

9

INHERITANCE: SUBTYPING AND CODE REUSE

Inheritance is the mechanism of deriving a new class from an old one. That is, the existing class can be added to or altered to create the derived class. This is a powerful code reuse mechanism. Inheritance allows creation of a hierarchy of related types that share code and interface.

Many useful types are variants of one another, and it can become tedious to produce the same code for each. A derived class inherits the description of the *base class*. It then can be altered by adding members, modifying existing member functions, and modifying access privileges. The usefulness of this concept can be seen by examining how taxonomic classification compactly summarizes large bodies of knowledge. For example, when we know the concept "mammal" and that an elephant and a mouse are both mammals, our descriptions of them can be considerably more succinct than they would be otherwise. The root concept "mammal" contains the information that mammals are warm-blooded animals and higher vertebrates and that they nourish their young using milk-producing mammary glands. This information is inherited by both the mouse and the elephant, but it is expressed only once: in the root concept "mammal." In C++ terms both classes, elephant and mouse, are derived from the base class, "mammal."

In OOP terms, the statement "elephant ISA mammal" describes the relationship. If one owned a circus and had a number of elephants, then the object circus might have members that were type elephant. In this case, the "class circus HASA elephant" describes a subpart relationship.

C++ supports `virtual` member functions, which are functions declared in the base class and redefined in a derived class. A class hierarchy defined by public inheritance creates a related set of user types, all of whose objects may be pointed at by a base class pointer. By accessing the virtual function through this pointer, C++ selects the appropriate function definition at run-time. The object being pointed at must carry around type information so that this distinction can be made dynamically, a feature typical of OOP code. Each object "knows" how it is to be acted on. This is a form of polymorphism called *pure polymorphism*.

Inheritance should be designed into software to maximize reuse and to allow a natural modeling of the problem domain. With inheritance, the key elements of the OOP design methodology become

- Decide on an appropriate set of types.
- Design in their relatedness, and use inheritance to share code.
- Use virtual functions to process related objects polymorphically.

9.1   A DERIVED CLASS

A class can be derived from an existing class using the form:

```
class   class-name :   (public|protected|private)opt base-class-name
{
    member   declarations
};
```

As usual, the keyword `class` can be replaced by the keyword `struct`, with the implication that members are `public` by default. One aspect of the derived class is the visibility of its inherited members. The keywords `public`, `protected`, and `private` are used to specify how the base class members are to be accessible to the derived class.

An example of deriving a class is

```
enum year { fresh, soph, junior, senior, grad};
class student {
protected:
    int        student_id;
    double     gpa;
    year       y;
    char       name[30];
public:
    student(char* nm, int id, double g, year x);
    void print();
};


enum support { ta, ra, fellowship, other};
class grad_student: public student {
protected:
    support    s;
    char       dept[10];
    char       thesis[80];
public:
    grad_student (char* nm, int id, double g, year x,
                support t, char* d, char* th);
    void print();
};
```

In this example, grad_student is the derived class and student is the base class. The use of the keyword public following the colon in the derived class header means that the protected and public members of student are to be inherited as protected and public members of grad_student, respectively. Private members are inaccessible. Public inheritance also means that the derived class grad_student is a subtype of student. Thus a graduate student is a student, but a student does not have to be a graduate student.

A derived class is a modification of the base class that inherits the public and protected members of the base class. Thus, in the example of grad_student, the student members—student_id, gpa, name, year, and print—are inherited. Frequently a derived class adds new members to existing class members. This is the case with grad_student, which has three new data members and a redefined member function print. The member function `print` is *overridden*, which means the derived class has a different implementation of the member function than the base class. This is different from overloading, where the same function name can have different meanings for each unique signature.

The benefits of such a mechanism include the following:

- Code is reused. The `grad_student` type uses existing tested code from `student`.
- The hierarchy reflects a relationship found in the problem domain. When speaking of students the special grouping called graduate student is an outgrowth of the real world and its treatment of this group.
- Various polymorphic mechanisms allow client code to treat `grad_student` as a subtype of `student`, thus simplifying client code while granting it the benefits of maintaining these distinctions among subtypes.

9.2   TYPING CONVERSIONS AND VISIBILITY

A publicly derived class is a *subtype* of its base class. A variable of the derived class can in many ways be treated as if it were the base class type. A pointer whose type is pointer to base class can point to objects having the derived class type. This can be confusing because subtle implicit conversions are occurring between the base and the derived type, and it is sometimes difficult to follow what member is being accessed if the base and the derived class overloaded the same member name.

Let us examine our example of `student` and `grad_student`. We first examine the base and derived class constructors.

```
student::student(char* nm, int id, double g, year x)
                :student_id(id), gpa(g), y(x)
{
    strcpy(name, nm);
}
```

The constructor for the base class does a series of simple initializations. It then calls `strcpy()` to copy over the student's name.

```
grad_student::grad_student(
   char* nm, int id, double g, year x,
   support t, char* d, char* th)
   :student(nm, id, g, x), s(t)
{
   strcpy(dept, d);
   strcpy(thesis, th);
}
```

Notice that the constructor for student is invoked as part of the initializer list. This is usual, and logically the base class object needs to be constructed first before the complete object can be completed.

The grad_student is a publicly derived type whose base class is student. In the class student the members student_id and gpa are protected. This makes them visible to the derived class but otherwise treated as private.

A reference to the derived class may be implicitly converted to a reference to the public base class. For example, in

```
grad_student gs("Morris Pohl", 200, 3.2564, grad, ta, "Pharmacy",
                "Retail Pharmacies");
student& rs = &gs;
```

the variable rs is a reference to student. The base class of grad_student is student. Therefore this reference conversion is appropriate.

The print member functions are overloaded. Let us implement the print functions.

```
void student::print()
{
   cout << "\n" << name << " , " << student_id << " , "
        << yr << " , " << gpa << endl;
}
```

```
void grad_student::print()
{
   student::print();    //base class information is printed
   cout << dept << " , " << s << "\n" << thesis << endl;
}
```

For `grad_student::print` to invoke the `student::print` function, the scope-resolved identifier `student::print` must be used. Otherwise, an infinite loop occurs. To see which versions of these functions get called and to demonstrate some of the conversion relationships between base and publicly derived classes, we write a simple test program.

```
//Test pointer conversion rules.
#include "student.h"  //include relevant declarations

main()
{
    student       s("Mae Pohl", 100, 3.425, fresh), *ps = &s;
    grad_student  gs("Morris Pohl", 200, 3.2564, grad, ta,
                     "Pharmacy", "Retail Pharmacies"), *pgs;
    ps -> print();        //student::print
    ps = pgs = &gs;
    ps -> print();        //student::print
    pgs -> print();       //grad_student::print
}
```

This function declares both class variables and pointers to them. The conversion rule is that a pointer to a publicly derived class may be converted implicitly to a pointer to its base class. In our example, the pointer variable `ps` can point at objects of both classes, but the pointer variable `pgs` can point only to objects of type `grad_student`. We wish to study how different pointer assignments affect the invocation of a version of `print`. The first instance of the statement

```
ps -> print();
```

invokes `student::print`. It is pointing at the variable `s1` of type `student`. The multiple assignment statement

```
ps = pgs = &gs;
```

has both pointers pointing at an object of type `grad_student`. The assignment to `ps` involves an implicit conversion. The second instance of the statement

```
ps -> print();
```

again invokes `student::print`. The fact that this pointer is pointing at a `grad_student` variable `gs` is not relevant. The statement

```
pgs -> print();    //grad_student::print
```

invokes `grad_student::print`. The variable `pgs` is of type pointer to `grad_student` and, when invoked with an object of this type, selects a member function from this class.

9.3   CODE REUSE: DYNAMIC ARRAY BOUNDS

In Chapter 7 we developed the `vect` safe array class. We want to reuse that code and extend this type into a safe array whose upper and lower bounds are dynamic. This style of array declaration is more flexible and allows the indices to correspond directly to a problem domain. For example, the Fahrenheit temperatures of water in its liquid state are 32–212 degrees at sea level. So if we were to collect data on this range of temperatures, it would be appropriate to use a lower bound of 32 and an upper bound of 212.

Recall that the dynamic safe array type `vect` checked array bounds for being in range and created arrays using free store. The class declaration follows:

```
//Implementation of a safe array type vect
class vect {
private:
    int *p;                        //base pointer
    int size;                      //number of elements
public:
    //constructors and destructor
    vect();                        //create a size 10 array
    vect(int l);                   //create a size l array
    vect(vect& v);                 //initialization by vect
    vect(int a[], int l);          //initialization by array
    ~vect() { delete [] p; }
    int ub()  { return (size - 1); } //upper bound
    int& operator[](int i);        //obtain range checked element
    vect& operator=(vect& v);
    vect operator+(vect& v);
};
```

The derived type will have members l_bnd and u_bnd that privately store the lower and upper bounds of the constructed safe array. The derived type reuses the base type's representation and code.

```
//Derived safe array type vect_bnd
class vect_bnd: public vect {
private:
    int l_bnd, u_bnd;
public:
    vect_bnd();
    vect_bnd(int, int);
    int& operator[](int);
    int ub() { return (u_bnd); }
    int lb() { return (l_bnd); }
};
```

The derived class constructors invoke the base class constructors. The syntax for this is the same as initialization syntax of members.

function header: base-class-name(argument list)

On early C++ compilers, the *base-class-name* could be omitted and was understood implicitly in the single inheritance case. This is considered anachronistic.

```
vect_bnd::vect_bnd() :vect(10)
{
    l_bnd = 0;
    u_bnd = 9;
}

vect_bnd::vect_bnd(int lb, int ub) :vect(ub - lb + 1)
{
    l_bnd = lb;
    u_bnd = ub;
}
```

Notice how the derived class constructors call the base class constructors. The additional code initializes the bound's pair. Alternatively, this could have been done in the initializing list.

```
vect_bnd::vect_bnd(int lb, int ub)
        vect(ub - lb + 1), l_bnd(lb), u_bnd(ub) {}
```

We also can reuse code in overloading the indexing operator [].

```
int& vect_bnd::operator[](int i)
{
    if (i < l_bnd || u_bnd < i) {
        cerr<<"index out of range\n";
        exit(1);
    };
    return (vect::operator[](i - l_bnd));
}
```

This would be very inefficient. Why? Because bounds checking is now done twice. To avoid this we must make two changes. First we must change the access privilege of the member vect::p to protected so the derived class has direct access to the previously private implementation of vect. This allows us to make the second change: we use p in the member function vect_bnd::operator[](). The more efficient code is

```
int& vect_bnd::operator[](int i)
{
    if (i < l_bnd || u_bnd < i) {
        cerr<<"index out of range\n";
        exit(1);
    };
    return (p[i - l_bnd]);
}
```

Notice the tradeoff in code reuse and efficiency. This is often the case. Also notice that inheritance requires us to think about three access boundaries. What is to be strictly private and what is to be protected depends on what is potentially reusable.

9.4   CODE REUSE: A BINARY TREE CLASS

Private inheritance does not have a subtype relationship. Private inheritance uses the base class for code and interface. Since this is not an ISA relationship, we will call it a REUSEA relationship. This comes in handy when diagramming the class relationships in a complicated software system. Because private (and protected) inheritance does not create a type hierarchy, it has more limited utility than public inheritance. In a first pass in understanding these concepts, nonpublic inheritance can be skipped.

Interface and code reuse are often all that is wanted from inheritance. Let us see how private inheritance is used by designing a generic container class that is a binary tree. The class stores void* data members. This class is inherited privately, thus turning the apparently useless container into one storing *useful-type** data.

```
//generic binary search trees
typedef void*    p_gen; //generic pointer type

class bnode {
private:
   friend  class gen_tree;
   bnode*  left;
   bnode*  right;
   p_gen   data;
   int     count;
   bnode(p_gen d, bnode* l, bnode* r)
        : data(d), left(l), right(r), count(1) {}
   friend int comp(p_gen a, p_gen b);
   friend void print(bnode* n);
};


class gen_tree {
protected:
   bnode* root;
   p_gen find(bnode* r, p_gen d);
   void print(bnode* r);
public:
   gen_tree() { root = 0; }
   void insert(p_gen d);
   p_gen find(p_gen d) { return (find(root, d)); }
   void print() { print(root); }
};
```

The individual nodes in this binary tree store a generic pointer data and an int count that counts duplicate entries. The pointer data matches a pointer type in the derived class. The tree is a binary search tree that stores nodes of smaller value to the left and larger or equal values to the right. We need a method of comparing values that is appropriate to the specific derived type. We use a friend function comp that is a friend of bnode and is coded appropriately for the derived class.

The insert function places nodes in a tree, and it must find the position in the tree for the new nodes. The function p_gen find(bnode* r, p_gen d) searches the subtree rooted at r for the information represented by d. The function p_gen find(p_gen d) searches the entire tree. The member function void print(bnode* r) walks around the subtree rooted at r, applying the friend function print(bnode* n) to each node in turn. This is done for the entire tree by void print().

```
void gen_tree::insert(p_gen d)
{
    bnode* temp = root;
    bnode* old;

    if (root == 0) {
        root = new bnode(d, 0, 0);
        return;
    }
    while (temp != 0) {
        old = temp;
        if (comp(temp -> data, d) == 0) {
            (temp -> count)++;
                return;
        }
        if (comp(temp -> data, d) > 0)
                temp = temp -> left;
        else
                temp = temp -> right;
    }
    if (comp(old -> data, d) > 0)
        old -> left = new bnode(d, 0, 0);
    else
        old -> right = new bnode(d, 0, 0);
}
```

The `insert` function creates a one-node tree if the tree is initially empty. If the information as represented by the pointer d matches existing information as determined by `comp`, then `count` is incremented. Otherwise `comp` navigates through the tree to the appropriate leaf position where the new node is constructed and attached. Note that the function `comp` can be computationally expensive, and multiple evaluations of it can be eliminated (see exercise 16).

```
p_gen gen_tree::find(bnode* r, p_gen d)
{
   if (r == 0)
      return (0);
   else if (comp(r -> data, d) == 0)
      return (r -> data);
   else if (comp(r -> data, d) > 0)
      return (find( r -> left, d));
   else
      return (find( r -> right, d));
}
```

This is a standard recursion. If the information as pointed at by d is not found, 0 is returned.

The `print()` function is also a standard recursion. At each node the external function `::print()` is applied.

```
void gen_tree::print(bnode* r)
{
   if  (r != 0) {
       print (r -> left);
       ::print(r);
       print (r -> right);
   }
}
```

We next derive a class capable of storing a pointer to `char` as its data member.

```
#include "gentree.h"
#include <string.h>

class s_tree: private gen_tree {
public:
    s_tree() {}
    void insert(char* d) { gen_tree::insert(p_gen(d)); }
    char* find(char* d)
            { return ((char*)gen_tree::find(p_gen(d))); }
    void print() { gen_tree::print(); }
};
```

The base class insertion function `gen_tree::insert` takes a generic pointer type as its argument. The derived class insertion function `s_tree::insert` takes a pointer to `char` as its argument. Therefore in the derived class `s_tree`,

```
void insert(char* d) { gen_tree::insert(p_gen(d)); }
```

uses the explicit conversion `p_gen(d)`.

We need a function to perform comparison: the promised `friend` function to `class bnode`.

```
int comp(p_gen i, p_gen j)
{
    return (strcmp((char*)i, (char*)j));
}
```

We also need an external `print()` that can properly print the values stored in a single node to be used recursively by `s_tree::print()` to output the entire tree.

```
void print(bnode* n)
{
    cout << (char*)n -> data << "\t" ;
    cout << n -> count << "\t";
}
```

The design of s_tree has a good deal more abstraction than would a like structure written in C. The payoff for this is the ease with which further classes can be derived that utilize the underlying binary tree structure. See the exercises to show how to test these routines.

9.5   VIRTUAL FUNCTIONS

Overloaded member functions are invoked by a type-matching algorithm that includes having the implicit argument matched to an object of that class type. All of this is known at compile-time and allows the compiler to select the appropriate member directly. As will become apparent, it would be nice to dynamically select at run-time the appropriate member function from among base and derived class functions. The keyword virtual is a function specifier that provides such a mechanism, but it may be used only to modify member function declarations. The combination of virtual functions and public inheritance is our most general and flexible way to build a piece of software. This is a form of *pure polymorphism*.

An ordinary virtual function must be executable code. When invoked its semantics are the same as other functions. In a derived class, it can be *overridden*, and the function prototype of the derived function must have matching signature and return type. The selection of which function definition to invoke for a virtual function is dynamic. The typical case is where a base class has a virtual function and derived classes have their versions of this function. A pointer to base class can point at either a base class object or a derived class object. The member function selected depends on the class of the object being pointed at, not on the pointer type. In the absence of a derived type member, the base class virtual function is used by default.

Note well that the difference between selection of the appropriate over-ridden virtual function and selection of an overloaded member function. The overloaded member function is compile-time selected based on sig-nature. It can have distinct return types. Also, once declared virtual, this property is carried along to all redefinitions in derived classes. It is unnecessary in the derived class to use the function modifier virtual.

The ANSI C++ committee is considering relaxing the constraint on return type match for virtual function overriding. The proposed rule would allow the return type of the virtual function to be a derived class pointer or reference in the case that the base class virtual function was declared with a corresponding form of the base class type.

Consider the following example:

```
//virtual function selection.
#include <iostream.h>

class B {
public:
   int  i;
   virtual void print_i() { cout << i << " inside B\n"; }
};

class D: public B {
public:
   void print_i() { cout << i << " inside D\n"; } //virtual as well
};

main()
{
    B    b;
    B*   pb = &b;
    D    f;

    f.i = 1 + (b.i = 1);
    pb -> print_i();
    pb = &f;
    pb -> print_i();
}
```

The output from this program is

```
1 inside B
2 inside D
```

In each case, a different version of print_i is executed. Selection depends dynamically on the object being pointed at. In OOP terminology "the object is sent the message print_i and selects its own version of the corresponding method." Thus the pointer's base type is not determining method (function) selection. Different class objects are processed by different functions determined at run-time. Facilities that allow the implementation of ADTs, inheritance, and the ability to process objects dynamically are the essentials of OOP.

Member function overloading and virtual functions cause mixups and confusion. Consider the following:

```
class B {
public:
   virtual foo(int);
   virtual foo(double);
   . . .
};

class D: public B {
public:
   foo(int);
   . . .
};

main()
{
   D d;
   B b, *pb = &d;

   b.foo(9);          //selects B::foo(int);
   b.foo(9.5);        //selects B::foo(double);
   pb -> foo(9.5);    //selects D::foo(int);
}
```

The base class member function B::foo(int) is overriden in the derived class. The base class member function B::foo(double) is hidden in the derived class. The double value 9.5 is converted to an integer value 9.

Only non-static member functions can be virtual. The virtual characteristic is inherited. Thus the derived class function is automatically virtual and the presence of the virtual keyword is usually a matter of taste.

Special restrictions: Constructors cannot be virtual. Destructors can be virtual.

The virtual functions allow run-time decisions. Consider a computer-aided design application where the area of the shapes in a design has to be computed. The different shapes are derived from the shape base class.

```
class shape {
protected:
   double x, y;
public:
   virtual double area() { return (0); } //default behavior
};

class rectangle: public shape {
private:
   double height, width;
public:
   double area() { return (height * width); }
};

class circle: public shape {
private:
   double radius;
public:
   double area() { return (PI * radius * radius); }
};
```

In such a class hierarchy, the derived classes correspond to important, well-understood types of shapes. The system is readily added to by deriving further classes. The area calculation is a local responsibility of a derived class.

Client code that uses the polymorphic area calculation looks like

```
shape* p[N];


. . .
for (i = 0; i < N; ++i)
   tot_area += p[i] -> area();
```

A major advantage here is that the client code need not change if new shapes are added to the system. Change is managed locally and propagated automatically by the polymorphic character of the client code.

9.6   ABSTRACT BASE CLASSES

The root class of a type hierarchy usually contains a number of virtual functions, which provide for dynamic typing. Often these virtual functions in the root class are dummy functions. They have an empty body in the root class, but they are given specific meanings in the derived classes. In C++, the *pure virtual function* is introduced for this purpose. A pure virtual function is a virtual member function whose body normally is undefined. Notationally it is declared inside the class as follows:

```
virtual  function prototype = 0;
```

The pure virtual function is used to defer the implementation decision of the function. In OOP terminology it is called a *deferred method*.

A class that has at least one *pure virtual* function is an *abstract class*. It is useful to have a root class for a type hierarchy be an abstract class. It has the basic common properties of its derived classes but cannot itself be used to declare objects. Instead it is used to declare pointers that can access subtype objects derived from the abstract class.

Let us explain this concept while developing a primitive form of ecological simulation. OOP was developed originally as a simulation methodology using Simula 67. Hence, conceptually, many of its ideas are understandable as an attempt to model a particular reality.

In our example our world will have different forms of life interacting. The abstract base class is living. Its interface is inherited by various forms of life. We have fox as an archetypical predator and rabbit as its prey. The rabbit eats grass.

```
//A Predator-Prey simulation using class hierarchy living.
const int N = 40, STATES = 4;          //size of square board
enum state{ EMPTY , GRASS , RABBIT , FOX };

class living;                          //forward declaration
typedef living* world[N][N];           //world will be simulation

class living {                         //what lives in the world
protected:
    int        row, column;            //location
    void       sums(world w, int sm[]);  //sm[#states] used by next()
public:
    living (int r, int c): row(r), column(c){}
    virtual state who() = 0;           //state identification
    virtual living* next(world w) = 0; //compute next
};

void living::sums(world w, int sm[])
{
    int i, j;
    sm[EMPTY] = sm[GRASS] = sm[RABBIT] = sm[FOX] = 0;

    for (i = -1; i <= 1; ++i)
       for ( j = -1; j <= 1; ++j)
           sm[w[row + i][column +j] -> who()]++;
}
```

This program has two pure virtual functions and one ordinary member function, sums(). Virtual functions incur a small added run-time cost over normal member functions. Therefore we use them only when necessary to our implementations. Our simulation has rules for deciding on who goes on living in a next cycle based on the populations in the neighborhood of a given square. These populations are computed by sums(). This is akin to Conway's "Game of Life" simulation.

The inheritance hierarchy is one level deep.

```
//currently only predator class
class fox:public living {
protected:
    int age;                          //used to decide on dying
public:
    fox(int r, int c, int a = 0): living (r,c), age(a) {}
    state who() {return (FOX);}    //deferred method for foxes
    living* next(world w);         //deferred method for foxes
};


//currently only prey class
class rabbit:public living {
protected:
    int age;
public:
    rabbit(int r, int c, int a = 0): living (r,c), age(a) {}
    state who() {return (RABBIT);}
    living* next(world w);
};


//currently only plant life
class grass:public living {
public:
    grass(int r, int c): living (r,c) {}
    state who() {return (GRASS);}
    living* next(world w);
};


//nothing lives here
class empty:public living {
public:
    empty(int r, int c): living (r,c) {}
    state who() {return (EMPTY);}
    living* next(world w);
};
```

Notice how the design allows other forms of predator, prey, and plant life to be developed using a further level of inheritance. The characteristics of how each life form behave are captured in its version of next().

```
living* grass::next(world w)
{
    int sum[STATES];
    sums(w, sum);

    if (sum[GRASS] > sum[RABBIT]) //eat grass
        return (new grass(row, column));
    else
        return (new empty(row, column));
}
```

Grass can be eaten by rabbits. If the neighborhood has more grass than rabbits, the grass remains; otherwise grass is eaten up. (Feel free to substitute your own rules as these are highly limited and artificial.)

```
living* rabbit::next(world w)
{
    int sum[STATES];
    sums(w, sum);

    if (sum[FOX] >= sum[RABBIT] )       //eat rabbits
        return (new empty(row, column));
    else if (age > DRAB)                //rabbit is too old
        return (new empty(row, column));
    else
        return (new rabbit(row, column, age + 1));
}
```

Rabbits die of old age if they exceed the defined limit DRAB, or they can be eaten if there are an appropriate number of foxes in the neighborhood.

```
living* fox::next(world w)
{
    int sum[STATES];
    sums(w, sum);

    if (sum[FOX] > 5)                    //too many foxes
        return (new empty(row, column));
    else if (age > DFOX)                 //fox is too old
        return (new empty(row, column));
    else
        return (new fox(row, column, age + 1));
}
```

Foxes die of overcrowding or of old age.

```
//how to fill an empty square
living* empty::next(world w)
{
    int sum[STATES];
    sums(w, sum);

    if (sum[STATES] > 1)
        return (new fox(row, column));
    else if (sum[RABBIT] > 1)
        return (new rabbit(row, column));
    else if (sum[GRASS])
        return (new grass(row, column));
    else
        return (new empty(row, column));
}
```

The various life forms competed for empty squares. The various rules in the different versions of next determine a possibly complex set of interactions. Of course, to make the simulation more interesting, other behaviors such as sexual reproduction, where the animals have gender and can mate, can be simulated.

The array type `world` is a container for the life forms. This container has the responsibility for creating its current pattern. It needs to have ownership of the `living` objects so as to allocate new ones and delete old ones.

```
//world is all empty
void init(world w)
{
   int i, j;

   for (i = 0; i < N; ++i)
      for (j = 0; j < N; ++j)
         w[i][j] = new empty(i,j);
}


//new world w_new is computed from old world w_old
void update(world w_new, world w_old)
{
   int i, j;

   for (i = 1; i < N - 1; ++i) //borders are taboo
      for (j = 1; j < N - 1; ++j)
         w_new[i][j] = w_old[i][j] -> next(w_old);
}


//clean world up
void dele(world w)
{
   int i, j;

   for (i = 1; i < N - 1; ++i)
      for  (j = 1; j < N - 1; ++j)
         delete (w[i][j]);
}
```

The simulation has an **odd** and **even** world. Each alternates as the basis for the next cycle's calculations.

```
main()
{
   world odd, even;
   int   i

   init(odd);  init(even);

   //we initialize inside part of world to non-empty types
   eden(even);              //generate initial world
   pr_state(even);          //print garden of eden state

   for (i = 0; i < CYCLES; ++i) { //simulation
      if (i % 2) {
         update(even, odd);
         pr_state(even);
         dele(odd);
      }
      else {
         update(odd, even);
         pr_state(odd);
         dele(even);
      }
   }
}
```

We leave as exercises the writing of `pr_state()` and `eden()`.

9.7   MULTIPLE INHERITANCE

The examples in the text thus far require only single inheritance; that is, they require that a class be derived from a single base class. This feature can lead to a chain of derivations wherein class B is derived from class A, class C is derived from class B, ..., and class N is derived from class M. In effect, N ends up being based on A, B, ..., M. This chain must not be circular, however, so a class cannot have itself as an ancestor.

Multiple inheritance allows a derived class to be derived from more than one base class. The syntax of class headers is extended to allow a list of base classes and their privacy designations. An example is

```
class tools {
   . . .

};

class parts {
   . . .

};

class labor {
   . . .

};

class plans: public tools, public parts, public labor {
   . . .

};
```

In this example the derived class plans publicly inherits the members of all three base classes. This parental relationship is described by the inheritance *directed acyclic graph (DAG)*. The DAG is a graph structure whose nodes are classes and whose directed edges point from base to derived class. To be legal it cannot be circular, so no class may, through its inheritance chain, inherit from itself.

In deriving an identically named member from different classes, ambiguities may arise. These derivations are allowed, provided the user does not make an ambiguous reference to such a member. For example,

```
class tools {
public:
    int cost();
    . . .
};

class labor {
public:
    int cost();
    . . .
};

class parts {
public:
    int cost();
    . . .
};

class plans: public tools, public parts, public labor {
public:
    int tot_cost() { return (parts::cost() + labor::cost()); }
    . . .
};

int foo()
{
    int  price;
    plans* ptr;

    price = ptr -> cost();
    . . .
}
```

In the body of foo, the reference to cost is inherently ambiguous. It can be resolved by either properly qualifying cost using the scope resolution operator or adding a member cost to the derived class plans.

One further modification to the original inheritance scheme has been made: `virtual` inheritance. With multiple inheritance two base classes can be derived from a common ancestor. If both base classes are used in the ordinary way by their derived class, that class will have two subobjects of the common ancestor. This duplication, if not desirable, can be eliminated by using `virtual` inheritance. An example is

```
class under_grad: public virtual student {

   . . .

};

class grad: public virtual student {

   . . .

};

class attendee: public under_grad, public grad {

   . . .

};
```

Without the use of `virtual` in this example, `class attendee` would have objects of `class::under_grad::student` and `class::grad::student`.

The order of execution for initializing constructors in base and member constructors is

- Base classes are initialized in declaration order.
- Members are initialized in declaration order.

Virtual base classes have special precedence and are constructed before any of their derived classes. They are constructed before any non-`virtual` base classes. Their construction order depends on their DAG. It is a depth-first, left-to-right order. Destructors are invoked in reverse order of constructors. These rules, although complicated, generally conform to our intuition.

The old style of just using a parenthesized argument list that implicitly called the base class constructor is allowed for single inheritance, but it is poor style even for that case. Finally, the associated destructors are called in the reverse order from constructor invocation.

Let us illustrate by elaborating on a previous example.

```
class tools {
 . . .
public:
   tools(char*);
   ~tools();
 . . .
};

class parts {
 . . .
public:
   parts(char*);
   ~parts();
 . . .
};

class labor {
 . . .
public:
   labor(int);
   ~labor();
 . . .
};

class plans: public tools, public parts, public labor {
 . . .
   special a;    //member class with constructor
public:
   plans(int m): tools("lathe"), parts("widget"), labor(m), a(m)
      { . . . }
   ~plans();
 . . .
};
```

The constructor initializing list and the member initializing list appear in declaration order. This is good style as it avoids confusion and should match declaration order as a documentation aid. Since its constructor was last, the ~a() destructor is invoked first, followed by ~labor(), ~parts(), ~tools(), and ~plans().

On many systems, a concrete, worked-out example of multiple inheritance can be found in *iostream.h*. This contains the class `iostream`, which can be derived from `istream` and `ostream`.

9.8   INHERITANCE AND DESIGN

At one level inheritance is a code-sharing technique. At another level inheritance reflects an understanding of the problem. It reflects relationships between parts of the problem space. Much of public inheritance is the expression of an ISA relationship between the base and derived classes. Rectangle is a shape: This is the conceptual underpinnings for making shape a superclass and allowing the behavior described by its public member functions to be interpretable on objects within its type hierarchy; in other words, subclasses derived from it share its interface.

There is no way to specify a completely optimal design. Design involves tradeoffs between various objectives that one wishes to achieve. For example, generality is frequently at odds with efficiency. Using a class hierarchy that expresses ISA relationships increases our effort to understand how to compartmentalize coding relationships and potentially introduces coding inefficiencies by having various layers of access to the (hidden) state description of an object. However, a reasonable ISA decomposition can simplify the overall coding process. For example, a shape-drawing package need not anticipate future additional shapes that will be added. Through inheritance the class developer imports the base class "shape" interface and provides code that implements operations such as "draw." What is primitive or held in common remains unchanged. Also unchanged is the client's use of the package.

An undue amount of decomposition imposes its own complexity that ends up being self-defeating. There is a granularity decision, where classes that are highly specialized do not provide enough benefit and are better folded into a larger concept.

Single inheritance (SI) conforms to a hierarchical decomposition of the key objects in the domain of discourse. Multiple inheritance (MI) is more troubling as a modelling or problem-solving concept. In MI we are saying that the new object is composed of several preexisting objects and is usefully thought of as a form of each. The concept *mixin* is sometimes used to mean a class composed using MI, where each base class is orthogonal. Much of the time there is an alternate HASA formulation. For example, is a vampire bat a mammal that happens to fly, a flying machine that happens to be a mammal, or both a flying machine and a mammal? Depending on what code is available, developing a proper class for vampire bat might involve an MI derivation or an SI with appropriate HASA members.

MI presents problems for the type theorist. A student might be derived from person. An employee might be derived from person. What about a student-employee? Generally types are best understood as SI chains.

Saying all this does not diminish the attraction of MI as a code reuse technique. It clearly is a powerful generalization of SI. As such it probably fits in with some programmers' style. Just as some programmers prefer iteration to recursion, some programmers prefer SI and aggregation to MI and composition.

SUBTYPING FORM

ADTs are successful insofar as they behave like native types. Native types such as the integer types in C act as a subtype hierarchy. This is a useful model for publicly derived type hierarchies. This promotes ease of use through polymorphism.

```
class Abstract_Base {
private:
   //most often empty -avoid because it constrains
   //future designs
   . . .
protected:
   //used in place of private because of inheritance
   . . .
public:
   //interface - largely virtual
   Abstract_Base();  //default constructor
   Abstract_Base(const Abstract_Base&);  //copy constructor
   virtual ~Abstract_Base();  //should need run-time type
   virtual void print() = 0;  //usual print expectation
   . . .
};

class D_is_AB: virtual public Abstract_Base {
private:
   . . .
protected:
   //used in place of private if inheritance expected
   . . .
public:
   //interface - supports concrete instance
   D_is_AB();  //default constructor
   D_is_AB(const D_is_AB&);  //copy constructor
   D_is_AB& operator=(const D_is_AB&);  //assignment
   void print();  //usual print expectation
   . . .
};
```

It is usual to leave the root of the hierarchy as abstract. This yields the most flexible design. Generally no concrete implementation is developed at this point. By using pure virtual functions, we are precluded from declaring objects of this type. Notice that the print() function is pure.

This level of the design focuses on public interface. These are the operations expected of any subtype in the hierarchy. In general, basic constructors are expected and they may not be virtual. Also, most useful aggregates require an explicit definition of assignment that differs from default assignment semantics. The destructor is `virtual` because response must be at run-time and is dependent on the object's size, which can vary across the hierarchy. Finally, `virtual public` inheritance ensures that in MI schemes, we will not have multiple copies of the abstract base class.

9.9   DETAILED C++ CONSIDERATIONS

Learning C++ can be difficult because of the many distinctions and rules pertaining to the use of functions. We have now completed describing most of these extensions and can summarize some of them as follows:

1   A virtual function and its derived instances having the same signature must have the same return type. The virtual function redefinition is called *overriding*. Notice non-virtual member functions having the same signature can have different return types in derived classes (see exercise 17).

2   Constructors, destructors, and conversion functions do not have return types. The return type of an overloaded `new` operator must be `void*`. The return type of an overloaded `delete` operator must be `void`.

3   All member functions except constructors, and overloaded `new` and `delete` can be `virtual`.

4   Constructors, destructors, overloaded `operator=`, and friends are not inherited.

5   Overloading the operators `=`, `()`, `[]`, and `->` can be done only with non-static member functions. Overloading operators `new` and `delete` can be done only with static member functions. Other overloadable operators can be done with either friend, member, or ordinary functions.

6   A `union` may have constructors and destructors but not virtual functions. A `union` cannot serve as a base class, nor can it have a base class.

7   Access modification is possible, but using it with public inheritance destroys the subtype relationship. Access modification cannot broaden visibility. This can be seen in the following example:

```
//Access modification
class B {
private:
    int i;
protected:
    int j, n;
public:
    int k;
};

class D: public B {
private:
    B::j;  //otherwise default is protected
public:
    int m;
    B::n;  //illegal protected access cannot be widened
};
```

9.10   SUMMARY

1   *Inheritance* is the mechanism of *deriving* a new class from an old
     one. That is, the existing class can be added to or altered to create
     the derived class. Inheritance allows creation of a hierarchy of
     related ADTs that share code.

2   A class can be derived from an existing class using the form

```
class class-name :(public|protected|private)opt base-class-name
{
    member declarations
};
```

     As usual, the keyword `class` can be replaced by the keyword
     `struct`, with the usual implication that members are by default
     `public`.

3   The keywords `public`, `private`, and `protected` are available
     as visibility modifiers for class members. A `public` member is

visible throughout its scope. A `private` member is visible to other member functions within its own class. A `protected` member is visible to other member functions within its class and any class immediately derived from it. These visibility modifiers can be used within a class declaration in any order and with any frequency.

4   The derived class has its own constructors, which will invoke the base class constructor. There is a special syntax to pass arguments from the derived class constructor back to the base class constructor:

function   header : base-class-name   (argument   list)

5   A publicly derived class is a *subtype* of its base class. A variable of the derived class can in many ways be treated as if it were the base class type. A pointer whose type is pointer to base class can point to objects of the publicly derived class type.

6   A reference to the derived class may be implicitly converted to a reference to the public base class. It is possible to declare a reference to a base class and initialize it to a reference to an object of the publicly derived class.

7   The keyword `virtual` is a function specifier that provides a mechanism to dynamically select at run-time the appropriate member function from among base and derived class functions. It may be used only to modify member function declarations. This is called *overriding*. This is a form of polymorphism called *pure polymorphism*.

8   Inheritance provides for code reuse. The derived class inherits the base class code. Typically the derived class modifies and extends the base class. Public inheritance also creates a type hierarchy. It allows further generality by providing additional implicit type conversions. It also, at a run-time cost, allows for run-time selection of overridden virtual functions. Facilities that allow the implementation of ADTs, inheritance, and the ability to process objects dynamically are the essentials of OOP.

9.11   EXERCISES

1   Change the declaration of **grad_student** found in Section 9.1 to

```
class grad_student: student {
public:
    enum {ta, ra, fellowship, other} support;
    char dept[10];
    char thesis[80];
    void print();
};
```

Explain what goes wrong in the following code:

```
main()
{
    grad_student s;

    strcpy(s.name, "Charles Babbage");
    . . .
}
```

2   The safe array member **vect_bnd::operator[]** from Section 9.3 is guaranteed to be passed a properly indexed element in the **return** statement

```
return (vect::operator[](i - l_bnd));
```

This means that the array index is unnecessarily checked twice. Add an unchecked access function as a member function of **class vect**:

```
int& elem(int i);    //unchecked indexing
```

Use this to modify the **return** statement so as not to recheck the index.

3   Write a member function **print** that prints out a variable of type **vect_bnd**.

4   Write two new constructors for `vect_bnd`:

```
//initialize by vect_bnd
vect_bnd::vect_bnd(const vect_bnd& v);

//initialize by array
vect_bnd::vect_bnd(const int a[], int l, int u);
```

5   Develop a type `matrix_bnd`:

```
class matrix_bnd: public matrix {
   int lb1, lb2, ub1, ub2;
   int size1, size2;
public:
   matrix_bnd(const matrix_bnd& m); //copy existing matrix
   matrix_bnd();                          //5 x 5 matrix
   matrix_bnd(int l1, int u1, int l2, int u2);
   void print();
      . . .
};
```

This is a two-dimensional safe array type that has both upper and lower bounds for each index. Write constructors for this type and a print member function. You should write a member function

```
//reference to an individual element
int& element(int i, int j);
```

that accesses individual elements, because overloading `[]` will not work. *Hint*: You can start by modifying the basic `matrix` class from Chapter 5, exercise 4, or see the `matrix` code in Section 5.7.

6   For `student` and `grad_student`, as defined in Section 9.1, code respective input member functions `read` that input data for each data member in their class. Use `student::read` to implement `grad_student::read`.

7   Pointer conversions, scope resolution, and explicit casting create a wide selection of possibilities. Using `main` from Section 9.2, which of the following work and what is printed?

```
((grad_student *)ps) -> print();
((student *)pgs) -> print(); //grad_student::print
pgs -> student::print();
ps -> grad_student::print();
```

Print out and explain the results.

8   Modify class D from Section 9.5 to be

```
class D: private B {
public:
   B::i;
   void print_i()
   {
      cout << i << " inside D and B::i is "
           << B::i << endl;
   }
};
```

What is changed in the output from that program?

9   The following uses class s_tree:

```
main()
{
   s_tree t;
   char dat[80], *p;

   cout << "\nEnter strings; exit with an end-of-file\n";
   while ( cin >> dat && cin.good()) {
      p = new char[strlen(dat) + 1];
      strcpy(p, dat);
      t.insert(p);
    }
   t.print();
   cout << "\n\n\n";
}
```

Use this with redirection to produce an ordered count of each string occurrence in a file. The function cin.good() returns true if there is input to read. It is part of the iostream input/output library that is discussed in detail in Appendix D.

10   Change the code in exercise 9 so as to use an arbitrary input file. To accomplish this read a file name from a command-line argument and use that to open an `ifstream`. Appendix D shows how to use *fstream.h*.

11   For `class gen_tree` write a description. Remember, this must traverse and individually delete nodes.

12   Write a destructor for `class s_tree`.

13   The printing routine for `s_tree` as written in this chapter is an *inorder* tree traversal.

```
void gen_tree::print(bnode* r);
{
   if (r != 0) {
      print (r -> left);
      ::print(r);    //inorder
      print (r -> right);
   }
}
```

Run the program using both *preorder* and *postorder* traversal. For preorder, the statement `::print(r)` goes first, and for postorder it goes last.

14   Develop a class `gen_vect` that is a safe array of generic pointers. Derive a class `s_vect` that is a safe array of `char*`.

15   *(Tricky)* Using `gen_tree`, derive a class `itree` that stores a vector of type `int` pointed at by the `data` member of each node. You must write an appropriate `comp` function.

16   Rewrite the code for `gen_tree::insert` to be more efficient. Do this by assigning the value of `comp(temp ->data, d)` to a temporary variable. This avoids the recomputation of a potentially expensive function call.

17   For the following program explain when overriding takes place. Also explain when overloading takes place.

```
//Override v. Overload
#include <iostream.h>

class B {
private:
   int i;
public:
   B(int j = 0): i(j) {}
   virtual void print() { cout << " i = " << i << endl; }
   void print(char *s) { cout << s << i << endl; }
};

class D: public B {
private:
   int i;
public:
   D(int j = 0): B(5), i(j) {}
   void print() { cout << " i = " << i << endl; }
   int print(char *s) { cout << s << i << endl; return (i); }
};

main()
{
   B  b1, b2(10), *pb;
   D  d1, d2(10), *pd = &d2;

   b1.print();
   b2.print();
   d1.print();
   d2.print();
   b1.print("b1.i = ");
   b2.print("b2.i = ");
   d1.print("d1.i = ");
   d2.print("d2.i = ");
   pb = pd;
   pb -> print();
   pb -> print("d2.i = ");
   pd -> print();
   pd -> print("d2.i = ");
}
```

18   Define a base class `person` that contains information that is universal for all people. Include name, address, birthdate, and gender information. Derive from this class the following classes:

```
class student: virtual public person {
// . . . relevant additional state and behavior
};

class employee: virtual public person {
// . . . relevant additional state and behavior
};

class student_employee: public student, public employee {
// . . .
};
```

Write a program that reads a file of information and creates a list of persons. Process the list to create, in sorted order by last name, a list of all people, a list of people who are students, a list of people who are employees, and a list of people who are student-employees. On your system can you easily produce a list in sorted order of all students that are not employees?

19   **Project**: Design and implement a graphical interface for the predator-prey simulation. It should draw each iteration of the simulation on the screen. You should be able to directly input a "garden of Eden" starting position. You should also be able to provide other settings for the simulation, such as the size of the simulation. Try to give the user a way to define other life forms and their rules for existing, eating, and reproducing. Make the graphical interface convenient to use and easy to comprehend. The user should be able to position it on the screen and resize it. The user should have the ability to select icons for the various available life forms.

10

PARAMETRIC POLYMORPHISM

C++ uses the keyword `template` to provide *parametric polymorphism*. Parametric polymorphism allows the same code to be used with respect to different types, where *type is a parameter of the code body*. Parametric polymorphism is especially useful in defining container classes. Processing the data in a container class has the same form, regardless of type. Template class definitions and template function definitions give us the ability to reuse code in a simple, type-safe manner that allows the compiler to automate the process of type instantiation. Polymorphism is a wondrous mechanism providing code reuse. (See Figure 10.1.)

Webster's: "Capable of Assuming Various Forms"

Aladdin's Genie

FIGURE 10.1   Polymorphism

10.1   TEMPLATE CLASS STACK

We modify the `stack` type from Chapter 6 to have a parameterized type.

```
//template stack implementation
template <class TYPE>
class stack {
private:
   enum  { EMPTY = -1};
   TYPE* s;
   int   max_len;
   int   top;
public:
   stack() :max_len(1000)
       { s = new TYPE[1000]; top = EMPTY; }
   stack(int size) :max_len(size)
       { s = new TYPE[size]; top = EMPTY; }
   ~stack() { delete [] s; }
   void reset() { top = EMPTY; }
   void push(TYPE c) { s[++top] = c; }
   TYPE pop() { return (s[top--]); }
   TYPE top_of() { return (s[top]); }
   boolean empty() { return boolean(top == EMPTY); }
   boolean full() { return boolean(top == max_len - 1); }
};
```

The syntax of the class declaration is prefaced by

```
template <class identifier >
```

Where *identifier* is a template argument that essentially stands for an arbitrary type. Throughout the class definition the template argument can be used as a type name. This argument is instantiated in the actual declarations. An example of a `stack` declaration using this is

```
stack<char> stk_ch;          // 1000 element char stack
stack<char*>  stk_str(200);  // 200 element char* stack
stack<complex> stk_cmplx(100); // 100 element complex stack
```

This mechanism saves our rewriting class declarations when the only variation would be type declarations. It is an alternate scheme to using `void*` as a universal pointer type.

When processing such a type, the code must always use the angle brackets as part of the declaration.

```
//Reversing a series of char* represented strings
void reverse(char* str[], int n)
{
   stack<char*> stk(n);

   for (int i = 0; i < n; ++i)
      stk.push(str[i]);
   for (i = 0; i < n; ++i)
      str[i] = stk.pop();
}

//Initializing a stack of complex numbers from an array
void init(complex c[], stack<complex> stk, n)
{
   for (int i = 0; i < n; ++i)
      stk.push(c[i]);
}
```

Member functions declared and defined inside the class are inline, as usual. When defined externally the full angle bracket declaration must be used. So,

```
TYPE top_of() { return (s[top]); }
```

when defined outside the template class, would be written as

```
template<class TYPE> TYPE stack<TYPE>::top_of()
{ return (s[top]); }
```

Yes this is ugly and takes some getting used to, but the compiler otherwise would not know that `TYPE` was a template argument.

10.2   FUNCTION TEMPLATES

Many functions have the same code body regardless of type, for example, initializing the contents of one array from another of the same type. The essential code is

```
for (i = 0; i < n; ++i)
   a[i] = b[i];
```

Most C programmers automate this with a simple macro.

```
#define COPY(A, B, N)  { int i; for(i = 0; i < N; ++i) A[i] = B[i]; }
```

This works but is not type-safe. A user could readily mix types when conversions were inappropriate. C++ programmers can make use of various forms of conversion and overloading to achieve similar effects. However, in the absence of appropriate conversions and signatures, no action would be taken. Templates provide a further polymorphic language mechanism for this.

```
template<class TYPE>
void copy(TYPE a[], TYPE b[], int n)
{
    for (int i = 0; i < n; ++i)
       a[i] = b[i];
}
```

The invocation of copy() with specific arguments causes the compiler to generate the actual function based on those arguments. If unable to do so, it leads to a compile-time error. What are the effects of the following calls?

```
double f1[50], f2[50];
char   c1[25], c2[50];
int    i1[75], i2[75];
char* ptr1, *ptr2;
copy(f1, f2, 50);
copy(c1, c2, 10);
copy(i1, i2, 40);
copy(ptr1, ptr2, 100);
copy(i1, f2, 50);
copy(ptr1, f2, 50);
```

The last two invocations of copy fail to compile because their types cannot be unified—the syntax error issued by the *g++* compiler. The types of the actual arguments do not conform to the template. If we cast f2, as in the following, we would get compilation.

```
copy(i1, (int* )f2, 50);
```

However, this would get us an inappropriate form of copying. Instead, we need to have a generic copying procedure that accepts two distinct class type arguments.

```
template<class T1, class T2>
void copy(T1 a[], T2 b[], int n)
{
   for (int i = 0; i < n; ++i)
      a[i] = b[i];
}
```

In this form, there is an element-by-element conversion. This is usually the appropriate and most safe conversion.

SIGNATURE MATCHING AND OVERLOADING

Frequently a generic routine cannot work for a special case. The following form of swapping template works on basic types:

```
//generic swap
template <class T>
void swap(T& x, T& y)
{
    T temp;
    temp = x;
    x = y;
    y = temp;
}
```

A function template is used to construct an appropriate function for any invocation that matches its arguments unambiguously.

```
int       i, j;
char      str1[100], str2[100];
complex   c1, c2;

swap(i, j);                //i j int - okay
swap(c1, c2);              //c1, c2 complex -okay
swap(str1[50], str2[33]); //both char variables -okay
swap(i, ch);              //i int ch char - illegal
swap(str1, str2);          //illegal
```

We want to have **swap** work for strings represented as character arrays, so we write the following special case:

```
void swap(char* s1, char* s2)
{
    int max_len;

    max_len =  (strlen(s1) >= strlen(s2)) ? strlen(s1) : strlen(s2);
    char* temp = new char[max_len + 1];

    strcpy(temp, s1);
    strcpy(s1, s2);
    strcpy(s2, temp);
    delete [] temp;
}
```

With this explicit case added, this nontemplate version, when an exact match to the signature of a `swap()` invocation, takes precedence over the exact match found by a template substitution.

The overloading function selection algorithm is as follows:

1   Exact match on a nontemplate function.
2   Exact match using a function template.
3   Ordinary argument resolution on a nontemplate function.

Note well that this algorithm is not universally used. ATT C++ Release 3.0 relaxes the exact-match condition on function templates, allowing both trivial conversions and base/derived pointer conversions.

10.3 CLASS TEMPLATES

In the `stack<T>` example we have an ordinary case of class parameterization. In this section we discuss various special features of parameterizing classes.

FRIENDS

Template classes can contain friends. A friend function that does not use a template specification is universally a friend of all instantiations of the template class. A friend function that incorporates template arguments is specifically a friend of its instantiated class.

```
template <class T>
class matrix {
private:
   friend void foo_bar();  //universal
   friend vect<T> product(vect<T> v); //instantiated
   . . .
};
```

STATIC MEMBERS

Static members are not universal but are specific to each instantiation.

```
template <class T>
class foo {
public:
   static int count;
   . . .
};
template <class T> int foo::count = 0;


. . .
foo<int> a;
foo<double> b;
```

The static variables foo<int>::count and foo<double>::count are distinct.

CLASS TEMPLATE ARGUMENTS

Both classes and functions can have several class template arguments. Let us write a function that converts one type of value to a second type, provided the first type is at least as wide as the second.

```
template <class T1, class T2>
boolean coerce(T1& x, T2 y)
{
   if (sizeof(x) >= sizeof(y))
      x = (T1)y;
   else
      return (false);
   return (true);
}
```

In this template function there are two possibly distinct types specified as template arguments.

Other template arguments include constant expressions, function names, and character strings.

```
template <int n, class T>
class assign_array {
public:
    T a[n];
};

assign_array<50, double> x, y;
x = y;   //should work efficiently
```

The benefits of this parameterization include allocation from the system stack as opposed to allocation from free store. On many systems this is the more efficient regime. The type is bound to the particular integer constant, so operations involving compatible length arrays are type-safe and checked at compile-time.

10.4   PARAMETERIZING THE CLASS *vect*

The class vect is a natural candidate for parameterization. It is a simple exercise to parameterize it and its associated iterator class.

```
//Template based safe array type

enum boolean { false, true};

template <class T> class  vect_iterator;
template <class T>
class vect {
private:
  T* p;                              //base pointer
  int size;                          //number of elements
  friend class vect_iterator<T>;
public:
  vect();                            //create a size 10 array
  vect(int n);                       //create a size n array
  vect(const vect& v);               //initialization by vect
  vect(const T a[], int n);          //initialization by array
  ~vect() { delete [] p; }           //destroy T's
  int  ub() { return (size - 1); }   //upper bound
  T& operator [] (int i);            //range checked element
  vect& operator =(const vect& v);
  void print();
};
```

Basically, everywhere the previous vect class used int as the value to be stored in individual elements, the template definition uses T. So the declaration of the private base pointer p is now of type T.

Note the need for a forward declaration of the associated iterator class vect_iterator. It also follows template syntax.

```
template<class T>
class vect_iterator {
private:
  vect<T>* pv;
  int cur_ind;
public:
  vect_iterator(vect<T>& v):cur_ind(0),pv(&v) {}
  boolean successor();
  boolean predecessor();
  T& item() { return (pv -> p[cur_ind] ); }
  void reset(int n = 0) {cur_ind = n % pv -> size; }
  int position() { return (cur_ind); }
};
```

Obviously, the associated iterator class also requires parameterization. The member function syntax, when defined outside of the class declaration, requires the preface `template<class T>`.

```
template<class T>
boolean vect_iterator<T>::successor()
{
  if (cur_ind >= pv -> size - 1)
    return (false);
  else {
    ++cur_ind;
    return (true);
  }
}


template<class T>
boolean vect_iterator<T>::predecessor()
{
  if (cur_ind <= 0)
    return (false);
  else {
    --cur_ind;
    return (true);
  }
}
```

A member function's definition in file scope includes the scope resolved label *class name*`<T>`. The following constructors for `vect<T>` use `T` as the type specification to `new`.

```
template<class T>
vect<T>::vect()
{
  size = 10;
  p = new T[size];
}


template<class T>
vect<T>::vect(int n)
{
  if (n <= 0) {
     cerr << "illegal vect size: " << n << endl;
     exit(1);
  }
  size = n;
  p = new T[size];
}


template<class T>
vect<T>::vect(const T a[], int n)
{
  if (n <= 0) {
     cerr << "illegal vect size: " << n << endl;
     exit(1);
  }
  size = n;
  p = new T[size];
  for (int i = 0; i < size; ++i)
     p[i] = a[i];
}


template<class T>
vect<T>::vect(const vect<T>& v)
{
  size = v.size;
  p = new T[size];
  for (int i = 0; i < size; ++i)
     p[i] = v.p[i];
}
```

The return type for the bracket operator is again T, as this is an item value stored in the container cell.

```
template<class T>
T& vect<T>::operator [](int i)
{
  if (i < 0 || i > ub()) {
    cerr << "illegal vect index: " << i << endl;
    exit(1);
  }
  return (p[i]);
}


template<class T>
vect<T>& vect<T>::operator =(const vect<T>& v)
{
  int s = (size < v.size) ? size : v.size;

  if (v.size != size)
    cerr << "copying different size arrays "
         << size << " and " << v.size << endl;
  for (int i = 0; i < s; ++i)
    p[i] = v.p[i];
  return (*this);
}
```

Client code is almost as simple as with nonparameterized declarations. To use these declarations we add within angle brackets only the specific type that instantiates the template. This type can be a native type, such as int in the example, or a user-defined type. We leave as an exercise writing template<class T> void vect<T>::print() (see exercise 5).

The following code uses these templates:

```
main()
{
  vect<int> v(8);  vect_iterator<int> a(v);

  for (int i = 0; i < 8; ++i)
    v[i] = i * i;
  do
      cout << a.item() << '\t';
  while (a.successor());
  cout << endl;
  v.print();
}
```

10.5 PARAMETERIZING *quicksort()*

These mechanisms build on each other. We use the `vect<T>` and
`vect_iterator<T>` templates to build a parameterized `quicksort()`
routine. Each piece of the traditional `quicksort` is parameterized.

```
//QUICKSORT using an iterator class

template<class T>
void swap(T& i, T& j) { T temp = i; i = j; j = temp; }
```

At the heart of any sorting routine is the reordering of elements. In this
case `swap()` is parameterized to accept an arbitrary type.

The `quicksort` routine itself is a simple recursion. It uses a partitioning
routine to divide the parameterized array `vect<T>` into two parts. The
elements in `v[from]` to `v[mid - 1]` are smaller than the elements in
`v[mid + 1]` to `v[to]`.

```
template<class T>
void quicksort(vect<T>& v, int from, int to)
{
   int mid;

   if (from < to) {
      if (from == to - 1) { //2 elements
         if (v[from] > v[to])
            swap(v[from], v[to]);
      }
      else {
         mid = partition(v, from, to);
         quicksort(v, from, mid - 1);
         quicksort(v, mid + 1, to);
      }
   }
}
```

The partition() routine is parameterized and uses iterators to track where it is when exchanging out-of-order elements. The iterators front and back maintain the current position in their respective parts of the array being partitioned.

```
template<class T>
int partition(vect<T>& v, int from, int to)
{
    vect_iterator<T> front(v), back(v);
    T   compare;

    back.reset(to); front.reset(from);
    compare = front.item(); front.successor();
    while (front.position() < back.position()) {
        while ((front.position() < back.position())
            && (compare >
            front.item()))
          front.successor(); //find first item larger
        while ((front.position() < back.position())
            && (compare <=
            back.item()))
          back.predecessor();
        swap(front.item(), back.item());
  }

  if (compare >= front.item()) {
      swap(v[from], front.item());
      return(front.position());
  }
  else {
      swap(v[from], v[front.position() - 1]);
      return(front.position() - 1);
  }
}
```

Using this in client code is very easy. We instantiate the angle brackets
with the desired type and invoke quicksort().

```
main()
{
    vect<int> v(8);   vect_iterator<int> a(v);
    v[0] = -6; v[1] = -7; v[2] = -8; v[3] = -9;
    v[4] = -6; v[5] = -7; v[6] = -8; v[7] = -9;

    v.print();
    cout << endl;
    quicksort(v, 0, 7);
    v.print();
    cout << endl;
}
```

Note that the parameterized type being sorted needs to have the comparison operators defined for it.

10.6   PARAMETERIZED BINARY SEARCH TREE

Parametric polymorphism is achievable with void* generic pointers. We saw this in Section 9.4. For comparison purposes, in this section, we develop the same code as a parameterized binary search tree type.

We start by parameterizing b_node. The key is to change the p_gen variables into a parameterized type.

```
//Template Version of GenTree.
#include <iostream.h>
template <class T> class gen_tree; //forward decl

template <class T>
class bnode {
private:
    friend  class gen_tree<T>;
    bnode<T>*  left;
    bnode<T>*  right;
    T        data;
    int      count;
    bnode(T d, bnode<T>* l, bnode<T>* r)
        : data(d), left(l), right(r), count(1) {}
    void print() { cout << data << " : " << count << '\t'; }
};
```

Notice the tree stores type T data, which need not be a pointer type. Notationally the internal self-referential pointers left and right are of type bnode<T>*. The notation is ugly but necessary. The inline bnode<T>::print() function is expected to have operator<<() defined as an output operator. If this is not the case, the instantiation fails at compile-time.

```
template <class T>
class gen_tree {
private:
    bnode<T>* root;
    T find(bnode<T>* r, T d);
    void print(bnode<T>* r);
public:
    gen_tree() { root = 0; }
    void insert(T d);
    T find(T d) { return (find(root, d)); }
    void print() { print(root); }
};
```

The generic tree type gentree<T> is instantiated to store T data, using the insertion routine insert() to build the binary sorted tree. Because this class is not designed for inheritance, as was the case with the corresponding class in Section 9.4, auxiliary functions can be given private access.

The friend function mono() is a parameterized external function. We have two forms of it. In its general form it uses existing or user-supplied meanings for == and <. Lexicographic comparisons on char* require a specific implementation of this function.

```
#include <string.h>
template <class T>   //general case
int comp(T i, T j)
{
   if (i == j)     //assumes == and < defined for T
      return (0);
   else
      return  ((i < j)? -1 : 1) ;
}

int comp(char* i, char* j) //specific case for char*
{
   return (strcmp(i, j));
}
```

The implementation of specific generic member functions requires little modification from the code in Section 9.4. Notice that the new operator needs to create a bnode<T> object.

```
template <class T>
void gen_tree<T>::insert(T d)
{
   bnode<T>* temp = root;
   bnode<T>* old;

   if (root == 0) {
      root = new bnode<T>(d, 0, 0);
      return;
   }
   while (temp != 0) {
      old = temp;
      if (comp(temp -> data, d) == 0) {
         (temp -> count)++;
         return;
      }
      if (comp(temp -> data, d) > 0)
         temp = temp -> left;
      else
         temp = temp -> right;
   }
   if (comp(old -> data, d) > 0)
      old -> left = new bnode<T>(d, 0, 0);
   else
      old -> right = new bnode<T>(d, 0, 0);
}
```

Other member functions require simple modifications to accommodate parameterization. Almost all changes to the concrete case occur in declarations.

```
template <class T>
T gen_tree<T>::find(bnode<T>* r, T d)
{
   if (r == 0)
      return (0);
   else if (comp(r -> data, d) == 0)
      return (r -> data);
   else if (comp(r -> data, d) > 0)
      return (find( r -> left, d));
   else
      return (find( r -> right, d));
}

template <class T>
void gen_tree<T>:: print(bnode<T> *r)
{
   if (r != 0) {
      print( r -> left);
      r -> bnode<T>::print();
      print ( r -> right);
   }
}
```

Client code needs only instantiation of the particular type to be stored in the binary trees. Here we show two uses. One to sort char* strings and the second to sort integers.

```
main()
{
    char dat[256];
    gen_tree<char*>    t;
    char*    p;

    while (cin>>dat && cin.good()) {
        p = new char[strlen(dat) + 1];
        strcpy(p, dat);
        t.insert(p);
    }
    t.print();
    cout << "EOF\n\n";

    gen_tree<int>   i_tree;

    for (int i = 15; i > -5; --i)
        i_tree.insert(i), i_tree.insert(i);
    i_tree.print();
}
```

10.7 INHERITANCE

Parameterized types can be reused through inheritance. Such use parallels the use of inheritance in deriving ordinary classes. Templates and inheritance are both mechanisms for code reuse, and both can involve polymorphism. They are distinct features of C++ and as such combine in different forms. A template class can be derived from an ordinary class. An ordinary class can be derived from an instantiated template class. A template class can be derived from a template class. Each of these possibilities leads to different relationships.

In some situations templates lead to unacceptable cost in the size of the object module. Each instantiated template class requires its own compiled object module. Consider the **gen_tree** class in Chapter 9. It provided reuse with code that was readily converted through inheritance and casting to specifically useful pointer types. Its drawback was that each pointer type required individual coding of its class definition. This can be remedied by using a template to inherit the base class.

```
//Base class is used to keep code body small.

template <class T>
class pointer_tree : private gen_tree {
public:
   pointer_tree() {}
   void  insert(T* d) { gen_tree::insert(p_gen(d)); }
   T* find(T* d)
       { return ((T*)gen_tree::find(p_gen(d))); }
   void  print() { gen_tree::print(); }
};
```

The object code for gen_tree is relatively large and is needed only once. The interface pointer_tree<*type*> requires only a small object module for each instantiation. This is a major saving vis-a-vis the template solution of Section 10.6. This implementation has the drawback of requiring hand coding of each friend function.

The derivation of a class from an instantiated template class is basically no different than ordinary inheritance. In the following example we reuse stack<char> as a base class for a safe character stack.

```
//safe character stack
#include <assert.h>

class safe_char_stack : public stack<char> {
public:
   // test push and pop
   void push(char c) { assert (!full()); stack<char>::push(c); }
   char pop() { assert (!empty()); return (stack<char>::pop()); }
};
```

The instantiated class stack<char> is generated and reused by safe_char_stack.

This last example can be usefully generalized to a template class.

```
//parameterized safe stack
template <class TYPE>
class safe_char_stack : public stack<TYPE> {
public:
   void push(TYPE c) { assert (!full()); stack<TYPE>::push(c); }
   TYPE pop() { assert (!empty()); return (stack<TYPE>::pop()); }
};
```

It is important to notice the link between base class and derived class. Both require the same instantiated type. Each pair of base and derived classes is independent of all other pairs.

10.8   OWNERSHIP AND DESIGN ISSUES

In the stack<> example we have a destructor invoking delete [] s. This means that upon exit the stack would invoke destructors on each object stored in the stack. If these objects are stored in the stack by an assignment routine invoked by push() that anticipates this destruction, then this can be appropriate. In essence stack<> owns the values stored in it. If this were not the case, then a danger would exist that an object would be multiply deleted, a prescription for a serious run-time error.

```
//template stack implementation
template <class TYPE>
class stack {
private:
   enum  { EMPTY = -1};
   TYPE* s;
   int   max_len;
   int   top;
public:
   stack() :max_len(1000)
        { s = new TYPE[1000]; top = EMPTY; }
   stack(int size) :max_len(size)
        { s = new TYPE[size]; top = EMPTY; }
   ~stack() { delete [] s; }
   . . .
};
```

If we change the destructor to

```
~stack() { if (owned) delete [] s; }
```

it does not delete unless owned is true. As a consequence many libraries give the user the choice of how to treat ownership.

What parameterized container classes expect from object behavior is an important design issue. If they expect a key set of behaviors, such as the objects are comparable using the relational operators < and >, then they intrude on the design of the objects or limit their utilization to conforming objects. If they expect too little, then they limit their effectiveness. Choices such as these lead to tradeoffs that preclude a universal solution. Just as there is no universally best automobile, there can be no universally best list ADT.

Parametric polymorphism provided by `template` allows strongly typed compile-time container classes. This form of programming is generally more robust and more efficient than the use of either unions or generic pointers to provide similar code.

10.9   DETAILED CONSIDERATIONS

Orthogonality is the property of a design that chooses independent, interacting features together to form its basis. One favorable characteristic of an orthogonal design is that a feature works in the same way with other features without special restrictions. Orthogonality is a form of minimalism. It is a useful guideline in assessing a class or language design.

Among the nonorthogonal features of C++ is the distinction between what can be a template parameter for functions versus what can be a template parameter for classes. Recall that for functions only class arguments are possible. Furthermore these class arguments must occur in the template function as part of the type description of at least one of the function parameters. Therefore this is legal:

```
template <class TYPE>
void maxelement(TYPE a[], TYPE& max, int size);

template <class TYPE>
int find(TYPE* data);
```

but this is illegal:

```
template <class TYPE>
TYPE convert(int i) { TYPE temp(i); return (temp); }
```

This restriction exists because the compiler must use the arguments at function invocation to deduce which functions actually will be created. An argument in favor of this restriction is that a function definition allows for parameters that are not type parameters already. We can work around the restriction by creating a class whose sole member is a static function appropriately parameterized.

```
template <class TYPE>  //also other arguments are possible
class conversion {
public:
   static TYPE convert(int i) { TYPE temp(i); return (temp); }
};
```

10.10 SUMMARY

1   C++ uses the keyword `template` to provide *parametric polymorphism*. Parametric polymorphism allows the same code to be used with respect to different types where *type is a parameter of the code body*.

2   The syntax of the class declaration is prefaced by

```
template <class identifier >
```

where *identifier* is a template argument that essentially stands for an arbitrary type. Throughout the class definition the template argument can be used as a type name. This argument is instantiated in the actual declarations.

3   Templates provide a further polymorphic language mechanism for parameterizing function definitions. For example,

```
template<class TYPE>
void swap(TYPE& a, TYPE& b)
{
    TYPE temp = a;

    a = b;
    b = temp;
}
```

can be used to generate any simple swapping function for two variables.

4   Both classes and functions can have several class template arguments. In addition to class template arguments, class template definitions can include constant expressions, function names and character strings as template arguments. A common case is to have an `int` argument that parameterized an important size characteristic within the class definition, as in

```
template <int n, class T>
class assign_array {
public:
   T a[n];
};
assign_array<50, double> x, y;
```

5   Parameterized types can be reused through inheritance. Such use parallels the use of inheritance in deriving ordinary classes. Templates and inheritance are both mechanisms for code reuse, and both can involve polymorphism. A template class can be derived from an ordinary class. An ordinary class can be derived from an instantiated template class. A template class can be derived from a template class.

6   The overloading function selection algorithm is as follows:

1 Exact match on a nontemplate function.

2 Exact match using a function template.

3 Ordinary argument resolution on a nontemplate function.

Note that this algorithm is not universally used. ATT C++ Release 3.0 relaxes the exact-match condition on function templates, allowing both trivial conversions and base/derived pointer conversions.

7   *Orthogonality* is the property of a design that chooses independent, interacting features to form its basis. One favorable characteristic of an orthogonal design is that a feature of a design works in the same way with other features without special restrictions. Orthogonality is a form of minimalism. It is a useful guideline in assessing a class or language design.

10.11   EXERCISES

1   Rewrite `stack < T >` to accept an integer value for the default size
     of the stack. Now client code can use declarations such as

```
stack<int, 100> s1, s2;
stack<char, 5000> sc1, sc2, sc3;
```

     Discuss the pros and cons of this additional parameterization.

2   Define a template for fixed-length stacks that allocate a compile-
     time determined size array to store the stacked values.

3   Write a generic `cycle()` function with the following definition,
     and test it:

```
template<class TYPE>
void cycle(TYPE& a, TYPE& b, TYPE& c)
{
    // replace a's value by b's and b's by c's and c's by a's

}
```

4   Write a generic function that, given an arbitrary array and its size,
     rotates the array's values with

```
a[1] = a[0] , a[1] = a[2], ...,
a[size - 1] = a[size - 2], a[0] = a[size - 1]
```

5   Write the member function

```
template<class T>void vect<T>::print().
```

6   Write a generic function that requires that two arrays of differ-
     ent type be swapped. You can assume that both array types have
     elements that are assignment convertible.

7   In the following code, using the safe character stack s, will an assertion fail? If it fails, what will be the last value of i before the error exit?

```
main()
{
    safe_char_stack s;
    int i = 0;

    while ( 1 ) {
        cout << ++i << endl;
        s.push('a');
        s.push('a');
        cout << s.pop();
    }
}
```

8   Write a parameterized set type whose parameter is the size of the set. Create a set conversion operator that works between different-sized sets. A larger-sized set should be truncated in a "natural" way by being converted to a smaller set type. Are there any reasons to prefer this design to one that allows a universal set type that can handle arbitrary size sets? In this case the size parameter would be an argument to the set constructor.

9   Write a complete class definition using the boolean variable owned that provides appropriate behavior for stack < >. Have a member function owns(boolean) be the manipulator function of the private member owned. For example, pop() of a stack-owned object should destroy its local copy, and correspondingly push() should have a local copy created.

10   **Project:** Create a parametric string type. The basic type is to act as a container class that contains a class T object. The prototype case is when the object is a char. The normal *end-of-string* sentinel will be 0. The standard behavior should model the functions found in *string.h*. The class definition could parameterize the sentinel as well.

EXCEPTIONS

11

EXCEPTIONS

This chapter describes exception handling in C++. It is based on the proposed ANSI standard and as such may not be currently released with your compiler. *Exceptions* generally are unexpected error conditions, for example, floating point divided by zero. Normally these conditions terminate the user program with a system-provided error message. C++ gives the programmer the opportunity to recover from these conditions and continue program execution.

We discuss *assertions* as a means to cope with error conditions and exceptions. One point of view is that an exception is based on a breakdown of a contractual guarantee given by the provider of a code concerning what the code is to be applied to. In this model the client guarantees that the conditions for applying the code exist, and the manufacturer guarantees that the code under these provisions works correctly. In this methodology, assertions provide the various guarantees.

We also discuss the ANSI C package *signal.h*, which handles asynchronous hardware exceptions. These exceptions are system-dependent and usually are raised by hardware detection of a special condition. The *signal.h* file also handles synchronous exceptions using the `raise()` function. While not as sophisticated as C++ language exception handling, *signal.h* has a long history as a useful library.

11.1   USING *assert.h*

Program correctness can be viewed in part as proof that the computation terminated with correct output dependent on correct input. The invoker of the computation had the responsibility of providing correct input. This was a precondition. The computation, if successful, satisfied a postcondition. The intention of providing a fully formal proof of correctness is an idealization that is not usually done. Nevertheless, such assertions can be monitored at run-time to provide very useful diagnostics. Indeed, the discipline of thinking out appropriate assertions frequently causes the programmer to avoid bugs and pitfalls.

The C and C++ communities increasingly emphasize the use of such assertions. The standard library *assert.h* provides the macro

```
void assert(int expression);
```

If the `expression` evaluates as false, then execution is aborted with diagnostic output. The assertions are discarded if the macro `NDEBUG` is defined.

Consider allocation to our safe array type `vect` (see Chapter 6):

```
vect::vect(int n)
{
    if (n <= 1) {
        cerr << "illegal vect size " << n << endl;
        exit(1);
    }
    size = n;
    p = new int[size];
}
```

We replace this with

```
vect::vect(int n)
{
    assert (n > 0);  //contractual precondition
    size = n;
    p = new int[size];
    assert (p != 0); //contractual postcondition
}
```

The use of assertions replace the ad hoc use of conditional tests with a more uniform methodology. This is conducive to better practice. The down side is that the assertion methodology does not allow a retry or other repair strategy to continue program execution.

It is possible to make this a slightly more sophisticated scheme by providing different testing levels, as found in the Borland *checks.h* file. Under this package the flag _DEBUG can be set to

```
_DEBUG 0    no testing
_DEBUG 1    PRECONDITION tests only
_DEBUG 2    CHECK tests also
```

Once the library functions are thought to be correct, the level of checking is reduced to only testing preconditions. Once the client code is debugged, all testing can be suspended.

11.2   USING *signal.h*

The *signal.h* file provides a standard mechanism for handling system-defined exceptions in a straightforward manner. Exceptions are defined within this library and are system-dependent integer values. Some examples are

```
#define   SIGINT    2        /*interrupt signal */
#define   SIGFPE    8        /*floating point exception */
#define   SIGABRT   22       /*abort signal */
```

The system can raise these exceptions. For example, hitting control-C on the keyboard, on many systems, generates an interrupt, usually killing the current user process.

The raise() function, prototyped in *signal.h*, can be used to generate an explicit exception.

```
raise(SIGFPE);    //floating point exception signal raised
```

These exceptions can be handled by use of the signal() function. It associates a *handler* function with a *signal*. It can also be used to ignore the signal or to reinstall the default action.

```
signal(SIGABRT, my_abort);   //call my_abrt() if SIGABRT is raised
signal(SIGABRT, SIG_DFL);    //default action if SIGABRT is raised
signal(SIGFPE, SIG_IGN);     //ignore SIGFPE
```

This is called *installing* the handler. It replaces the normal system action with the user-defined handler.

Let us use these ideas to write a loop that is interrupted from the keyboard. Upon interruption, the handler requests from the user whether or not the program should continue executing.

```
//Interrupts handled using signal.h.
#include <signal.h>
#include <time.h>
#include <iostream.h>
#include <stdlib.h>

void cntrl_c_handler(int sig);

main()
{
    int i = 0, j;

    cout << "COUNT TO J MILLION, Enter j: ";
    cin >> j;
    j *= 1000000;
    signal(SIGINT, cntrl_c_handler);
    cout << (double)clock()/CLOCKS_PER_SEC << " start time\n";
    while (1) {
        ++i;
        if (i > j) {
            cout << (double)clock()/CLOCKS_PER_SEC << " end loop\n";
            cout << " HIT " << j/1000000 << "  MILLION" << endl;
            raise(SIGINT);
            cout << "\nEnter j: ";
            cin >> j;
            j *= 1000000;
            i = 0;
            cout << (double)clock()/CLOCKS_PER_SEC << " start loop\n";
        }
    }
}
```

```
void cntrl_c_handler(int sig)
{
    char   c;

    cout << "INTERRUPT";
    cout << "\ntype y to continue: ";
    cin >> c;
    if (c == 'y')
        signal(SIGINT, cntrl_c_handler);
    else
        exit(0);
}
```

DISSECTION OF THE *interrupt* PROGRAM

■ `signal(SIGINT, cntrl_c_handler);`

The handler function is associated with the interrupt SIGINT. Upon detecting the next interrupt, the system invokes `cntrl_c_handler()` instead of a default system action.

■ `cout << (double)clock()/CLOCKS_PER_SEC << " start time\n";`

The function `clock()` is found in *time.h*. It reads out elapsed cpu cycles in local units. Divided by the integer constant CLOCKS_PER_SEC, it gives times in seconds for executing the computation.

■ `while (1) {`
    `++i;`
    `if (i > j) }`
      `. . .`
      `raise(SIGINT);`

The interrupt signal is raised by an explicit call. Implicitly `cntrl_c_handler()` is invoked.

■ `void cntrl_c_handler(int sig)`

This routine handles a `SIGINT` exception.

■ `cout << "INTERRUPT";`
  `cout << "\ntype y to continue: ";`

An interrupt has been detected and the user is asked whether the program is to be continued.

■ `if (c == 'y')`
    `signal(SIGINT, cntrl_c_handler);`

On this request to continue execution, the exception handler is reinstalled. Without the handler being reinstalled, the system would revert to its default handling of the interrupt.

■ `else`
    `exit(0);`

The `exit()` function from the *stdlib.h* is invoked to terminate execution.

Let us apply this technique to handling exceptions for the `vect` type. We begin by replacing the assertions with conditions that raise user-defined signals.

```
const int SIGHEAP = SIGUSR1;
const int SIGSIZE = SIGUSR2;


vect::vect(int n)
{
   if (n <= 0) {
      raise(SIGSIZE);
      cout << "\nEnter vect size n: ";
      cin >> n; //retry with user provided value
   }
   p = new int[n];
   if (p == 0) {
      raise(SIGHEAP);
      p = new int[n];
   }
}
```

Now we can define handlers that can provide appropriate action. For example,

```
void vect_size_handler(int sig)
{
   char c;

   cout << "\nSIZE ERROR\nENTER y to continue with default: ";
   cin >> c;
   if (c == 'y') {
      signal(SIGSIZE, vect_size_handler);
   }
   else
      exit(0);
}

void vect_heap_handler(int sig)
{
   //Possible action to reclaim store for heap
   //or exit gracefully
   . . .
}
```

Contrast this complicated technique with the standard technique for handling heap exhaustion using the `set_new_handler()` mechanism described in Chapter 8.

Note that both signals and assertions can often be replaced by local tests and function calls that have greater flexibility. However, assertions and signals provide a uniform methodology. Also, they mitigate against trying to be overly fault-tolerant. In many cases overdoing recovery is a prescription for incorrect programming and sloppy habits. Assertions test that agreed-to conditions are met. Signals and handlers give a global recovery context for unanticipated conditions. Signals are restricted to a number of asynchronous, system-dependent conditions. However, the scheme is readily extended by setting up global data that is reset at the time the `raise` condition is invoked.

11.3   C++ EXCEPTIONS

C++ introduces an exception handling mechanism that is sensitive to context. As such it can be more informed than a *signal.h* handler and can provide more sophisticated recovery. It is not intended to handle the asynchronous exceptions defined in *signal.h*. The context for raising an exception is a `try` block. Handlers are declared at the end of a `try` block using the keyword `catch`.

C++ code is allowed to directly raise an exception in a `try` block by using the `throw` expression. The exception is handled by invoking an appropriate handler selected from a list of handlers found immediately after the handler's `try` block. A simple example of this technique is

```
vect::vect(int n)
{
    if (n < 1)
        throw (n);
    p = new int[n];
    if (p == 0)
        throw ("FREE STORE EXHAUSTED");
}

void g()
{
    try {
        vect  a(n), b(n);
        . . .

    }
    catch (int n) { . . .} //catches an incorrect size
    catch (char* error) { . . .} //catches free store exhaustion
}
```

The first throw() has an integer argument and matches the catch(int n) signature. When an incorrect array size has been passed as an argument to the constructor, this handler is expected to perform an appropriate action, for example, an error message and abort. The second throw() has a pointer to character argument and matches the catch(char* error) signature.

11.4   THROWING EXCEPTIONS

Syntactically throw expressions come in two forms:

```
throw
throw expression
```

The throw expression raises an exception. The innermost try block in which an exception is raised is used to select the catch statement that processes the exception. The throw expression with no argument rethrows the current exception. It is used typically when a second handler called from the first handler is needed to further process the exception.

The expression thrown is a static, temporary object that persists until exception handling is exited. The expression is caught by a handler that may use this value.

```
void foo()
{
    int i;
    . . .
    throw i;
}

main()
{
    try {
        foo();
    }
    catch(int n) { . . . }
}
```

The integer value thrown by throw i persists until the handler with integer signature catch(int n) exits. This value is available for use within the handler as its argument.

When a nested function throws an exception, the process stack is "unwound" until an exception handler is found. This means that block exit from each terminated local process causes automatic objects to be destroyed.

```
void foo()
{
    int i, j;
    . . .
    throw i;
    . . .
}

void call_foo()
{
    int k;
    . . .
    foo();
    . . .
}

main()
{
    try {
        call_foo();  //foo is exited with i and j destroyed
    }
    catch(int n { . . . }
}
```

An example of rethrowing of an exception is as follows:

```
catch(int n)
{
    . . .
    throw;   //rethrown
}
```

Assuming the thrown expression was of integer type, the rethrown exception is the same persistent integer object that is handled by the nearest handler suitable for that type.

Conceptually the thrown expression passes information into the handlers. Frequently the handlers do not need this information. For example, a handler that prints a message and aborts needs no information from its environment. However, the user might want additional information printed or additional information that can be used to select or help decide the handler's action. In this case it is appropriate to package the information as an object.

```
enum error { bounds, heap, other};
class vect_error {
private:
   error  e_type;
   int  ub, index, size;
public:
   vect_error(error, int, int); //package out of bounds
   vect_error(error, int);      //package out of memory
   . . .
};
```

Now a throw expression using an object of type vect_error can be more informative to a handler than just throwing expressions of simple types.

```
. . .
throw vect_error(bounds, i, ub);
. . .
```

11.5   *try* BLOCKS

Syntactically a try block has the form

> try
> *compound statement*
> *handler list*

The try block is the context for deciding which handlers are invoked on a raised exception. The order in which handlers are defined determines the order in which handlers for a raised exception of matching type are tried.

```
try {
    . . .
    throw ("SOS");
    . . .
    io_condition eof(argv[i]);
    throw (eof);
    . . .
}
catch (const char*) { . . .}
catch (io_condition& x) { . . .}
```

A throw expression matches the catch argument if it is

■   An exact match.
■   A public base class of a derived type which is what is thrown.
■   A thrown object type that is a pointer type convertible to a pointer type that is the catch argument.

It is an error to list handlers in an order that prevents them from being called. An example would be

```
catch(void*)   //any char* would match
catch(char*)
catch(BaseTypeError&)   //would always be called for DerivedTypeError
catch(DerivedTypeError&)
```

In C++, try blocks can be nested. If no matching handler is available in the immediate try block, a handler is selected from its immediately surrounding try block. If no handler can be found that matches, then a default behavior is used.

11.6   HANDLERS

Syntactically a handler has the form

catch (*formal argument*)
compound statement

The `catch` looks like a function declaration of one argument without a return type.

```
catch (char* message)
{
   cerr << message << endl;
   exit(1);
}

catch( . . . )   //default action to be taken
{
   cerr << "THAT'S ALL FOLKS." << endl;
   abort();
}
```

An ellipses signature that matches any argument is allowed. Also, the formal argument can be an abstract declaration, meaning it can have type information without a variable name.

The handler is invoked by an appropriate `throw` expression. At that point the `try` block in effect is exited. The system calls cleanup functions that include destructors for any objects that are local to the `try` block. A partially constructed object will have destructors invoked on any parts of them that are constructed subobjects.

11.7   EXCEPTION SPECIFICATION

Syntactically an exception specification is part of a function declaration and has the form

function header `throw` (*type list*)

The *type list* is the list of types that a `throw` expression within the function can have. If the list is empty, the compiler may assume that no `throw` will be executed by the function, either directly or indirectly.

```
void foo() throw(int, over_flow);
void noex(int i) throw();
```

If an exception specification is left off, then the assumption is that an arbitrary exception can be thrown by such a function. It is good programming practice to indicate through specifications what exceptions are to be expected. Violations of these specifications are a run-time error.

11.8   *terminate()* AND *unexpected()*

The system-provided handler `terminate()` is called when no other handler has been provided to deal with an exception. By default the `abort()` function is called. Otherwise a `set_terminate()` can be used to provide a handler.

The system-provided handler `unexpected()` is called when a function throws an exception that was not in its exception specification list. By default the `abort()` function is called. Otherwise a `set_unexpected()` can be used to provide a handler.

11.9   EXAMPLE EXCEPTION CODE

In this section we discuss some examples of exception code and their effects. Let us return to catching a size error in our `vect` constructor.

```
vect::vect(int n)
{
   if (n < 1)
      throw (n);
   p = new int[n];
   if (p == 0)
      throw ("FREE STORE EXHAUSTED");
}

void g(int m)
{
   try {
      vect a(m);
      . . .

   }
   catch (int n)
   {
      cerr << "SIZE ERROR " << n << endl;
      g(10);   //retry g with legal size
   }
   catch (const char* error)
   {
      cerr << error << endl;
      abort();
   }
}
```

The handler has replaced an illegal value with a default legal value. This may be reasonable in the debugging phase for a system, when many routines are being integrated and tested. The system attempts to continue providing further diagnostics. It is analogous to a compiler attempting to continue to parse an incorrect program after a syntax error. Frequently the compiler provides further additional error messages that prove useful.

The above constructor checks that only one variable has a legal value. It looks artificial in that it replaces code that could directly replace the illegal value with a default by throwing an exception and allowing the handler to repair the value. However, in this form the separation of what is an error and how it is handled is clear. It is a clear methodology for developing fault-tolerant code.

More generally, one could have an object's constructor look like

```
Object::Object(arguments)
{
    if (illegalargument1 )
        throw expression1 ;
    if (illegalargument2 )
        throw expression2 ;
    . . .
    //attempt to construct
    . . .
}
```

The `Object` constructor now provides a set of thrown expressions for an illegal state. The `try` block can now use the information to repair or abort incorrect code.

```
try {

    //. . . fault tolerant code

    }
catch(declaration1) { /* fixup this case */ }
catch(declaration2) { /* fixup this case */ }
    . . .
catch(declarationK ) { /* fixup this case */ }
//correct or repaired - state values are now legal
```

When many distinct error conditions are useful for a given object's state, a class hierarchy can be used to create a selection of related types to be used as `throw` expressions.

```
Class Object_Error {
public:
   Object_Error(arguments); //capture useful information
   members that contain thrown expression state
   virtual void repair()
      { cerr << "Repair failed in Object " << endl; abort(): }
};

Class Object_Error_S1 : public Object_Error {
public:
   Object_Error_S1(arguments);
   added members that contain thrown expression state
   void repair(); //override to provide suitable repair
};

   . . . //other derived error classes as needed
```

These hierarchies allow an appropriately ordered set of catches to handle exceptions in a logical sequence. Recall that a base class type should come after a derived class type in the list of catch declarations.

11.10   THE PHILOSOPHY OF ERROR RECOVERY

Error recovery is chiefly and paradoxically concerned with writing a correct program. Exception handling is about error recovery and secondarily a transfer of the control mechanism. Following the client/manufacturer model, the manufacturer must guarantee that, for an acceptable input state, its software produces correct output. The question for the manufacturer is how much error-detection and conceivably correction should be built in. The client is often better served by fault-detecting libraries and can decide on whether to attempt to continue the computation.

Error recovery is based on transfer of control. Undisciplined transfer of control leads to chaos. In error recovery one assumes an exceptional condition has corrupted the computation. It becomes dangerous to continue the computation. It is analogous to driving a car after an indication that the steering is damaged. The disciplined recovery when damage happens is what useful exception handling entails.

In most cases programming that raises exceptions should print a diagnostic message and gracefully terminate. In special forms of processing, such as real-time processing, and in fault-tolerant computing, the requirement exists that the system not go down. In these cases heroic attempts at repair are legitimate.

What can be agreed upon is that classes can usefully be provided with error conditions. Many of these conditions are that the object has member values in illegal states—values they are not allowed to have. The system raises an exception for these cases, with the default action being program termination. This is analogous to the native types raising system-defined exceptions, such as `SIGFPE`.

The controversy focuses on the question, What kind of intervention is reasonable to keep the program running, and where should the flow of control be returned to? C++ uses a termination model that forces the current `try` block to terminate. Under this regime the client either retries the code, ignores the exception, or substitutes a default result and continues. Retrying the code seems the most likely to give a correct result.

Experience shows that code is usually too thinly commented. It is hard to imagine the program that would be too rich in assertions. Assertions and simple throws and catches that terminate the computation are parallel techniques. A well-planned set of error conditions detectable by the user of an ADT is an important part of a good design. An over reliance on exception handling in normal programming, beyond error detection and termination, is a sign that a program was ill-conceived with too many holes in its original form.

11.11   SUMMARY

1   *Exceptions* are generally unexpected error conditions. Normally these conditions terminate the user program with a system-provided error message. An example is floating point divide-by-zero.

2   The standard library *assert.h* provides the macro

```
void assert(int expression);
```

If the `expression` evaluates as false, then execution is aborted with diagnostic output. The assertions are discarded if the macro `NDEBUG` is defined.

3   The *signal.h* file provides a standard mechanism for handling system-defined exceptions in a straightforward manner. Some examples are

```
#define  SIGINT   2      /*interrupt signal */
#define  SIGFPE   8      /*floating point exception */
#define  SIGABRT  22     /*abort signal */
```

The system can *raise* these exceptions. For example, on many systems hitting control-C on the keyboard generates an interrupt. The normal action is to kill the current user process. These exceptions can be handled by use of the `signal()` function. It associates a *handler* function with a signal.

4   C++ code is allowed to directly raise an exception in a `try` block by using the `throw` expression. The exception is handled by invoking an appropriate handler selected from a list found immediately after the handler's `try` block.

5   Syntactically `throw` expressions come in two forms:

```
throw
throw expression
```

The `throw` expression raises an exception in a `try` block. The `throw` expression with no argument rethrows the current exception.

6   Syntactically a `try` block has the form

```
try
compound statement
handler list
```

The `try` block is the context for deciding which handlers are invoked on a raised exception. The order in which handlers are defined determines the order in which handlers for a raised exception of matching type are tried.

7   Syntactically a handler has the form

```
catch ( formal argument )
compound statement
```

The `catch` looks like a function declaration of one argument without a return type.

8   Syntactically an exception specification is part of a function decla-
     ration and has the form

     function header throw (*type list*)

     The *type list* is the list of types that a throw expression within the
     function can have. If the list is empty, the compiler may assume
     that no throw will be executed by the function, either directly or
     indirectly.

9   The system-provided handler terminate() is called when no other
     handler has been provided to deal with an exception. The system-
     provided handler unexpected() is called when a function throws
     an exception that was not in its exception specification list. By
     default each of these call the abort() function.

11.12 EXERCISES

1   The following bubble sort does not work correctly.

```
//Incorrect bubble sort.
#include <iostream.h>

void swap(int a, int b)
{
    int temp = a;
    a = b;
    b = temp;
}

void bubble(int a[], int size)
{
    int i, j;

    for (i = 0; i != size; ++i)
        for (j = i ; j != size; ++j)
            if (a[j] < a [j + 1])
                swap (a[j], a[j + 1]);
};

main()
{
    int t[10] = { 9, 4, 6, 4, 5, 9, -3, 1, 0, 12};

    bubble(t, 10);
    for (int i = 0; i < 10; ++i)
        cout << t[i] << '\t';
    cout << "\nsorted? " << endl;
}
```

Place assertions in this code to test that the code is working properly. Use this technique to write a correct program.

2   Use templates to write a generic version of the correct bubble sort,
complete with assertions. Use a random number generator to generate test data. On what types can this be made to work generically?

3   Replace the `cntrl_c_handler()` with

```
void cntrl_c_handler(int sig)
{
    char   c;
    static int count = 0;

    cout << "INTERRUPT";
    cout << "\ntype y to continue:";
    cin >> c;
    if (c == 'y' && count++ < N)
        signal(SIGINT, cntrl_c_handler);
    else
        abort();
}
```

The variable N is an integer constant provided to the program. What is the difference in behavior between this version and the one in Section 11.2?

4   Remove `raise(SIGINT)` from `main()` in the previous program. The intended effect is to allow the user to interrupt the running program and decide to discontinue it if it is running too long. Make sure that this is how it works on your system. Now modify the code to accept a distinct new value of j at each completion of a timing run. Can you use these values to estimate the MIPS rate of your processor?

5   In many instances thread of control should not be resumed at the point where a signal is raised. Also, the system default action of termination may be too drastic. On ANSI systems the file *setjmp.h* provides declarations that allow nonlocal resumption of processing.

```
//setjmp.h definitions
typedef long jmp_buf[16];         //space to hold environment
int setjmp(jmp_buf env);          //save calling environment
void longjmp(jmp_buf env, int v); //restore environment
```

Rewrite the code in Section 11.2 to return to the beginning of the timing loop anytime an interrupt is caught. Again, only allow this for N times so that repeated interrupts can cancel the routine. Note that using *setjmp.h* bypasses a normal block exit and can be dangerous because objects can be left undestroyed.

6   The following code often results in an abort.

```
//Default behavior on sqrt of a negative number.
//Compile with -lm flag for math library on many systems.
#include <math.h>
#include <iostream.h>

main()
{
   for (int i = 10; i >= -1; --i)
      cout << " I = " << i << " , sqrt = " << sqrt(i) << endl;
}
```

Catch the interrupt and allow the user to decide for a negative value of i what should be computed.

7   Compute 1/x as a floating point number.

```
double reciprocal(double x);   //return 1/x
```

If the computation raises a floating point exception because of division by zero, then return the value **DBL_MAX** in *float.h*. Can you code this so that other floating point exceptions not thrown or raised from within reciprocal() are treated by the system default behavior? Notice that this is easy when using C++ try blocks.

8   Code the member function vect::operator[](int) to throw an out-of-range exception if an incorrect index is used. Also code a reasonable catch that prints out the incorrect value and terminates. Execute a try block in which the exception occurs to test the code. Write a catch that would allow user intervention at the keyboard to produce a correct index and continue or retry the computation. Can this be done in a reasonable manner?

9   Recode the stack class of Chapter 6 to throw exceptions for as many conditions as you think are reasonable. Use an enumerated type to list the conditions

```
enum stack_error { overflow, underflow, . . . };
```

Write a catch that uses a switch statement to select an appropriate message and terminate the computation.

10   Write a `stack_error` class that replaces the enumerated type of the previous exercise. Have this be a base class for a series of derived classes that encapsulates each specific exception condition. The catches should be able to use overridden virtual functions to process the various thrown exceptions.

11   **Project:** Redo the text editor package project of Chapter 8 to add exception handling. For example, when processing a text search command that is incorrect, the application should return to a state that can receive a new command. The undo command in most editor packages is a critical example of fault tolerance. Also, the writing of a backup file in case of irreversible failure is another example. To the extent that you can, add these to your software.

12

OOP USING C++

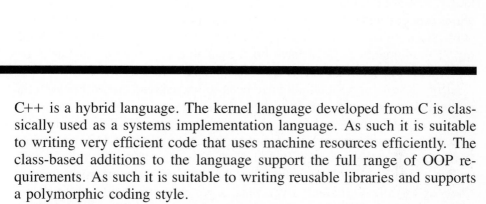

C++ is a hybrid language. The kernel language developed from C is classically used as a systems implementation language. As such it is suitable to writing very efficient code that uses machine resources efficiently. The class-based additions to the language support the full range of OOP requirements. As such it is suitable to writing reusable libraries and supports a polymorphic coding style.

Object-oriented programming (OOP) and C++ have been embraced by industry in a very short time frame. C++ is a hybrid OOP language. As such, it allows a multiparadigmatic approach to coding. What surfaces as new is the use of polymorphism and inheritance. The traditional advantages of the C language as an efficient and powerful programmer's language are not lost. The key new secret ingredient is polymorphism—"to be capable of assuming many forms."

12.1 OOP LANGUAGE REQUIREMENTS

An OOP language has

1 Encapsulation with data hiding: The ability to distinguish an object's internal state and behavior from its external state and behavior.

2   Type extensibility: The ability to add user-defined types to augment native types.

3   Inheritance: The ability to create new types by importing or reusing the description of existing types.

4   Polymorphism with dynamic binding: The ability of objects to be responsible for interpreting function invocation.

These features cannot substitute for programmer discipline and community-observed convention, but they can be used to promote such behavior.

A typical procedural language, such as Pascal or C, has limited forms of type extensibility and encapsulation. Both languages have pointer and record types that provide these features. Additionally, C has an ad hoc scheme of file-oriented privacy, namely `static` global declarations. Languages such as Modula–2 and Ada have more complete forms of encapsulation, namely module and package, respectively. These languages readily allow users to build ADTs and provide significant library support for many application areas. A language such as pure LISP supports dynamic binding. The elements in OOP have been available in different languages for at least 25 years.

LISP, Simula, and Smalltalk have been in widespread use within both the academic and research communities. These languages are in many ways more elegant than C and C++. However, not until OOP elements were added to C was there any significant movement to using OOP in industry. In the face of the notorious software crisis, this is quite mystifying. Indeed, we have in the US a *bandwagon effect* that cuts across companies, product lines, and application areas. Even Ada, a government-mandated language, has not been so received. Our thesis is that industry needed to couple OOP with the ability to program effectively at a low level.

Also crucial is the ease of migration from C to C++. Unlike PL/1, whose heritage was Fortran and Cobol, and Ada, which is rooted in Pascal, C++ had C as a nearly proper subset. As such the installed base of C code need not be abandoned. These other languages required nontrivial conversion processes to modify existing code from their ancestor languages.

The conventional academic wisdom is that excessive concern with efficiency is detrimental to good coding practices. This concern misses the obvious—product competition is based on performance. Consequently, industry values low-level technology. In this environment C is a very effective tool.

12.2   ADTs IN NON-OOP LANGUAGES

Existing languages and methodology supported much of the OOP methodology by combining language features with programmer discipline. Programmer discipline and community conventions do work. It is possible in
a non-OOP language to create and use ADTs. Three examples in the C
community are the use of the pseudotypes string, boolean, and file. They
are pseudotypes in that they do not enjoy the same privileges as true types.
What is gained by looking at these examples is a better understanding of
the limits of extensibility in the non-OOP context.

A boolean type is implicit in C. Namely, logical expressions treat zero
as false and nonzero as true. Since zero is a universal value, available for
all native types, it is by convention used as a sentinel value. An idiom in
pointer-based processing is zero used to represent an end-of-list condition.

```
while (p) {          //p == 0  NULL pointer
   . . .             //process list
   p = p -> next;    //traverse
}
```

Frequently an enumerated type is used explicitly to provide better documentation.

```
enum boolean {FALSE, TRUE};

boolean search(int table[], int x, int& where)
{
   where = -1;
   for (int i = 0; i < N; ++i)
      if (x == table[i] {
         where = i;
         break;
      }
   return boolean(where != -1);
}
```

The string type is a combination of programmer discipline and community convention in using the library *string.h*. This library is applicable to the
type pointer-to-character. The end-of-string is again the zero value. Concatenation, copying, length, and other operations are given by functions

in *string.h*. A measure of this success is the extent to which C is used for string processing applications.

The file type is based on the use of *stdio.h*. A system-dependent type is defined with the name FILE. Functions such as file opening, closing, and seeking are given in *stdio.h*. These routines expect file pointers as parameters. Specific structure members are not directly manipulated when the programmer stays with these conventions. Again C has been very successfully used in writing operating systems and code that manipulates file systems.

These successes do not argue for the status quo. Instead they argue for OOP as implemented in a language that ensures that library conventions are not circumvented. By hiding implementation, C++ does not allow access to the non-public representation of such types. C++ allows user-defined types to be more universally reused by giving them the look-and-feel of a native type.

12.3   CLIENTS AND MANUFACTURERS

To fully appreciate the OOP paradigm, we must view the overall coding process as an exercise in shared and distributed responsibilities. We have used the term *client* to mean a user of a class. We have used the term *manufacturer* to mean the provider of the class.

A client of a class expects an approximation to an abstraction. A stack, to be useful, has to be of reasonable size. A complex number must be of reasonable precision. A deck of cards must be shufflable with random outcome in dealing hands. The internals of how these behaviors are computed is not a direct concern of the client. The client is concerned with cost, effectiveness, and ease of operation, but not with implementation. This is the *black box* principle.

A Black Box for the client should be

1   Simple to use, easy to understand, and familiar

2   Cheap, efficient, and powerful

3   In a component relationship within the system

A Black Box for the manufacturer should be

1   Easy to reuse and modify, and hard to misuse and reproduce

2   Cheap, efficient and powerful

3   Profitable to produce with a large client base

The manufacturer competes for clients by implementing an ADT product that is reasonably priced and efficient. It is in the manufacturer's interest to hide details of an implementation. This simplifies what the manufacturer needs to explain to the client. It frees the manufacturer to allow internal repairs or improvements that do not affect the client's use. It restrains the client from dangerous and inadvertent tampering with the product.

Structures and ordinary functions in C allow us to build useful ADT but do not support a client/manufacturer distinction. The client has ready access to internal details and may modify them in unsuitable ways. Consider a stack in C represented as an array with an integer variable `top`. A client of such a stack in C can extract an internal member of the array used to represent the stack. This violates the LIFO abstraction that the stack is implementing.

Encapsulation of objects prevents these violations. A data hiding scheme that restricts access of implementation detail to manufacturers guarantees client conformance to the ADT abstraction. The private parts are hidden from client code, and the public parts are available. It is possible to change the hidden representation, but not to change the public access or functionality. If done properly, client code need not change when the hidden representation is modified.

The keys to fulfilling these conditions are encapsulation, inheritance, and polymorphism.

12.4   REUSE AND INHERITANCE

Library creation and reuse are crucial indicators of successful language strategies. Inheritance is used both for code sharing and reuse, and for developing type hierarchies. Inheritance is the mechanism of deriving a new class from an old one. That is, the existing class can be added to or altered to create the derived class. Through inheritance, a hierarchy of related ADTs can be created that share code and a common interface, a feature critical to the ability to reuse code.

Inheritance influences overall software design by providing a framework that captures conceptual elements that become the focus for system building and reuse. For example, InterViews (Linton et al. 1989) is a C++ library that supports building graphical user interfaces. Major categories of objects include interactive objects, text objects, and graphics objects. These categories are readily composed to produce different applications, such as a CAD system, browser, or WYSIWYG editor.

The OOP design methodology becomes

- Decide on an appropriate set of ADTs.
- Design in their relatedness, and use inheritance to share code and interface.
- Use virtual functions to process related objects dynamically.

Inheritance also facilitates the black box principle. It is an important mechanism for suppressing detail. As it is hierarchical, each level provides functionality to the next level built on it. In retrospect structured programming methodology with its process-centered view relied on step-wise refinement to nest routines, but did not adequately appreciate the need for a corresponding view of data.

12.5 POLYMORPHISM

Polymorphism is the genie in OOP taking instruction from a client and properly interpreting its wishes. A polymorphic function has many forms. Following Cardelli and Wegner (1985), we make the following distinctions:

- *ad hoc polymorphism—coercion* A function or operator works on several different types by converting their values to the expected type. An example in ANSI C is assignment conversions of arithmetic types upon function call.
- *ad hoc polymorphism—overloading* A function is called based on its *signature* defined as the list of argument types in its parameter list. The C integer divide operator and float divide operator are distinguished based on their argument list.
- *pure polymorphism—inclusion* A type is a subtype of another type. Functions available for the base type will work on the subtype. Such a function can have different implementations that are invoked by a run-time determination of subtype.
- *pure polymorphism—parametric* The type is left unspecified and is later instantiated. Manipulation of generic pointers and templates provide this in C++.

```
//polymorphism-various contexts

a / b        //divide behavior determined by native coercions

cout << a    //ad-hoc polymorphism through function overloading

p -> draw()  //pure polymorphism through virtual function call

stack <window*> win[40]   //parametric polymorphism using templates
```

Polymorphism localizes responsibility for behavior. The client code frequently requires no revision when additional functionality is added to the system through manufacturer-provided code additions.

Polymorphism directly contributes to the black box principle. The virtual functions specified for the base class are the interface used by the client throughout. The client knows that an overridden member function takes responsibility for a specific implementation of a given action relevant to the object. The client need not know different routines for each calculation or different forms of specification. These details are suppressed.

12.6 LANGUAGE COMPLEXITY

C++ extracts a major price for all of its advantages. Language complexity is substantial. This leads to additional training costs and to subtle misuse. Also, the rapid evolution of the language while in major use is nearly unprecedented. C is a small, elegant language. The syntax of C++ is similar to that of C, but its semantics are complex. To appreciate these difficulties, we compare some characteristics of Pascal, Modula–2, C++, and Ada.

	Keywords	Statements	Operators	Pages
Pascal	35	9	16	28
Modula-2	40	10	19	25
C	29	13	44	40
C++ v1.0	42	14	47	66
C++ v3.0	48	14	52	155
Ada	63	17	21	241

These numbers are only suggestive. Modula-2 by these measures is slightly more complicated than its ancestor Pascal; and both are on a par with C. C++ is intentionally constructed as an extension of C and follows C style manual explanations. C++ v3.0 adds 19 keywords to the 29 found in traditional C, a two-thirds increase. The C++ v3.0 reference manual has 155 pages compared with 40 pages in the C reference manual, a quadrupling. These two measures suggest that C++ is much more complicated than C. Furthermore many C++ constructs are orthogonal, so that their interactions greatly affect complexity.

An example of this occurs in Ellis and Stroustrup (1990, p. 306), where a thirteen by five table is used to outline distinct cases and features of different function types. The five function characteristics are inherited, virtual, return type, member or friend, and default generation. For example, constructors, destructors, and conversion functions cannot have return type declarations, and `new()` and `delete()` must have `void*` and `void` respectively. C has effectively one form of function semantics. This 65-fold expansion is awe inspiring; and while regularities exist in this table, and many characteristics are derivable from a conceptual understanding of the language design, Stroustrup still felt it advisable to list these distinctions.

C++ overloads key concepts with several meanings. This causes a great deal of conceptual confusion. A candidate for the worst offender is the keyword `static`. There can be a local static variable—meaning a variable that retains value upon block exit. There can be a static global identifier—meaning a name that has visibility restricted to that file. There can be a class variable that is static—meaning a variable whose existence is independent of the class. There can be static member functions—meaning member functions that do not receive the `this` pointer arguments. These meanings are related, but they also are distinct enough to prevent us from successfully understanding them all as derived from a single concept.

C++ as a hybrid OOP language can cause the programmer a *dialectical tension headache*. The penchant of C programmers to focus on efficiency and implementation conflicts with the penchant for objectivists to focus on elegance, abstraction, and generality. The two demands on the coding process are reconcilable, but require a measure of coordination and respect that must be brought to the process.

12.7   C++ OOP BANDWAGON

OOP using C++ has had dazzling acceptance in industry, in spite of acknowledged flaws. The reason for this is that it brings OOP technology to industry in an acceptable way. Namely, it is based on an existing successful language in widespread use. It allows portable code to be written that is tight and efficient. Type safety is retained and type extensibility is general. C++ coexists with standard languages and does not require special resources from the system.

C was initially designed as a systems implementation language and as such allows coding that is readily translated to efficiently use machine resources. Software products gain competitive advantage from such efficiency. Hence, despite complaints that traditional C was not a safe or robust language in which to code, C grew in its range of application. The C community by convention and discipline used, in ad hoc ways, structured programming and ADT extensions. OOP as such made inroads into this professional community only when it was wedded to C within a conceptual framework that maintained its traditional point of view and advantages. Key to the bandwagon changeover to C++ has been the understanding that inheritance and polymorphism gain important advantages over traditional coding practice.

Polymorphism in C++ allows a client of an ADT to use it as a black box. Success in OOP is characterized by the extent to which a user-defined type can be made indistinguishable from a native type. Polymorphism allows coercions to be specified that integrate the ADT with the coercion rules of the kernel language. Polymorphism permits objects from subtype hierarchies to respond dynamically to function invocation—the messaging principle in OOP. Polymorphism simplifies client protocols. Name proliferation is controlled by function and operator overloading. The availability of all four forms of polymorphism in C++ encourages the programmer to design with encapsulation and data hiding in mind.

OOP is many things to many people. Attempts at defining it are reminiscent of the blind sages' attempts to describe the elephant. We offer one more equation:

$$OOP \ = \ type\text{-}extensibility \ + \ polymorphism$$

In many languages and systems, the cost of this detail suppression was run-time inefficiency or undue rigidity in the interface. C++ has a range of choices that allow both efficiency and flexibility. As a consequence of this, industry will increasingly adopt it.

12.8   PLATONISM: TABULA RASA DESIGN

C++ gives the programmer a tool to implement an OOP design. But how do you develop such a design? Given an empty slate—a *tabula rasa*—no simple methodology exists because each design must be strongly tied to the problem domain and reflect its abstractions. Discovering these abstractions is a design philosophy we call *Platonism*.

In the Platonic paradigm, there is an ideal object. For example, imagine an ideal chair in the heavens and attempt to describe its characteristics. These would be characteristics shared by all chairs. Such a chair would be a subcategory of another ideal—furniture. Chair would have subcategories, such as swivel chair, beach chair, reclining chair, rocking chair, and so on. Useful descriptions would require expertise on chairs and agreement on the nature of "chairness" among producers and users of chairs. The Platonic chair would be easily modified to describe most commonly occurring chairs. The Platonic chair would be described in terms consistent with existing chair terminology. (See Figure 12.1.)

C++ was influenced by Simula 67, a language specifically invented for simulations. The Platonic paradigm is a modeling or simulation of the concrete world. It involves extra effort in determining a design. The design typically provides a public interface that is convenient, general, and efficient. These considerations can be in conflict. Again there are no simple rules for deciding such tradeoffs.

The extra effort should be very beneficial to offset the increased initial design cost. First and foremost, it imposes an additional level of discipline

FIGURE 12.1   The Ideal Chair

to the programming process. Increasing programmer discipline always pays dividends. Second, it encapsulates into classes meaningful related pieces of code. Encapsulation and decomposition always pays dividends. Third, it enhances code reuse through inheritance and ADTs. Code reuse always pays dividends. Fourth, it improves prototyping by deferring implementation decisions and providing access to large conveniently used general libraries. Cheap prototyping always pays dividends.

The Platonic paradigm using OOP techniques is quietly revolutionizing the programming process. It does not displace older techniques, such as structured programming, but instead uses them in the small to effectively manage the composition of large and more robust software.

12.9   DESIGN PRINCIPLES

Most programming should involve the use of existing designs. For example, the mathematical and scientific community have standard definitions of complex numbers, rationals, matrices, and polynomials. Each of these can be readily coded as ADTs. The expected public behavior of these types is widely agreed to.

The programming community has widespread experience with standard container classes. Reasonable agreement exists as to the behavior of stack, associative array, binary tree, and queue. Also, the programming community has many examples of specialized programming language oriented around a particular domain. For example, SNOBOL and its successor language ICON have very powerful string processing features. These can be captured as ADTs in C++.

Useful design principles include Occam's razor—"Entities should not be multiplied beyond necessity"—completeness, invertibility, orthogonality, consistency, simplicity, efficiency, and expressiveness. These principles can be in conflict and frequently involve tradeoffs in arriving at a design.

Invertibility means that one should have member functions that are inverses. In mathematical types, addition and subtraction are inverses. In a text editor, add and delete are inverses. Some commands are their own inverses, such as negation. The importance of invertibility in a nonmathematical context can be seen by the brilliant success of the undo command in text editing and the recover commands in file maintenance.

Completeness is best seen in Boolean algebra, where the *nand* operation suffices to generate all possible Boolean expressions. But Boolean algebra is usually taught with negation, conjunction, and disjunction as the basic operations. Completeness by itself is not enough to judge a design. A large set of operators is frequently more expressive.

Orthogonality is a principle that says each element of a design should integrate and work with all other elements. Also, elements of the basic design should not overlap or be redundant. For example, on a system that manipulates shapes, you should have a horizontal move, a vertical move, and a rotate operation. In effect, these would be adequate to position the shape at any point on the screen.

Designs should be hierarchical. Hierarchy is captured through inheritance. It is a reflection of two principles—decomposition and localization. Both principles are methods of suppressing detail, a key idea in coping with complexity. There is a scale problem in such a design. How much detail is enough to make a concept useful as its own class? It is important to avoid a proliferation of specialized concepts. How much detail renders it hard to master?

12.10 SCHEMA, DIAGRAMS, AND TOOLS

Designs can be aided by a diagramming process. Several OO-design (OOD) notations exist, and a number have been incorporated in software CASE (computer assisted software engineering) tools. We will describe two different schemes that we have found useful. The first is the CRC notecard scheme (Budd 1991), and the second is the Wasserman-Pircher diagram (Wasserman et al. 1990; Booch 1991, for an alternative).

CRC stands for class, responsibility, and collaboration. A CRC notecard is used to design a given class. What initially is described are the responsibilities of the class and the collaborators for that class. The back of the card is used to describe implementation detail. The front of the card corresponds to public behavior (see Figure 12.2).

As the design process proceeds, the cards are rewritten and refined. They become more detailed and closer to a set of member function headers. The back of the card can be used to show implementation details, including ISA and HASA relationships.

The attractiveness of this scheme is its flexibility. In effect it represents a pseudo-code refinement process that can reflect local tastes. The number of revisions and the level of detail and rigor is a matter of taste (Budd 1991).

CRC card

Class Responsibility Collaborator—state index cards

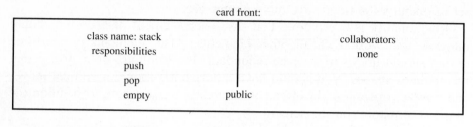

card front:

class name: stack responsibilities push pop empty	collaborators none

public

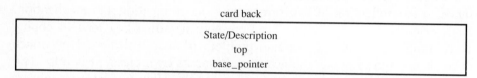

card back

State/Description
top
base_pointer

FIGURE 12.2   CRC Cards

Wasserman-Pircher diagrams are derived from entity-relation modeling and structured design. A sophisticated integrated software environment that uses these to develop OOP code is provided by Interactive Development Environments, San Francisco, California. The software design is captured in Figures 12.3 and 12.4. The level of detail is such that code stubs can be automatically produced from this design. Also documentation and style rules can semiautomatically be tested for or generated.

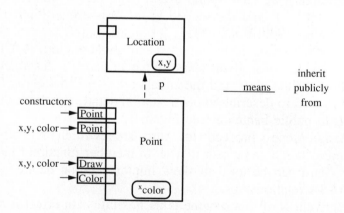

A Wasserman-Pircher diagram of a C++ Inheritance Relationship

FIGURE 12.3   Design Tools

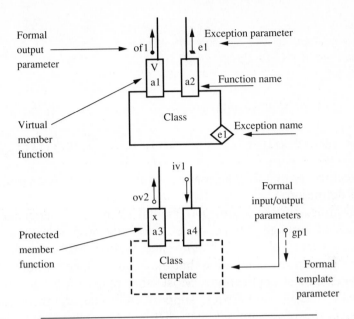

FIGURE 12.4   IDE's C++ Design Templates

12.11 LAST WORDS

C++ is to an extent the 1990s version of PL/1 (1965) or Ada (1980). It is an attempt within the professional programming community to provide a nearly universal programming language. The defect of PL/1 is its attempt to mix too many styles—namely COBOL, FORTRAN, and elements of ALGOL—into the same language. The defects of ADA are its size, complexity, and inefficiency. C++ has problems with size and complexity, but very importantly it builds on existing resources and practice. It also emphasizes efficiency—sometimes to a fault.

Some of its complexity problems can be avoided by keeping to a conceptual view of its features. An example is the fact that a pure virtual function can be defined with executable code.

```
class ABC {
public:
   virtual void f() = 0;
};
```

```
void ABC::f() { cout << "pure virtual foo " << endl }
```

```
//must be called with qualified name, e.g.  x.ABC::f();
```

It is an eccentricity that this is possible. Conceptually a pure virtual is used to defer a definition.

Other complexity issues are fundamental to the C++ language design, such as lack of garbage collection (GC). Several proposals exist (Edelson 1992; Edelson and Pohl 1991; Boehm and Weiser 1988) and their implementations support the contention that they can be done without degrading performance in most applications. Most other major OPP languages, such as Smalltalk, CLOS, and Eiffel, support GC. The argument for GC is that it makes the programmer's task distinctly easier. Memory leaks and pointer errors are common when each class provides for its own storage management. These are very hard errors to find and debug. GC is a well-understood technology—so why not?

The argument against GC is that it extracts a hidden cost from all users when employed universally. Also, GC manages memory but not other resources. This would still require destructors for *finalization*. Finalization is the return of resources and other behavior when an object's lifetime is over. For example, the object might be a file, and finalization might require closing the file. Finally, it is not in the tradition of the C community to have free store managed automatically.

OOP attempts to emphasize reuse. Reuse is possible on different scales. The grandest scale is the development of libraries that are effective for an entire problem domain. The up side is reuse contributes in the long run to more easily maintained code. The down side is a particular application does not need costly library development.

OOP requires more programmer sophistication. More sophisticated programmers are better programmers. The down side is training cost and potential misuse of sophisticated tools.

OOP lets client code be simpler and more readily extensible. Polymorphism can be used to incorporate local changes into a large-scale system without the need for global modification. The down side can be run-time overhead.

C++ provides programming encapsulations through classes, inheritance, and templates. Encapsulations hide and localize. As systems get bigger and more complex, encapsulations are increasingly needed. Simple block structure and functional encapsulation of languages such as FORTRAN and ALGOL are not enough. The 1970s taught us the need for the module as a programming unit. The 1980s taught us that the module needs to have a logical coherence supported in the language, and that modules need to be derivable from each other. When supported by a programming language, these encapsulations and relationships lead to increased programmer discipline. The art of programming is to blend rigor and discipline with creativity.

12.12   REFERENCES

1.   Boehm, Hans-J., and Mark Weiser. 1988. "Garbage collection in an uncooperative environment," *Software—Practice and Experience*, September, 807–820.

2.   Booch, Grady. 1991. *Object-Oriented Design with Applications*. Redwood City, CA: Benjamin/Cummings Publishing.

3.   Budd, Timothy. 1991. *An Introduction to Object-Oriented Programming*. Reading, MA: Addison-Wesley Publishing.

4.   Cardelli, Luca, and Peter Wegner. 1985. "On understanding types, data abstraction, and polymorphism." *Computing Surveys*. 17: 471–522.

5.   Edelson, Daniel. 1992. "A mark and sweep collector for C++." *Proc. Princ. Prog. Lang.* January.

6.   Edelson, Daniel, and Ira Pohl. 1991. "A copying collector for C++." *Usenix C++ Conf. Proc.* 85–102.

7.   Ellis, Margaret, and Bjarne Stroustrup. 1990. *The Annotated C++ Reference Manual*. Reading, MA: Addison-Wesley Publishing.

8.   Linton, Mark; John Vlissides; and Paul Calder. 1989. "Composing user interfaces with InterViews." IEEE *Computer*. 22, no. 2:8–22.

9.   Wasserman, Anthony; P.A. Pircher; and R. Muller. 1990. "The object-oriented structured design notation for software design representation." IEEE *Computer*. 23, no. 3: 50–63.

12.13   SUMMARY

1   Object-oriented Programming (OOP) and C++ have been embraced by industry in a very short time. C++ is a hybrid OOP language. As such it allows a multiparadigmatic approach to coding. The traditional advantages of the C language as an efficient powerful programmer's language are not lost. The key new secret ingredient is polymorphism—"to be capable of assuming many forms."

2   Existing languages and methodology supported much of the OOP methodology by combining language features with programmer discipline. It is possible in a non-OOP language to create and use ADTs. Three examples in the C community are the use of the pseudotypes string, boolean, and file. They are pseudotypes in that they do not enjoy the same privileges as true types. What is gained by looking at these examples is a better understanding of the limits of extensibility in non-OOP languages.

3   A *black box* for the *client* should be simple to use, easy to understand and familiar; cheap, efficient and powerful; and in a component relationship within the system. A *black box* for the *manufacturer* should be easy to reuse and modify, and hard to misuse and reproduce; cheap, efficient and powerful; and profitable to produce with a large client base.

4   The OOP design methodology becomes

   ■ Decide on an appropriate set of ADTs.
   ■ Design in their relatedness, and use inheritance to share code and interface.
   ■ Use virtual functions to process related objects dynamically.

5   Polymorphism directly contributes to the black box principle. The virtual functions specified for the base class are the interface used by the client throughout. The client knows that an overridden member function takes responsibility for a specific implementation of a given action relevant to the object.

6   C++ as a hybrid OOP language can cause the programmer a *dialectical tension headache*. The penchant of C programmers to focus on efficiency and implementation conflicts with the penchant for objectivists to focus on elegance, abstraction, and generality. The two demands on the coding process are reconcilable but require a

measure of coordination and respect that must be brought to the process.

7   OOP is many things to many people. We offer one more equation:

$$OOP = type\text{-}extensibility + polymorphism$$

In many languages and systems, the cost of this detail suppression is run-time inefficiency or undue rigidity in the interface. C++ has a range of choices that allow both efficiency and flexibility.

8   Given an empty slate—a *tabula rasa*—no simple methodology exists for OOP design, because each design must be strongly tied to the problem domain and reflect its abstractions. Discovering these abstractions is a design philosophy we call *Platonism*. In the Platonic paradigm there is an ideal object. For example, imagine an ideal chair in the heavens and attempt to describe its characteristics. These would be characteristics shared by all chairs.

9   Useful design principles include Occam's razor—"Entities should not be multiplied beyond necessity"—completeness, invertibility, orthogonality, consistency, simplicity, efficiency, and expressiveness. These principles can be in conflict and frequently involve tradeoffs in arriving at a design.

12.14 EXERCISES

1   Consider the following three ways to provide a `boolean` type:

```
//Traditional C using the preprocessor
#define TRUE  1
#define FALSE 0
#define Boolean int

//ANSI C and C++ using enumerated types
enum Boolean { false, true};

//C++ as a class
class Boolean {
   . . .
public:
  //various member functions
  //including overloading  !  &&  ||  ==  !=
};
```

Discuss the advantages and disadvantages of each style. Keep in mind scope, naming, and conversion problems.

2   C++ originally allowed the `this` pointer to be modifiable. One use was to have user-controlled storage management by assigning directly to the `this` pointer. The assignment of zero meant that the associated memory could be returned to free store. Discuss why this is a bad idea.

3   The rules for deciding which definition of an overloaded function to invoke have changed since the first version of the C++ language. One reason for this has been to reduce the number of ambiguities. Investigate how these rules have changed. One criticism is that the rules allow matching through conversions that possibly are unintended by the programmer. This can cause run-time bugs that are difficult to detect. One strategy is to have the compiler issue a diagnostic warning in such cases. Another is to use casting defensively to inform the compiler as to the intended choice. Discuss these alternatives.

4   List three things that you would drop from the C++ language. Argue why they would not be missed. For example, it is possible to have protected inheritance. It was never used in this text. Should it be in the language for completeness sake?

5   Describe at least two separate concepts for the keyword virtual as used in C++. Does this cause conceptual confusion?

6   The package *string.h* is a pseudo-type. It employs traditional C technology and programmer discipline to provide the ADT string. Why is it preferable to provide class string?

7   Using CRC notation, diagram class string as you would design it.

8   Using Wasserman-Pircher diagrams, rework exercise 7. The level of detail should give you a coding specification.

9   Write and test out your design for class string.

10   **Project:** A drawback for C++ is its lack of automated garbage collection. Program a smart pointer class that, if used in building an associated ADT, is automatically garbage collected. When storage associated with these smart pointers is exhausted, GC is invoked and an attempt is made to collect garbage. If available free store is adequate for creating further objects, the application is resumed. Do some performance testing to see how such a scheme compares to an ADT using reference counting that is coded specifically for the class.

APPENDIX A: ASCII CHARACTER CODES

Left/Right Digits	ASCII American Standard Code for Information Interchange									
	0	1	2	3	4	5	6	7	8	9
0	nul	soh	stx	etx	eot	enq	ack	bel	bs	ht
1	nl	vt	np	cr	so	si	dle	dc1	dc2	dc3
2	dc4	nak	syn	etb	can	em	sub	esc	fs	gs
3	rs	us	sp	!	"	#	$	%	&	'
4	(	)	*	+	,	-	.	/	0	1
5	2	3	4	5	6	7	8	9	:	;
6	<	=	>	?	»	A	B	C	D	E
7	F	G	H	I	J	K	L	M	N	O
8	P	Q	R	S	T	U	V	W	X	Y
9	Z	[	\	]	^	_	'	a	b	c
10	d	e	f	g	h	i	j	k	l	m
11	n	o	p	q	r	s	t	u	v	w
12	x	y	z	{	|	}	~	del		

Some Observations

1	Character codes 0–31 and 127 are nonprinting.
2	Character code 32 prints a single space.
3	Character codes for digits 0 through 9 are contiguous.
4	Character codes for letters A through Z are contiguous.
5	Character codes for letters a through z are contiguous.
6	The difference between a capital letter and the corresponding lowercase letter is 32.

The meaning of some of the abbreviations

nul	null	nl	newline
ht	horizontal tab	esc	escape
cr	carriage return	bs	backspace
bel	bell	vt	vertical tab

B

APPENDIX B: OPERATOR PRECEDENCE AND ASSOCIATIVITY

The following is the precedence and associativity table for all the C++ operators.

Operators	*Associativity*
:: (global scope) :: (class scope)	left to right
() [] -> . sizeof *postfix* ++ *postfix* --	left to right
++ -- ! ~ *(type)* + (unary) - (unary) * (indirection) & (address) new delete	right to left
* -> * * / %	left to right
+ -	left to right
<< >>	left to right

Operators	Associativity
< <= > >=	left to right
== !=	left to right
&	left to right
^	left to right
|	left to right
&&	left to right
||	left to right
?:	right to left
= += -= *= /= *etc*	right to left
, (comma operator)	left to right

In case of doubt, parenthesize.

C++ LANGUAGE GUIDE

This appendix is a concise guide to C++. It summarizes many of the key language elements of C++ that are not found in older procedural languages, such as Pascal and C. It is intended as a convenient guide to the language.

C.1   LEXICAL ELEMENTS

A C++ program is a sequence of characters that are collected into *tokens*, which comprise the basic vocabulary of the language. There are six categories of tokens: keywords, identifiers, constants, string constants, operators, and punctuators.

Among the characters that can be used to construct tokens are

```
a b c d e f g h i j k l m n o p q r s t u v w x y z
A B C D E F G H I J K L M N O P Q R S T U V W X Y Z
0 1 2 3 4 5 6 7 8 9
+ - * / = ( ) { } [ ] < > ' " ! @ # $ % ^ & _ : ; , . ? \ |
```
white space characters such as blank and tab

When producing tokens the compiler selects the longest string of characters that constitutes a token.

COMMENTS

C++ has a one-line comment symbol //.

```
//Compile with version 1.2 or later
const float pi = 3.14159;  //pi accurate to six places
```

C-style comments are also available.

```
/*   * * * * *
   C++
   Demonstrate Multiple-Inheritance
   OOP - Platonic Designs
 *   * * * * * */
```

Comments do not nest.

IDENTIFIERS

An identifier can be one or more characters. The first character must be a letter or underscore. Subsequent characters can be either letters, digits, or an underscore.

```
speed Speed speedy    //are all distinct
_ c _                 //reserved for library use
q213                  //opaque
multi_word            //normal style
MultiWord             //pascal style
```

Good programming style is to pick meaningful identifier names that help document a program. Avoid using underscore as a starting character, as many system programs and libraries use these.

KEYWORDS

Keywords are explicitly reserved identifiers that have a strict meaning in C++. They cannot be redefined or used in other contexts.

Keywords

asm	continue	float	new	signed	try
auto	default	for	operator	sizeof	typedef
break	delete	friend	private	static	union
case	do	goto	protected	struct	unsigned
catch	double	if	public	switch	virtual
char	else	inline	register	template	void
class	enum	int	return	this	volatile
const	extern	long	short	throw	while

Other keywords are specific to different implementations, such as near and far, which are in Borland C++, and typeof, which is in GNU C++.

C.2   CONSTANTS

C++ has constants for each basic type. These include integer, character, and floating constants. These constants also can be long and unsigned. String constants are character sequences surrounded by double quotes. There is one universal pointer constant, namely 0. Some examples follow:

```
156   0156  0x156        //int constants: decimal, octal, hexadecimal
156l  156ul              //int constants: long, unsigned long
3.14f 3.1415 3.14159L    //float constants of different precision
"A string."              //string constant
```

Suffixes such as u, l, and f are used to indicate unsigned, long, and float, respectively. They can be uppercase.

The character literals are usually given as '*symbol.*' Some nonprinting and special characters require an escape sequence.

```
L'oop'  //wchar_t or wide character literal
```

The floating point constants can be specified with or without signed integer exponents.

```
3.14f  1.234F    //float constant - smallest floating point type
0.1234567        //double constant
0.123456789L     //long double - either l or L
3.  3.0  0.3E1   //all express double 3.0
300e-2           //also 3.0
```

String literals are considered static char[] constants. A string literal is a contiguous array of characters with the null character at its end.

```
""               //empty string  is '\0'
"OOP 4ME"        // 'O' 'O' 'P' ' ' '4' 'M' 'E' '\0'
"my \"quote \"is escaped"     // \" used for"
"a multi-line string \
is also \
possible"
```

Enumerations define named int constants. The constants are a list of identifiers that are implicitly consecutive integer values starting with 0. They can be anonymous, as in

```
enum {false, true};   //false == 0 true == 1
```

They can be their own type, as in

```
enum color {red, blue, white, green, orange}; //color is a type
```

They can have specifically initialized values, as in

```
enum {BOTTOM = 50, TOP = 100, OVER}; //OVER == 101
enum grades {F = 60, D = 60, C = 70, B = 80, A = 90};
```

The keyword const is used to declare that an object's value is constant throughout its scope.

```
const int N = 100;
double w[N];       //N may be used in a constant expression

const  int bus_stops[5] = {23, 44, 57, 59, 83};
//The element values, bus_stops[i], are constant.
```

The use of `const` differs from the use of constant definitions by `#define`, as in

```
#define N   100
```

In the `const` case, N is a nonmodifiable *lvalue*. In the `define` case, N is a literal. Also, the macro replacement of N occurs regardless of scope.

C.3 DECLARATIONS AND SCOPE RULES

Declarations associate meaning with a given identifier. The syntax of C++ declarations is highly complex because they incorporate many disparate elements that are context-dependent. A declaration provides an identifier with a type, a storage class, and a scope. A simple declaration is often a definition as well. For a simple variable, this means the object is created and possibly initialized.

```
void foo()          //foo is declared and defined
{
    int  i = 5;     //i is declared and defined and initialized
                    //i is automatic and local to foo
    . . .
}
```

Complex declarations, such as class, function, and template declarations, are described in their own sections.

C++ has file scope, function scope, block scope, class scope, and function prototype scope. File scope extends from the point of declaration in a file to the end of that file. Function prototype scope is the scope of identifiers in the function prototype argument list and extends to the end of the declaration. Blocks nest in a conventional way, but functions cannot be declared inside other functions or blocks.

Declarations can occur almost anywhere in a block. A declaration can also be an initializing statement of a `for` statement.

```
for (int i = 0; i < N; ++i) {
    . . .
```

Declarations cannot occur as initializing statements within nested loops. Selection statements, such as the `if` or `switch` statement, cannot merely control a declaration. In general, jumps and selections cannot bypass an initialization. This is not true of ANSI C.

```
if (flag)
   int j = 6;        //illegal
else
   j = 19;

if (flag) {
  int j = 6;         //legal within block
  cout << j ;
}
```

C++ introduces the operator `::`, called the scope resolution operator. When used in the form `::` *variable,* it allows access to the externally named variable. Other uses of this notation are important for classes.

Class member identifiers are local to that class. The scope resolution operator `::` can be used to resolve ambiguities. When used in the form *class name* `::` *variable,* it allows access to the named variable from that class.

```
class A {
public:
   int  i;
   static void foo();
};

class B {
public:
   char i;
   void foo() {  A :: foo(); . . .}
};
```

A hidden external name can be accessed by using the scope resolution operator.

```
int  i;
void foo(int  i)
{
    i = ::i;
    . . .
}
```

A hidden `class`, `struct`, `union`, or `enum` identifier can be accessed by using its respective keyword.

```
static union u {
    . . .
};

void foo(int u)
{
    union u U;
    . . .
}
```

Classes can be nested. C++ rules make the inner class scoped within the outer class. This is a source of confusion, since the rules have changed and are different from ANSI C rules.

Enumerations declared inside a class, as in

```
class foo_bool {
public:
    enum boolean { false, true} flag;
};

main()
{
    foo_bool c;
    c.flag = foo_bool::false;
    . . .
}
```

make the enumerators have class scope.

C.4   LINKAGE RULES

Modern systems are built around multifile inclusion, compilation, and linkage. For C++, it is necessary to understand how multifile programs are combined. Linking separate modules requires resolving external references. The key rule is that external non-static variables must be defined in exactly one place. Use of the keyword extern together with an initializer constitutes defining a variable. Using the keyword extern without an initializer constitutes a declaration but not a definition. If the keyword extern is omitted, the resulting declaration is a definition, with or without an initializer. The following example illustrates these rules:

```
//file prog1.c
   char c;              //definition of c
   . . .

//file prog2.c
   extern char c;       //declaration of c
   . . .

//file prog3.c
   extern int n = 5;    //definition of n
   . . .

//file prog4.c
   char         c;      //illegal second definition
   extern float n;      //illegal type mismatch
   extern int   k;      //illegal no definition
   . . .
```

Static definitions at file scope are local to that file. Constant definitions and inline definitions are implicitly static. Constant definitions can be explicitly declared extern. It is usual to place such definitions in a header file to be included with any code that needs these definitions.

A typedef declaration is local to its file. It is a synonym for the type it defines.

```
typedef int  BOOLEAN;     //one way to produce BOOLEAN
typedef char *c_string;   //c_string is pointer to char
typedef void (*ptr_f)();  //pointer to function
                          //of no arguments returning void
```

An enumerator declaration is local to its file. Enumerators and typedefs that are needed in a multifile program should be placed in a header file. Enumerators defined within a class are local to that class. Access to them requires the scope resolution operator.

```
//types.h    header file
typedef char *c_string;    //c_string is pointer to char
typedef void (*ptr_f)();   //pointer to function

void foo(c_string s);      //function prototypes
void title();
void pr_onoff();

enum { OFF, ON };
extern int x;



//fcns.c to be separately compiled
#include <iostream.h>
#include "types.h"

void foo(c_string s)
{
    cout <<"\noutput: " << s;
}

void title()
{
    cout << "\nTEST TYPEDEFS";
}

void pr_onoff()
{
    if (x == OFF)
        cout << "\nOFF";
    else
        cout << "\nON";
}
```

```
//linkage_ex.c    main program file   CC fcns.o linkage_ex.c
#include <iostream.h>
#include "types.h"
int x = 0;
main()
{
    c_string f = "foo on you";
    ptr_f     pf = &pr_onoff;

    foo("ENTER 0 or 1: ");
    cin >> x;
    if ( x == ON)
        pf = &title;
    pr_onoff();
    pf();
    x = !x;
    pf();
    foo(f);
}
```

C.5 TYPES

The fundamental types in C++ are integral types and floating point types.
The char type is the shortest integral type. The long double type is the
longest floating point type.

The following table lists these types, shortest to longest.

Simple data types

char	signed char	unsigned char
short	int	long
unsigned short	unsigned	unsigned long
float	double	long double

Types can be derived from the basic types. A simple derived type is
the enumeration type. The derived types allow pointer types, array types,
and structure types. A generic pointer type void* is allowed. Both anonymous unions and anonymous enumerations are allowed, and there is also a
reference type. An anonymous union can have only public data members. A

file scope anonymous union has to be declared `static`. The `class` type is another extension, and the `struct` is extended to be a variant of the `class`. Union, enumeration, and class names are type names.

```
void*   gen_ptr;                  //a generic pointer
int     i, &ref_i = i;            //ref_i is an alias for i
enum    boolean { false, true };  //enumeration
boolean flag;                     //boolean is now a type name
boolean set[10];                  //array type

class   card {                    //user-defined type
private:
   int  cd;                       //private data member
public:
   suit s;                        //public data member
   pips p;
   void pr_card();                //member function
};
suit card::* ptr_s = &card::s;    //pointer to member
```

There are five storage class keywords.

```
auto            //local to blocks and implicit
register        //optimization advice and automatic
extern          //global scope
static          //within blocks - value retained
typedef         //creates synonyms for types
```

The keyword `auto` can be used within blocks, but is redundant and is normally omitted. Automatic variables are created at block entry and destroyed at block exit. The keyword `register` can be used within blocks and for function parameters. It advises the compiler that for optimization purposes the program wants a variable to reside in a high-speed register. Register variables have behavior that is semantically equivalent to automatic variables.

The keyword `extern` can be used within blocks and at file scope. It indicates a variable is linked in from elsewhere. The keyword `static` can be used within blocks and at file scope. Inside a block it indicates that a variable's value is retained after block exit. At file scope it indicates that declarations have internal linkage.

The type qualifier keywords are

```
const          //non-modifiable
volatile       //suppresses compiler optimization
```

We discuss `const` in a number of contexts. It is used to indicate a variable or function parameter has a nonmodifiable value. The `volatile` keyword implies that an agent external to the program can change the variable's value.

```
volatile const gmt;  //expect external time signal
```

C.6 CONVERSION RULES

C++ has numerous conversion rules. Many of these conversions are implicit, which makes C++ convenient but potentially dangerous for the novice. Implicit conversions can induce run-time bugs that are hard to detect.

The general rules are straightforward.

Automatic conversion in an arithmetic expression   x op y

First:

Any `char`, `short`, or `enum` is promoted to `int`
Integral types unrepresentable as `int` are promoted to `unsigned`

Second:

If, after the first step, the expression is of mixed type,
then, according to the hierarchy of types,

`int` < `unsigned` < `long` < `unsigned long`
    < `float` < `double` < `long double`

the operand of lower type is promoted to that of the higher type,
and the value of the expression has that type.
Note: `unsigned` is promoted to `unsigned long`,
if `long` cannot contain all values of `unsigned`.

Implicit pointer conversions also occur in C++. Any pointer type can be converted to a generic pointer of type `void*`. However, unlike ANSI C, a generic pointer is not assignment-compatible with an arbitrary pointer type. This means that C++ requires that generic pointers be cast to an explicit type for assignment to a nongeneric pointer variable.

```
char* mem;
void* gen_p;
gen_p = mem;            //C and C++
mem   = (char*)gen_p; //C and C++
mem   = gen_p;          //legal C and illegal C++
```

The name of an array is a pointer to its base element. The null pointer value can be converted to any type. A pointer to a class can be converted to a pointer to a publicly derived base class. This also applies to references.

Explicit conversions are forced by *casts*. Traditional C casts are augmented in C++ by a functional notation as a syntactic alternative. The cast notation has the form

   (*type*) *expression*

A functional notation of the form

   type-name (*expression*)

is equivalent to a cast. The *type-name* in functional notation must be expressible as an identifier. Thus the two expressions

```
x = float(i);    //C++ functional notation
x = (float) i;  //C  cast notation
```

are equivalent. Functional notation is the preferred style.

A constructor of one argument is de facto a type conversion from the argument's type to the constructor's class type. Consider an example of a `string` constructor.

```
string::string(const char* p)
{
    len = strlen(p);
    s = new char[len + 1];
    strcpy(s, p);
}
```

This is automatically a type transfer from `char*` to `string`. These conversions are from an already defined type to a user-defined type. However, it is not possible for the user to add a constructor to a built-in type—for example, to `int` or `double`. In the `string` example a conversion from `string` to `char*` also can be done by defining a special conversion function inside the `string` class as follows:

```
operator char*() { return s; }   //recall char *s; is a member
```

The general form of such a member function is

```
operator type() { . . . }
```

These conversions occur implicitly in assignment expressions and in argument and return conversions from functions.

Temporaries can be created by the compiler to facilitate these operations. This can require constructor invocation. This is system- and compiler-dependent. It may dramatically and unexpectedly affect execution speeds.

C.7   EXPRESSIONS AND OPERATORS

C++ is an operator rich language that is expression oriented. The operators have 17 precedence levels. Operators also can have side effects. Appendix B lists their precedence and associativity.

There is a great variety of expressions. For example, assignment is an expression. The following is legal C++:

```
a = b + (c = d + 3);
```

The equivalent multistatement code is

```
c = d + 3;
a = b + c;
```

sizeof EXPRESSIONS

The `sizeof` operator can be applied to an expression or a parenthesized type name. It gives the size in bytes of the type that it is applied to.

```
int   a, b[10];

sizeof(a)            //4 on gnu C++ running on a DECSTATION
sizeof(b)            //40 the array storage
sizeof(b[1])         //4
sizeof(5)            //4
sizeof(5.5L)         //8
```

AUTOINCREMENT AND AUTODECREMENT EXPRESSIONS

C++ provides autoincrement (++) and autodecrement (--) operators in both prefix and postfix form. In prefix form the autoincrement operator adds 1 to the value stored at the lvalue it acts upon. Similarly the autodecrement operator subtracts 1 from the value stored at the lvalue it acts upon.

> ++i; *is equivalent to* i = i + 1;
> --x; *is equivalent to* x = x - 1;

The postfix form behaves differently than the prefix form by changing the affected lvalue after the rest of the expression is evaluated.

> j = ++i; *is equivalent to* i = i + 1; j = i;
> j = i ++; *is equivalent to* j = i; i = i + 1;
> i = ++i + i++; // hazardous practice: system dependent

Note that these are not exact equivalencies. The compound assignment operators evaluate their left-side expression once. Therefore, for complicated expressions with side effects, results of the two forms can be different.

ARITHMETIC EXPRESSIONS

Arithmetic expressions are consistent with expected practice. The following examples are grouped by precedence with highest first:

```
-i        +w                  //unary minus   unary plus
a * b     a / b    i % 5      //multiplication division modulus
a + b     a - b               //binary addition and subtraction
```

Note how the result of the division operator / depends on its argument types.

```
a = 3 / 2;    // a is assigned 1
a = 3 / 2.0;  // a is assigned 1.5
```

The modulus operator % is the remainder from the division of the first argument by the second argument.

RELATIONAL, EQUALITY, AND LOGICAL EXPRESSIONS

In C++ the values zero and nonzero are thought of as *false* and *true* and are used to effect flow of control in various statement types. The following table contains the C++ operators that are most often used to effect flow of control.

Relational, equality, and logical operators		*C++*
Relational operators:	less than:	<
	greater than:	>
	less than or equal:	<=
	greater than or equal:	>=
Equality operators:	equal:	==
	not equal:	!=
Logical operators:	(unary) negation:	!
	logical and:	&&
	logical or:	||

The negation operator ! is unary. All the other relational, equality, and logical operators are binary. They operate on expressions and yield either the int value 0 or the int value 1. The value for *false* can be either 0 or 0.0 (or the null pointer), and the value for *true* can be any nonzero value.

The logical operators !, &&, and ||, when applied to expressions, yield either the int value 0 or the int value 1. Logical negation can be applied to an arbitrary expression. If an expression has value 0 or 0.0, then its negation yields the int value 1. If the expression has a nonzero value, then its negation yields the int value 0.

In the evaluation of expressions that are the operands of && and ||, the evaluation process stops as soon as the outcome true or false is known.

This is called *short-circuit* evaluation. Suppose that *expr1* and *expr2* are expressions. If *expr1* has a zero value, then in

> *expr1* **&&** *expr2*

expr2 is not evaluated because the value of the logical expression is already determined to be 0. Similarly, if *expr1* has a nonzero value, then in

> *expr1* **||** *expr2*

expr2 is not evaluated because the value of the logical expression is already determined to be 1.

Some examples in C++ are STOPPED

```
a + 5 && b       parenthesized equivalent is   ((a + 5) && b
! (a < b) && c  parenthesized equivalent is   ((! (a < b)) && c)
1 || ( a !=  7) parenthesized equivalent is ( 1 || (a != 7))
```

Note that the last expression always short-circuits to value 1.

ASSIGNMENT EXPRESSIONS

In C++, assignment occurs as part of an assignment expression.

```
a = b + 1;  //assign (b + 1) to a
```

The effect is to evaluate the right-hand side of the assignment and convert it to a value compatible with the left-hand-side variable. Assignment conversions occur implicitly and include narrowing conversions.

```
int     i, *p = &i;
double w, *q = &w;

  i = w;              //legal w value converted to int
  *q = i;             //legal integer value promoted to double
  *q = *p;            //legal
  q = p;              //illegal conversion between pointer types
  q = (double *)p; //legal
```

Simple variables are lvalues.

C++ allows multiple assignment in a single statement.

```
a = b + (c = 3);
 is equivalent to c = 3; a = b + c;
```

C++ provides assignment operators that combine an assignment and some other operator.

```
a += b;      is equivalent to  a = a + b;
a *= a + b; is equivalent to  a = a * (a + b);
a op = b; is equivalent to  a = a op  b;
```

COMMA EXPRESSIONS

The comma operator has the lowest precedence. It is a binary operator with expressions as operands. In a comma expression of the form

expr1, expr2

expr1 is evaluated first, and then *expr2*. The comma expression as a whole has the value and type of its right operand. The comma operator is a control point. Therefore, each expression in the comma-separated list is evaluated completely before the next expression to its right. An example would be

```
sum = 0, i = 1
```

If i has been declared an int, then this comma expression has value 1 and type int. The comma operator associates from left to right.

CONDITIONAL EXPRESSIONS

The conditional operator ?: is unusual in that it is a ternary operator. It takes as operands three expressions. In a construct such as

expr1 ? expr2: expr3

expr1 is evaluated first. If it is nonzero (true), then *expr2* is evaluated and that is the value of the conditional expression as a whole. If *expr1* is zero (false), then *expr3* is evaluated and that is the value of the conditional expression as a whole. The following example uses a conditional operator to assign the smaller of two values to the variable x:

```
x = (y < z) ? y : z;
```

The parentheses are not necessary because the conditional operator has precedence greater than the assignment operator. However, parentheses are good style because they clarify what is being tested.

The type of the conditional expression

$$expr1 \ ? \ expr2 \ : \ expr3$$

is determined by *expr2* and *expr3*. If they are different types, then the usual conversion rules apply. The conditional expression's type cannot depend on which of the two expressions, *expr2* or *expr3*, is evaluated. The conditional operator ?: associates right to left.

BIT MANIPULATION EXPRESSIONS

C++ provides bit manipulation operators. They operate on the machine-dependent bit representation of integral operands.

Bitwise Operators	Meaning
~	unary one's complement
<<	left shift
>>	right shift
&	and
^	exclusive or
|	or

It is customary that the shift operators are overloaded to perform I/O.

ADDRESS AND INDIRECTION EXPRESSIONS

The address operator & is a unary operator that yields the address or location where an object is stored. The indirection operator * is a unary operator that is applied to an object of type pointer. It retrieves the value from the location being pointed at. This is also known as dereferencing.

```
int a = 5, *p = &a; //declarations

&a;         //address or location of a
*p;         //reference to object pointed at by p
*p = 7;     //lvalue in effect a is assigned 7
a = *p +1; //rvalue 7 is added to 1 and a is assigned 8
```

new AND *delete* EXPRESSIONS

The unary operators new and delete are available to manipulate *free store*. Free store is a system-provided memory pool for objects whose lifetime is directly managed by the programmer. The programmer creates the object by using new and destroys the object by using delete.

The operator new is used in the following forms:

> new *type-name*
> new *type-name initializer*
> new *(type-name)*

Each case has at least two effects. First, an appropriate amount of store is allocated from free store to contain the named type. Second, the base address of the object is returned as the value of the new expression. If new fails, the null pointer value 0 is returned. An initializer is a parenthesized list of arguments. For a simple type, such as an int, it would be a single expression. It cannot be used to initialize arrays, but it can be an argument list to an appropriate constructor.

The operator delete is used in the following forms:

> delete *expression*
> delete [] *expression*

In both forms the expression is typically a pointer variable used in a previous new expression. The second form is used when returning store that was allocated as an array type. The brackets indicate that a destructor should be called for each element of the array. The operator delete returns a value of type void.

The operator delete destroys an object created by new, in effect returning its allocated storage to free store for reuse. The following example uses these constructs to dynamically allocate an array:

```
//Use of new operator to dynamically allocate an array.

#include <iostream.h>

main()
{
   int* data;
   int  size;

   cout << "\nEnter array size: ";
   cin >> size;

   data = new int[size];      //return int* expression
   for (int j = 0; j < size; ++j)
      cout << (data[j] = j) << "\t";
   cout << "\n\n";
   delete [] data;
   . . .
}
```

The pointer variable `data` is used as the base address of a dynamically allocated array whose number of elements is the value of `size`. The `new` operator is used to allocate from free store sufficient storage for an object of type `int[size]`. The operator `delete` returns to free store the storage associated with the pointer variable `data`. This can be done only with objects allocated by `new`. There are no guarantees on what values will appear in objects allocated from free store. The programmer is responsible for properly initializing such objects.

PLACEMENT SYNTAX AND OVERLOADING

Operator `new` has the general form

$$::_{opt} \text{ new } placement_{opt} \text{ } type \text{ } initializer_{opt}$$

The global `operator new()` typically is used to allocate free store. The system implicitly provides a `sizeof( type)` argument to this function. Its function prototype is

```
void* operator new(size_t size);
```

The operators new and delete can be overloaded. This feature provides a simple mechanism for user-defined manipulation of free store. For example:

```
#include <stddef.h>     //size_t type defined
#include <stdlib.h>     //malloc() and free() defined
class X {
    . . .
public:
    void* operator new(size_t size) { return (malloc(size)); }
    void  operator delete(void* ptr) { free(ptr); }
    X(unsigned size) { new(size); }
    ~X() { delete(this); }
    . . .
};
```

In this example, the class X has provided overloaded forms of new() and delete(). When a class overloads operator new(), the global operator is still accessible using the scope-resolution operator ::.

The placement syntax provides for a comma-separated argument list is used to select an overloaded operator new() with a matching signature. These additional arguments are often used to *place* the constructed object at a particular address. One form of this can be found in *new.h*:

```
//overloaded new as found in <new.h>
 void* operator new(size_t size, void* ptr) { return (ptr); }

char*  buf1 = new char[1000];   //globally allocated memory
char*  buf2 = new char[1000];   //more global memory

class object {
    . . .
};

main()
{
    object *p = new(buf1) object; //place at beginning of buf1[]
    object *q = new(buf2) object; //place at beginning of buf2[]
    object *r = new(buf2 + sizeof(object)) object;
    . . .
}
```

These class new() and delete() member functions are always static.

OTHER EXPRESSIONS

Function call and array subscripting are expressions. They have the same precedence as pointer and `sizeof` expressions.

```
a[j + 6]            // means  *(a + j + 6)
sqrt(z + 15.5);  // returns a double
```

The global scope resolution operator is of highest precedence. The class scope resolution operator is used with a class name to qualify a local-to-class identifier.

```
::i              // access global i
A::foo()         // invoke member foo() defined in A
```

The pointer to member operators are

```
.*   and   ->*
```

Their precedence is below the unary operators and above the multiplicative operator. Their use is described in Section C.9.

C.8   STATEMENTS

C++ has a large variety of statement types. It uses the semicolon as a statement terminator. Braces are used to enclose multiple statements so they are treated as a single unit. Statements are control points. Before a new statement is executed, the previous statement's actions must be completed. Inside statements the compiler has some liberty in picking which parts of subexpressions are first evaluated. For example:

```
a = f(i) + f(j);  //compiler can evaluate as it wishes
a = f(i);
a += f(j);         //order is determined
```

EXPRESSION STATEMENTS

In C++, assignment occurs as part of an assignment expression. There is no assignment statement, but instead it is a form of expression statement.

```
a = b + 1;   //assign (b + 1) to a
++i;         //an expression statement
a + b;       //also a statement - but seemingly useless
```

C++ allows multiple assignment in a single statement.

> `a = b + (c = 3);` *is equivalent to* `c = 3; a = b + c;`

THE COMPOUND STATEMENT

A compound statement in C++ is a series of statements surrounded by the braces { and }. The chief use of the compound statement is to group statements into an executable unit. The body of a C++ function is always a compound statement. In C, when declarations come at the beginning of a compound statement, the statement is called a block. This rule is relaxed in C++ and declaration statements may occur throughout the statement list. Wherever it is possible to place a statement, it is also possible to place a compound statement.

THE *if* AND THE *if-else* STATEMENTS

The general form of an `if` statement is

> *if* (*expression*)
>   *statement*

If *expression* is nonzero (true), then *statement* is executed; otherwise *statement* is skipped. After the `if` statement has been executed, control passes to the next statement. In the example

```
if (temperature >= 32)
   cout << "Above Freezing!\n";
cout << "Fahrenheit is " << temperature << endl;
```

"Above Freezing!" is printed only when `temperature` is greater than or equal to 32. The second statement is always executed.

The `if-else` statement has the general form

```
if (expression)
    statement1
else
    statement2
```

If *expression* is nonzero, then *statement1* is executed and *statement2* is skipped; if *expression* is zero, then *statement1* is skipped and *statement2* is executed. After the `if-else` statement has been executed, control passes to the next statement.

```
if (temperature >= 32)
    cout << "Above Freezing!\n";
else if (temperature >= 212)
    cout << "Above Boiling!\n";
else
    cout << "Boy its cold " << temperature << endl;
```

Note that an `else` statement associates with its nearest `if`. This rule prevents the *dangling else* ambiguity.

THE *while* STATEMENT

The general form of a `while` statement is

```
while (expression)
    statement
```

First *expression* is evaluated. If it is nonzero (true), then *statement* is executed and control passes back to the beginning of the `while` loop. The effect of this is that the body of the `while` loop, namely *statement*, is executed repeatedly until *expression* is zero (false). At that point control passes to the next statement. The effect of this is that *statement* can be executed zero or more times.

An example of a `while` statement is the following:

```cpp
int  i = 1, sum = 0;

while (i <= 10) {
   sum += i;
   ++i;
}
```

When this `while` loop is exited, the value of `sum` is 55.

THE *for* STATEMENT

The general form of a `for` statement is

> `for` (*expression1*; *expression2*; *expression3*)
>   *statement*
> *next statement*

First *expression1* is evaluated. Typically *expression1* is used to initialize a variable used in the loop. Then *expression2* is evaluated. If it is nonzero (true), then *statement* is executed, *expression3* is evaluated, and control passes back to the beginning of the `for` loop again, except that evaluation of *expression1* is skipped. This iteration continues until *expression2* is zero (false), at which point control passes to *next statement*.

```cpp
for (int i = 1, sum = 0 ; i <= 10; ++i )
   sum += i;
```

When this `for` loop is exited, the value of `sum` is 55.

Any or all of the expressions in a `for` statement can be missing, but the two semicolons must remain. If *expression1* is missing, then no initialization step is performed as part of the `for` loop. If *expression3* is missing, then no incrementation step is performed as part of the `for` loop. If *expression2* is missing, then no testing step is performed as part of the `for` loop. The special rule for when *expression2* is missing is that the test is always true. Thus the `for` loop in the code

```
for (i = 1, sum = 0 ; ; sum += i++ )
   cout << sum << endl;
```

is an infinite loop.

THE *do* STATEMENT

The general form of a do statement is

```
do
   statement
while (expression);
next statement
```

First *statement* is executed and then *expression* is evaluated. If it is nonzero (true), then control passes back to the beginning of the do statement and the process repeats itself. If the value of *expression* is zero (false), then control passes to *next statement*. An example is the following:

```
do {
   sum += i;
   cin >> i;
} while (i > 0);
```

TRANSFER STATEMENTS

C++ has several statements that transfer flow of control. C++ has the invidious goto statement. Of course, we recommend against its use unless it is unavoidable. The break and continue statements are used to interrupt ordinary iterative flow of control in loops. In addition, the break statement can be used within a switch statement. A switch statement can select among several different cases. The return statement is a transfer statement that exits a function call.

THE *break* AND *continue* STATEMENTS

To interrupt normal flow of control within a loop, the programmer can use the two special statements `break;` and `continue;`

In addition to its being used in loops, the `break` statement can be used in a `switch` statement. It causes an exit from the innermost enclosing loop or `switch` statement.

The following example illustrates the use of a `break` statement. A test for a negative value is made, and if the test is true, the `break` statement causes the `for` loop to be exited. Program control jumps to the statement immediately following the loop.

```
for (i = 0; i < 10; ++i) {
   cin >> x;
   if (x < 0.0) {
      cout << "All done\n";
      break;      // exit loop if value is negative
   }
   cout << sqrt(x) << endl;
}
// break jumps to here
   . . .
```

The `continue` statement causes the current iteration of a loop to stop and causes the next iteration of the loop to begin immediately. The following code processes all characters except digits.

```
for (i = 0; i < MAX; ++i) {
   cin.get(c);
   if (isdigit(c))
      continue;
   . . .   // process other characters
// continue jumps to here
}
```

In this example, all characters except digits are processed. When the `continue` statement is executed, control jumps to just before the closing brace, causing the loop to begin execution at the top again. Notice that the `continue` statement ends the current iteration, whereas a `break` statement would end the loop.

A `break` statement can occur only inside the body of a `for`, `while`, `do`, or `switch` statement. The `continue` statement can occur only inside the body of a `for`, `while`, or `do` statement.

THE *switch* STATEMENT

The `switch` statement is a multiway conditional statement generalizing the `if-else` statement. Its general form is given by

> `switch` (*expression*)
>   *statement*

where *statement* typically is a compound statement containing `case` labels and optionally a `default` label. Typically a `switch` is composed of many cases, and the expression in parentheses following the keyword `switch` determines which, if any, of the cases get executed.

The following switch statement counts the number of test scores by category:

```
switch (score) {
case 9: case 10:
   ++a_grades; break;
case 8:
   ++b_grades; break;
case 7:
   ++c_grades; break;
default:
   ++fails;
}
```

A `case` label is of the form

> `case`
>   *constant integral expression*:

In a `switch` statement, the `case` labels must all be unique.

If no `case` label is selected, then control passes to the `default` label, if there is one. A `default` label is not required. If no `case` label is selected, and there is no `default` label, then the `switch` statement is exited. To detect errors, programmers frequently include a `default`, even when all the expected cases have been accounted for.

The keywords `case` and `default` cannot occur outside of a `switch`.

The effects of a `switch`

1   Evaluates the integral expression in the parentheses following `switch`.
2   Executes the `case` label having a constant value that matches the value of the expression found in step 1, or, if a match is not found, executes the `default` label, or, if there is no `default` label, terminates the `switch`.
3   Terminates the `switch` when a `break` statement is encountered, or terminates the `switch` by "falling off the end."

THE *goto* STATEMENT

The `goto` statement is an unconditional branch to an arbitrary, labeled statement in the function. The `goto` statement is considered a harmful construct in most accounts of modern programming methodology.

A label is an identifier. By executing a `goto` statement of the form

```
goto
   label;
```

control is unconditionally transferred to a labeled statement. An example would be

```
if (d == 0.0)
   goto error;
else
   ratio = n / d;
 . . .
error:  cerr << "ERROR:  division by zero\n";
```

Both the `goto` statement and its corresponding labeled statement must be in the body of the same function.

THE DECLARATION STATEMENT

The declaration statement can be placed nearly anywhere in a block. This lifts the C restriction that variable declarations are placed at the head of a block before executable statements. A declaration statement has the form

declaration

Normal block structure rules apply to a variable so declared. Some examples are

```
for (int i = 0; i < N; ++i) { //typical case within for
    a[i] = b[i] * c[i];
    int k = a[i];                    //k is local -possibly inefficient
    . . .
}
```

C++ imposes natural restrictions on transferring into blocks passed where declarations occur. These are disallowed, as are declarations that would only occur in one branch of a conditional statement.

C.9 CLASSES

C++ and C have structures; they are forms of heterogeneous aggregate types. C++ redefines structures to allow data hiding, inheritance, and member functions as major new extensions. In C++ the keywords `class` and `struct` are used to declare user-defined types. An example is

```
class vect {
private:
    int* p;                          //base pointer
    int size;                        //number of elements
public:
    //constructors and destructor
    vect() { size = 10; p = new int[10]} //create a size 10 array
    vect(int n);                     //create a size n array
    vect(vect& v);                   //initialization by vect
    vect(int a[], int n);            //initialization by array
    ~vect() { delete [] p; }         //destructor
    //other member functions
    int  ub() { return (size - 1); } //upper bound
    int& operator[](int i);          //range checked element
};
```

The keywords `public`, `private`, and `protected` indicate the visibility of members that follow. The default for `class` is `private`, and the default for `struct` is `public`. In the above example, the data members p and size are `private`. This makes them visible solely to member functions of the same class.

CONSTRUCTORS AND DESTRUCTORS

A constructor is a member function whose name is the same as the class name. It *constructs* objects of the class type. This involves initialization of data members and frequently free store allocation using `new`. For classes with constructors, if they have a constructor with a void argument list, or one where all its arguments have defaults, then they can be a base type of an array declaration, where initialization is not explicit. Such a constructor is called the *default constructor.*

```
foo::foo() { . . .}   //default constructor

hoo::hoo(int i = 0) { . . .} //default constructor
```

A destructor is a member function whose name is the class name preceded by the character ~ (tilde). Its usual purpose is to destroy values of the class type. This is typically accomplished by using `delete`.
    A constructor of the form

  type ::*type* (const *type* & x)

is used to perform copying of one *type* value into another when

    1 A *type* variable is initialized by a *type* value.
    2 A *type* value is passed as an argument in a function.
    3 A *type* value is returned from a function.

    This is called the *copy constructor,* and if not given explicitly it is compiler-generated. The default is member-by-member initialization of value.
    Classes with default constructors can have a derived array type. For example,

```
vect a[5];
```

is a declaration that uses the empty argument constructor to create an array a of five objects, each of which is a size 10 `vect`.

A class having members whose type requires a constructor may have these specified after the argument list for its own constructor. The constructor has a comma-separated list of constructor calls following a colon. The constructor is invoked by using the member name followed by a parenthesized argument list. Constructors cannot be virtual, but destructors can be virtual. Constructors and destructors are not inherited.

MEMBER FUNCTIONS

Member functions are functions declared within a class, and, as a consequence, have access to `private`, `protected`, and `public` members of that class. If defined inside the class, they are treated as `inline` functions and are also treated when necessary as overloaded functions. In the class `vect`, the member function

```
int  ub() { return (size - 1); }          //upper bound
```

is defined. In this example, the member function `ub` is `inline` and has access to the `private` member `size`.

Member functions are invoked normally by use of the "`.`" or `->` operators, as in

```
vect   a(20), b;           //invoke appropriate constructor
vect* ptr_v = &b;
int    uba = a.ub(), ubb;  //invoke member ub
ubb = ptr_v -> ub();       //invoke member ub
```

THE *this* POINTER

The keyword `this` denotes an implicitly declared self-referential pointer. It can be used only in a non-static member function. A simple illustration of its use is as follows:

```
// Use of the this pointer

class c_pair {
private:
    char      c1, c2;
public:
    c_pair(char b) { c1 = 1 + (c2 = b); }
    c_pair increment() { c1++; c2++; return (*this); }
    unsigned where_am_I() { return ((unsigned)this); }
    void print() { cout << c1 << c2 << "\t"; }
};
```

The member function `increment()` uses the implicitly provided pointer `this` to return the newly incremented value of both `c1` and `c2`. The member function `where_am_I()` returns the address of the given object. The `this` keyword provides for a built-in self-referential pointer. It is as if `c_pair` implicitly declared the private member `c_pair* const this`.

Early C++ systems allowed memory management for objects to be controlled by assignment to the `this` pointer. Such code is obsolete because the `this` pointer is nonmodifiable.

static AND *const* MEMBER FUNCTIONS

An ordinary member function invoked as

```
object.mem(i, j, k);
```

has an explicit argument list `i, j, k`, and an implicit argument list that consists of the members of `objecti`. The implicit arguments can be thought of as a list of arguments accessible through the `this` pointer. In contrast, a `static` member function cannot access any of the members using the `this` pointer. A `const` member function cannot modify its implicit arguments. The following example illustrates these differences:

```
//Salary calculation using
//static and constant member functions.

#include <iostream.h>

class salary {
private:
    int        b_sal;
    int        your_bonus;
    static int all_bonus;  //declaration
public:
    salary(int b) : b_sal(b) { }
    void calc_bonus(double perc) { your_bonus = b_sal * perc; }
    static void reset_all(int p) { all_bonus = p; }
    int comp_tot() const
         { return (b_sal + your_bonus + all_bonus); }
};

int salary::all_bonus = 100; //declaration and definition

main()
{
    salary w1(1000), w2(2000);

    w1.calc_bonus(0.2);
    w2.calc_bonus(0.15);
    salary::reset_all(400);    //equivalently w1.reset_all(400);
    cout << " w1 " << w1.comp_tot() << "   w2 " << w2.comp_tot()
           << "\n";
}
```

The `static` member `all_bonus` requires a file scope declaration. It exists independently of any specific variables of type `salary` being declared. The `static` member can also be referred to as

```
salary::all_bonus
```

The `const` modifier comes between the end of the argument list and the front of the code body. It indicates that no data members will have their values changed. As such it makes the code more robust. In effect it means that the self-referential pointer is passed as `const salary* const this`.

A `static` member function can be invoked using the scope resolution operator, or it can be invoked using a specific object. Therefore,

```
salary::reset_all(400);
w1.reset_all(400);
(&w2) -> reset_all(400);
```

are equivalent.

INHERITANCE

Inheritance is the mechanism of *deriving* a new class from an old one. The existing class can be added to or altered to create the derived class. A class can be derived from an existing class using the form

```
class class-name : (public|protected|private)opt base-class-name
{
    member  declarations
};
```

As usual, the keyword `class` can be replaced by the keyword `struct`, with the usual implication that members are default `public`. The keywords `public`, `private`, and `protected` are available as visibility modifiers for class members. A `public` member is visible throughout its scope. A `private` member is visible to other member functions within its own class. A `protected` member is visible to other member functions within its class and any class immediately derived from it. These visibility modifiers can be used within a class declaration in any order and with any frequency.

A base class having a constructor with arguments requires that a class derived from it have a constructor. The form of such a constructor is

```
class-name (argument list) : base-class-name (base-class argument list)
{
    . . .
};
```

The *base class argument list* is used when invoking the appropriate base class constructor and is executed before the body of the derived class constructor is executed.

A publicly derived class is a *subtype* of its base class. A variable of the derived class can in many ways be treated as if it were the base class type. A pointer whose type is pointer to base class can point to objects having the publicly derived class type. A reference to the derived class, when meaningful, may be implicitly converted to a reference to the public base class. It is possible to declare a reference to a base class and initialize it to an object of the publicly derived class.

The following is an example of a derived class:

```
class vect_bnd : public vect {
private:
    int l_bnd, u_bnd;
public:
    vect_bnd();
    vect_bnd(int, int);
    int& operator[](int);
    int  ub() { return (u_bnd); }
    int  lb() { return (l_bnd); }
};

vect_bnd::vect_bnd() : vect(10)
{
    l_bnd = 0;
    u_bnd = 9;
}

vect_bnd::vect_bnd(int lb, int ub) : vect(ub - lb + 1)
{
    l_bnd = lb;
    u_bnd = ub;
}
```

In this example the constructors for the derived class invoke a constructor in the base class with the argument list following the colon.

MULTIPLE INHERITANCE

Multiple inheritance allows a derived class to be derived from more than one base class. The syntax of class headers is extended to allow a list of base classes and their privacy designation. An example is

```
class tools {
  . . .

};

class parts {
  . . .

};

class labor {
  . . .

};

class plans : public tools, public parts, public labor {
  . . .

};
```

In this example the derived class plans publicly inherits the members of all three base classes. This parental relationship is described by the inheritance *directed acyclic graph* (DAG). The DAG is a graph structure whose nodes are classes and whose directed edges point from base to derived class.

In deriving an identically named member from different classes, ambiguities may arise. These derivations are allowed, provided the user does not make an ambiguous reference to such a member.

With multiple inheritance two base classes can be derived from a common ancestor. If both base classes are used in the ordinary way by their derived class, that class will have two subobjects of the common ancestor. This duplication, if not desirable, can be eliminated by using virtual inheritance.

CONSTRUCTOR INVOCATION

The early releases of C++ left unspecified the order of execution for initializing constructors in base and member constructors. Most of the time these constructions were independent of each other, and the results were independent of order. With the addition of multiple inheritance, however, it became unnecessarily hazardous to continue this laxness. Thus the current ordering is

1 Explicit reference to base class constructors in the order in which they are listed after the header colon.
2 Unmentioned base classes in the order in which they are declared.
3 Explicit reference to member class constructors in the order in which they are listed after the header colon.

Virtual base classes have special precedence and are constructed before any of their derived classes. They are constructed before any nonvirtual base classes. Their construction order depends on their DAG. It is a depth-first, left-to-right order. Destructors are invoked in reverse order of constructors.

Let us illustrate by elaborating on a previous example.

```
class tools {
    . . .
public:
    tools(char*);
    ~tools();
    . . .
};

class parts {
    . . .
public:
    parts(char*);
    ~parts();
    . . .
};

class labor {
    . . .
public:
    labor(int);
    ~labor();
    . . .
};

class plans : public tools, public parts, public labor {
    . . .
    special a;   //member class with constructor
public:
    plans(int m) : labor(m), tools("lathe"), a(m), parts("widget")
        { . . . }
    ~plans();
    . . .
};
```

In this case the member constructor a(m) appears before the base class constructor parts("widget") but by our rules is invoked last. Since its constructor was last, its destructor is invoked first, followed by ~parts, ~tools, ~labor, and ~plans.

ABSTRACT BASE CLASSES

A pure virtual function is a virtual member function whose body is undefined. Notationally it is declared inside the class as follows:

virtual *function prototype* = 0;

A derived class must define or declare each pure virtual function in its immediate base class. A class that has at least one *pure virtual* function is an *abstract class*.

POINTER TO CLASS MEMBER

C uses pointers to structures and a simple accessing scheme to pick off a member value. In C++, a pointer to class member is distinct from a pointer to class. A pointer to class member has type $T::*$, where T is the class name. C++ has two operators that act to dereference a pointer to class member. The pointer to member operators are

.*   *and*   å‹*

Think of *obj .* ptr_mem* as first dereferencing the pointer to obtain a member variable and then accessing the member for the designated *obj*.

```
class object { public: int a, b, c; } x, y, *q = &y;
int object::*p = &object::b;

x.*p            //gets x.b
y ->*p          //gets y.b
```

C.10   FUNCTIONS

In C, functions are strictly call-by-value. In C++, changes in how functions work include use of function prototypes, overloading, call-by-reference, default arguments, and the effects of the keywords `inline`, `friend`, and `virtual`.

PROTOTYPES

In C++, the prototype form is

type name (argument-declaration-list);

Examples are:

```
double sqrt(double x);
void   pr_int(char*, int);       //definition contains names
void   print(const char* s);     //contents s points at are const
int    printf(char* format, ...); //variable number of args.
```

With the above `sqrt` prototype definition, invoking `sqrt` guarantees that, if feasible, an argument is converted to type `double`. Prototypes are also found in ANSI C and greatly improve type checking.

OVERLOADING

The term *overloading* refers to use of the same name for multiple meanings of an operator or a function. The meaning selected depends on the types of the arguments used by the operator or function.

Consider a function that averages the values in an array of `double` versus one that averages the values in an array of `int`. Both are conveniently named `avg_arr`.

```
double    avg_arr(const double a[], int size);
double    avg_arr(const int a[], int size);

double avg_arr(const int a[], int size)
{
   int   sum = 0;

   for (int i = 0; i < size; ++i)
      sum += a[i];                   //performs int arithmetic
   return ((double) sum / size);
}

double avg_arr(const double a[], int size)
{
   double   sum = 0.0;

   for (int i = 0; i < size; ++i)
      sum += a[i];                   //performs double arithmetic
   return (sum / size);
}
```

In early systems, the keyword **overload** was used to declare a nonmember function name as overloadable. This practice is allowed but obsolete.

The function argument type list is called its *signature*. The return type is not a part of the signature, but the order of the arguments is crucial.

```
int   sqr(int i);               //signature is int
double  sqr(int i);             //signature is int
void print(int i = 0);          //signature is int
void print(int i, double x);    //signature is int, double
void print(double y, int i);    //signature is double, int
```

In this example sqr() is illegally redeclared, but print() has three distinct signatures. When the print() function is invoked, the compiler matches the actual arguments to the different signatures and picks the best match. In general, there are three possibilities: a best match, an ambiguous match, and no match. Without a best match, the compiler issues an appropriate syntax error.

```
print('A');              //converts and matches int
print(str[]);            //no match wrong type
print(15, 9);            //ambiguous
print(15, 9.0);          //matches int, double
print();                 //match  int by default
```

There are two parts to the signature-matching algorithm. The first part determines a best match for each argument. The second part sees if there is one function that is a uniquely best match in each argument. This uniquely best match is defined as being a best match on at least one argument, and a "tied-for-best" match on all other arguments.

For a given argument, a best match is always an exact match. An exact match also includes *trivial conversions*. For type T these are

From	*To*
//equally good	
T	T&
T&	T
T	const T
T	volatile T
T[]	T*
T (*args*)	(*T) (*args*)
//not as good	
T*	const T*
T*	volatile T*
T&	const T&
T&	volatile T&

The first six trivial conversions cannot be used to disambiguate exact matches. The last four are considered worse than the first six. Thus

```
void print(int i);
void print(const int& i);
```

can be unambiguously overloaded.

Whichever overloaded function is to be invoked, the invocation argument list must be matched to the declaration parameter list. The matching algorithm is as follows:

Overloaded Function Selection Algorithm

1   Use an exact match if found.
2   Try standard type promotions.
3   Try standard type conversions.
4   Try user-defined conversions.
5   Use a match to ellipsis if found.

The complete rule on promotions is a two-part rule that distinguishes promotions from other standard conversions. A promotion is going from a narrower type to a wider type. Thus going from char to int is a promotion. Promotions are better than other standard conversions. Among promotions, conversion from float to double and conversion from char, short, or enum to int are better than other promotions. Standard conversions also include pointer conversions.

An exact match is clearly best. Casts can be used to force such a match. The compiler will complain about ambiguous situations. Thus, it is poor practice to rely on subtle type distinctions and implicit conversions that obscure the overloaded function that is called. When in doubt use explicit conversions to provide an exact match.

CALL-BY-REFERENCE

Reference declarations allow C++ to have *call-by-reference* arguments. Let us use this mechanism to write a function greater that exchanges two values if the first is greater than the second.

```
int greater(int& a, int& b)
{
    if (a > b) {            //exchange
        int temp = a;
        a = b;
        b = temp;
        return (1);
    }
    else
        return (0);
}
```

Now, if i and j are two int variables, then

```
greater(i, j)
```

will use the reference to i and the reference to j to exchange, if necessary, their two values. In traditional C, this must be accomplished using pointers and indirection.

```
/* traditional C greater */
int greater(int* a, int* b)
{
    if (*a > *b) {        //exchange
        int temp = *a;
        *a = *b;
        *b = temp;
        return (1);
    }
    else
        return (0);
}
```

INLINE

The keyword inline suggests to the compiler that the function be converted to inline code. This keyword is used for the sake of efficiency, generally with short functions, and is implicit for member functions that are defined within their class. A compiler can ignore this directive for a variety of reasons, including the fact that the function is too long. In those cases the inline function is compiled as an ordinary function. An example is

```
inline float circum(float rad) { return (pi * 2 * rad); }
```

Inline functions are of internal linkage.

DEFAULT ARGUMENTS

A formal parameter can be given a default argument. However, this can be done only with contiguous formal parameters that are rightmost in the parameter list. A default value is usually an appropriate constant that occurs frequently when the function is called. The following function illustrates this point:

```
int mult(int n, int k = 2)        //k = 2 is default
{
    if (k == 2)
        return (n * n);
    else
        return (mult(n, k - 1) * n);
}
```

We assume that most of the time the function is used to return the value of n squared.

FRIEND FUNCTIONS

The keyword `friend` is a function specifier. It allows a nonmember function access to the hidden members of the class of which it is a friend. Its use is a method of escaping the strict strong typing and data hiding restrictions of C++. A `friend` function must be declared inside the class declaration of which it is a friend. It is prefaced by the keyword `friend` and can appear anywhere in the class. Member functions of one class can be `friend` functions of another class. In this case the member function is declared in the friend's class using the scope resolution operator to qualify its function name. If all member functions of one class are friend functions of a second class, this can be specified by writing `friend class` *class name*.

The following declarations are typical:

```
class tweedledee {
    . . .
    friend void alice();        //friend function
    int          cheshire();    //member function
    . . .
};

class tweedledum {
    . . .
    friend int tweedledee::cheshire();
    . . .
};

class tweedledumber {
    . . .
    friend class tweedledee;    //all member functions
                                //of tweedledee have access
    . . .
};
```

OPERATOR OVERLOADING

A special case of function overloading is operator overloading. The keyword `operator` is used to overload the built-in C operators. Just as a function name, such as `print`, can be given a variety of meanings that depend on its arguments, so can an operator, such as +, be given additional meanings. This allows infix expressions of both user types and built-in types to be written. The precedence and associativity remain fixed.

Operator overloading typically uses either member functions or friend functions because they both have privileged access. Overloading a unary operator using a member function has an empty argument list because the single operator argument is the implicit argument. For binary operators, member function operator overloading has, as the first argument, the implicitly passed class variable and, as a second argument, the lone argument list parameter. Friend functions or ordinary functions have both arguments specified in the parameter list.

We will demonstrate how to overload a unary operator using **++** as an example. We define the class `clock` that can store time as days, hours, minutes, and seconds.

```
class clock {
    unsigned long int  tot_secs, secs, mins, hours, days;
public:
private:
    clock(unsigned long int i); //constructor and conversion
    void print();                //formatted printout
    void tick();                 //add one second
    clock operator ++() { this -> tick(); return(*this); }
};
```

This class overloads the autoincrement operator. It is a member function and can be invoked on its implicit single argument. The member function `tick` adds one second to the implicit argument of the overloaded **++** operator.

The ternary conditional operator **?:**, the scope resolution operator **::**, and the two member operators **.** and **.*** cannot be overloaded.

C++ Release 2.1 distinguishes between prefix and postfix autoincrement and autodecrement operators. To stay compatible, use only the prefix version of this operator. In the future, postfix can be distinguished by defining the postfix overloaded function as having a single, unused integer argument, as in

```
class T {
public:
    void operator++(int);   //postfix invoked as t.operator++(0);
    void operator--(int);
};
```

There will be no implied semantical relationship between the postfix and prefix forms.

VIRTUAL FUNCTIONS

The keyword `virtual` is a function specifier that provides a mechanism for dynamically selecting at run-time the appropriate member function from among base and derived class functions. It may be used only to modify member function declarations. A virtual function must be executable code. When invoked its semantics are the same as other functions. In a derived class its name can be overloaded, and the function prototype of the derived function must have matching type. The selection of which function to invoke from among a group of overloaded virtual functions is dynamic. The typical case is a base class with a virtual function and derived classes that have their versions of this function. A pointer to a base class type can point at either a base class object or a derived class object. The member function to be invoked is selected at run-time. It corresponds to the object's type, not the pointer's type. In the absence of a derived type member, the base class virtual function is used by default.

Consider the following example:

```
//virtual function selection
#include <iostream.h>

class B {
public:
    int  i;
    virtual void print_i() { cout << i << " inside B\n"; }
};

class D : public B {
public:
    void print_i() { cout << i << " inside D\n"; }
};

main()
{
    B    b;
    B*   pb = &b;
    D    f;

    f.i = 1 + (b.i = 1);
    pb -> print_i();
    pb = &f;
    pb -> print_i();
}
```

The output from this program is

```
1 inside B
2 inside D
```

In each case a different version of `print_i` is executed. Selection depends dynamically on the object being pointed at.

TYPE-SAFE LINKAGE

Linkage rules for non-C++ functions can be specified using a *linkage specification*. Some examples are

```
extern "C" atoi(const char* nptr);   //C linkage
```

```
extern "C" {
#include <stdio.h>
}                        //C linkage for these prototypes
```

This specification is at file scope with "C" and "C++" always supported. It is system-dependent, if type-safe linkage for other languages is provided.

C.11   TEMPLATES

The keyword `template` is used to implement parameterized types. Rather than repeatedly recoding for each explicit type, its own class, the template feature allows a general formulation that can be explicitly instantiated for each type.

```
template <class T>       //parameterize T
class stack {
private:
    T*    item;
    int   top;
    int   size;
public:
    stack();
    stack(int s);
    T& pop();
    void push(T);
    . . .
};
typedef stack<string> str_stack;
str_stack s(100);    //an explicit variable used as a string stack
```

A template declaration has the form

```
template
  < template arguments > declaration
```

and a template argument can be

```
class
  identifier
argument declaration
```

The class *identifier* arguments are instantiated with a type. Other argument declarations are instantiated with constant expressions.

```
template<class T, int n>
class array_n {
private:
    T items[n];  //n will be explicitly instantiated
};

array_n<complex, 1000> w;  //w is an array of complex
```

Member function syntax when external to the class definition is as follows:

```
template <class T>
T& stack<T>::pop()
{
    return(item[top--]);
};
```

The class name used by the scope resolution operator includes the template arguments, and the member function declaration requires the template declaration as a preface to the function declaration.

FUNCTION TEMPLATE

Ordinary functions can be parameterized using a restricted form of template syntax. Only class *identifier* instantiation is allowed. It must occur inside the function argument list.

```
//generic swap
template <class T>
void swap(T& x, T& y)
{
    T temp;
    temp = x;
    x = y;
    y = temp;
}

//illegal
template <class T>
T foo()
{
    T temp;
    . . .
}
```

A function template is used to construct an appropriate function for any invocation that matches its arguments unambiguously.

```
swap(i, j);   //i, j int -  okay
swap(c1, c2); //c1, c2 complex -okay
swap(i, ch);  //i int, ch char - illegal
```

The overloading function selection algorithm is as follows:

1 Exact match on a nontemplate function.
2 Exact match using a function template.
3 Ordinary argument resolution on a nontemplate function.

Note well that this algorithm is not what is universally in use. AT&T C++ Release 3.0 relaxes the exact match condition on function templates, allowing both trivial conversions and base/derived pointer conversions.

In the previous example an ordinary function declaration whose prototype was

```
void swap(char, char);
```

would have been invoked on swap(i, ch).

FRIENDS

Template classes can contain friends. A friend function that does not use a template specification is universally a friend of all instantiations of the template class. A friend function that incorporates template arguments is specifically a friend of its instantiated class.

```
template <class T>
class matrix {
private:
    friend void foo_bar();   //universal
    friend vect<T> product(vect<T> v); //instantiated
    . . .
};
```

STATIC MEMBERS

Static members are not universal but are specific to each instantiation.

```
template <class T>
class foo {
public:
    static int count;
    . . .
};

foo<int> a;
foo<double> b;
```

The static variables `foo<int>::count` and `foo<double>::count` are distinct.

C.12 EXCEPTIONS

Exception handling is not yet incorporated in most available compilers. This description is based on the Andrew Koenig and Bjarne Stroustrup proposal that has been accepted by the C++ ANSI standards committee.

Classically an exception is an unexpected condition encountered by the program that it cannot cope with. An example is floating point divide-by-zero. Usually the system aborts the running program.

C++ code will be allowed to directly raise an exception in a try block by using the throw expression. The exception will be handled by invoking an appropriate *handler* selected from a list of handlers found in the handler's try block. A simple example of all this is

```
vect::vect(int n)
{  //fault tolerant constructor
    try {
        if (n < 1)
            throw (n);
        p = new int[n];
        if (p == 0)
            throw ("FREE STORE EXHAUSTED");
    }
    catch (int n) { . . .} //catches an incorrect size
    catch (const char* error) { . . .} //catches free store exhaustion
}
```

THROWING EXCEPTIONS

Syntactically *throw expressions* come in two forms:

```
throw
throw expression
```

The throw expression raises an exception in a try block. The innermost try block is used to select the catch statement that processes the exception. The throw expression with no argument rethrows the current exception. Typically it is used when second handler called from the first handler is needed to further process the exception.

The expression thrown is a static temporary object that persists until exception handling is exited. The expression is caught by a handler that may use this value.

```
void foo()
{
    int i;
    . . .
    throw i;
}

main()
{
    try {
        foo();
    }
    catch(int n) {   . . . }
}
```

The integer value thrown by throw i persists until the handler with integer signature catch(int n) exits. This value is available for use within the handler as its argument.

An example of rethrowing of an exception is as follows:

```
catch(int n)
{
    . . .
    throw;   //rethrown
}
```

Assuming the thrown expression was of integer type, the rethrown exception is the same persistent integer object that is handled by the nearest handler suitable for that type.

TRY BLOCKS

Syntactically a *try block* has the form

    try
    compound statement
    handler list

The try block is the context for deciding which handlers are invoked on a raised exception. The order in which handlers are defined is important, as they determine the order on which a handler for a raised exception of matching type will be tried.

```
try {
    . . .
    throw ("SOS");
    . . .
    io_condition eof(argv[i]);
    throw (eof);
    . . .
}
catch (const char*) {  . . .}
catch (io_condition& x) {  . . .}
```

A `throw` expression matches the `catch` argument, if it is

1 An exact match.
2 A public base class of a derived type, which is what is thrown.
3 A thrown object type that is a pointer type convertible to a pointer type that is the `catch` argument.

It is an error to list handlers in an order that prevents them from being called. An example would be

```
catch(void*)  //any char* would match
catch(char*)
catch(BaseTypeError&)  //would always be called for DerivedTypeError
catch(DerivedTypeError&)
```

HANDLERS

Syntactically a *handler* has the form

```
catch (
formal argument)
compound statement
```

The `catch` looks like a function declaration of one argument without a return type.

```
catch (const char* message)
{
    cerr << message << endl;
    exit(1);
}
```

An ellipsis signature that matches any argument is allowed. Also the formal argument can be an abstract declaration, meaning it can have type information without a variable name.

EXCEPTION SPECIFICATION

Syntactically an exception specification is part of a function declaration and has the form

function header) type list)

The type list is the list of types that a throw expression within the function can have. If the list is empty, the compiler may assume that no throw will be executed by the function, either directly or indirectly.

```
void foo() throw(int, over_flow);
void noex(int i) throw();
```

If an exception specification is left off, then the assumption is that an arbitrary exception can be thrown by such a function. It is good programming practice to indicate through specifications what exceptions are to be expected. Violations of these specifications are run-time errors.

terminate() AND *unexpected()*

The system-provided handler terminate() is called when no other handler has been provided to deal with an exception. By default the abort() function is called. Otherwise set_terminate() can be used to provide a handler.

The system-provided handler unexpected() is called when a function throws an exception that was not in its exception specification list. By default the abort() function is called. Otherwise set_unexpected() can be used to provide a handler.

C.13   CAUTION AND COMPATIBILITY

C++ is not completely upwardly compatible with C. In most cases of ordinary use, it is a superset of C. Also C++ is not a completely stable language design. It is at the beginning of the ANSI standards process, and several novel features are being experimented with, most notably exception handling and parameterized types. The following sections mention features of the language that are problematic.

NESTED CLASS DECLARATIONS

The original scoping of nested classes was based on C rules. In effect, nesting was cosmetic, with the inner class globally visible. In C++ the inner class is local to the outer class enclosing it. Accessing such an inner class could require multiple use of the scope resolution operator.

```
int outer::inner::foo(double w) //foo is nested
   . . .
```

It will also be possible to have classes nested inside functions. To avoid incompatibilities among C++ systems and between C++ and ANSI C, it may be best to avoid these forms of nesting.

TYPE COMPATIBILITIES

In general, C++ is more strongly typed than ANSI C. Some differences include

1 Enumerations are distinct types, with enumerators not being explicitly `int`. This means that enumerations must be cast when making assignments from integer types or other enumerations to each other. They are promotable to integer.

2 Any pointer type can be converted to a generic pointer of type `void*`. However, unlike ANSI C, a generic pointer is not assignment-compatible with an arbitrary pointer type. This means that C++ requires that generic pointers be cast to an explicit type for assignment to a nongeneric pointer variable.

3 A character constant in C++ is `char`, but in ANSI C it is an `int`.

MISCELLANEOUS

The old C function syntax in which the argument list is left blank is replaced in ANSI C by the explicit argument `void`. The signature `foo()` in C is considered equivalent to the use of ellipsis and in C++ is considered equivalent to the empty argument list.

In early C++ systems the `this` pointer could be modified. It could be used to allocate memory for class objects. Although this use is obsolete, a compiler can continue to allow it.

C++ allows declarations to be intermixed with executable statements. ANSI C allows declarations to be only at the heads of blocks or in file scope. However, in C++ `goto`, iteration, and selection statements are not allowed to bypass initialization of variables. This rule differs from ANSI C.

In C++ a global data object must have exactly one definition. Other declarations must use the keyword `extern`. ANSI C allows multiple declarations without the keyword `extern`.

Currently overriding virtual functions require the same return type. It is expected that this restriction will be relaxed where a derived class replaces the base class as the return type.

```
class Base {
public:
   virtual Base compute(int n);
};

class Derived : public Base {
public:
   virtual Derived compute(int n); //override Base::compute
};
```

Currently garbage collection is not directly supported by the language. Various proposals exist to provide or support garbage collectible classes.

Mechanisms that dynamically determine object type may enter the language.

UNIMPLEMENTED FEATURES

Exception handling using the keywords `catch`, `throw`, and `try` may not yet be implemented.

C.14   STYLE EXAMPLES AND PRAGMATICS

Our style follows the original Kernighan and Ritchie C style of indentation and brace matching.

```
// Code exhibiting style characteristics
#include <iostream.h>
#define MAX   16000

int sum(int n)
{
   int i, total = 0;

   for (i = 0; i < n; ++i) {
      total += i;
      if (total > MAX) {
         cout << "too large" << endl;
         exit(1);
      }
   }
   return (total);
}
```

1   One statement to a line.

2   A blank line after initial declarations.

3   A compound statement brace comes on the same line as its controlling expression. Its matching terminating brace is lined up under the initial letter of the keyword starting the statement.

4   A pure compound statement, such as a function definition, starts on its own line.

5   Everything after the opening (left) brace is indented a standard number of spaces; for example, three spaces is used in this text. The matching closing (right) brace causes subsequent statements to be lined up under it.

6   Return expressions are parenthesized.

7   With the exception of semicolon, a space is added after each token for readability.

8   Preprocessor identifiers are capitalized. Ordinary identifiers are lowercase.

9   Preprocessor commands and file level declarations and statements start in column 1.

Frequently found variations from these practices include

1 Brace alignment is Algol-style with the initial brace always on its own line.

2 Return expressions are not parenthesized.

3 Very short statements that are conceptual related can be on the same line.

```
//Algol style matching braces
int order(int& y, int& z)
{
   int temp;

   if (z < y)
   {
      temp = z; z = y; y = temp;
   }
   return z;
}
```

CLASS DEFINITION STYLE

C++ class style derives from Stroustrup's writing and defaults that were historically needed.

```
//Traditional C++ class style
class vect {
private:
    int *p;                          //base pointer
    int size;                        //number of elements
public:
    //constructors and destructor
    vect();                          //create a size 10 array
    vect(int l);                     //create a size l array
    vect(vect& v);                   //initialization by vect
    vect(int a[], int l);            //initialization by array
    ~vect() { delete [] p; }
    int  ub() { return (size - 1); } //upper bound
    int& operator[](int i);          //obtain range checked element
    vect& operator=(vect& v);
    vect operator+(vect& v);
};
```

Style rules include

1 Access privileges are in order—private, protected, and public. This conforms to early practice when, by default, private members came first in a class declaration.

2 Indentation is as follows: class, access keywords, and closing brace all line up and are placed on separate lines. Member declarations are indented and line up.

3 One-line member declarations that are inline can be defined inside the class.

4 Constructors come first, then a destructor, then other member functions.

5 Data members are to be private or protected. They are to be accessed and modified using member functions.

Alternate style rules include

1 Access privileges are in order—`public`, `protected`, and `private`. This conforms to the most visible first rule. Clients of a class need not know about nonpublic members; therefore, it is logical to place public members first.

2 Member functions are declared but not defined.

```
//C++ Need to know access - widest first
class string {
public:
   string();                       //default
   string(int n);
   string(const char* p);          //useful conversion
   string(const string& str);      //copy
   ~string();
   string& operator=(string&str);  //overload =
   operator char*();               //inverse conversion
   friend class string_iterator;
   friend ostream& operator<<(ostream& out, const string& str);
protected:
   void assign(const string& str);
   void print() const;
private:
   str_obj* st;                    //implementation
};

//A friend function of class string.
//This is a typical method for overloading << "put to".
ostream& operator<<(ostream& out, const string& str)
{
   out << str.st -> s;
   return (out);
}
```

D

INPUT/OUTPUT

This appendix describes input/output practice in C++ using *iostream.h* and its associated libraries. The software for C++ includes a standard library that contains functions commonly used by the C++ community. The standard input/output library for C, described by the header *stdio.h*, is still available in C++. However, C++ introduces *iostream.h*, which implements its own collection of input/output functions. The header *stream.h* was used on systems before Release 2.0 and is still available under many C++ systems.

The stream I/O is described as a set of classes in *iostream.h*. These classes overload the put-to and get-from operators << and >>. Streams can be associated with files, and examples of file processing using streams are given and discussed in this chapter. Much of file processing requires character handling macros that are found in *ctype.h*. These also are discussed here.

In OOP, objects should know how to print themselves, and we frequently have made `print` a member function of a class. Notationally it is also useful to overload << for user-defined ADTs. In this appendix we develop output functions for `card` and `deck` that illustrate these techniques.

D.1   THE OUTPUT CLASS *ostream*

Output is returned to an object of type `ostream` as described in *iostream.h*. The operator `<<` is overloaded in this class to perform output conversions from standard types. The operator is left associative and returns a value of type `ostream&`. The standard output `ostream` corresponding to `stdout` is `cout`, and the standard output `ostream` corresponding to `stderr` is `cerr`.

The effect of executing a simple output statement such as

```
cout << "x = " << x << "\n";
```

is to print to the screen first a string of four characters, then an appropriate representation for the output of x, and then a newline. The representation depends on which overloaded version of `<<` is invoked.

The class `ostream` contains public members such as

```
ostream& operator<<(int i);
ostream& operator<<(long i);
ostream& operator<<(double x);
ostream& operator<<(char c);
ostream& operator<<(const char* s);
ostream& put(char c);
ostream& write(const char* p, int n);
ostream& flush();
```

The member function `put` outputs the character representation of c. The member function `write` outputs the string of length n pointed at by p. The member function `flush` forces the stream to be written. Since these are member functions, they can be used as follows:

```
int c = 'A';
cout.put(c);        //output A
cout.put(66);       //output B   ascii value 66
cout.put(c + 2);    //output C
char* str = "ABCDEFGHI";
cout.write(str + 2, 3);  //output CDE
cout.flush();       //write contents of buffered stream
```

D.2   FORMATTED OUTPUT AND *iomanip.h*

As given, the *put-to* operator << produces by default the minimum number of characters needed to represent the output. Consequently output can be confusing, as seen in the following example:

```
int  i = 8, j = 9;
cout << i << j ;                   //confused: prints 89
cout << i << "   " << j;           //better: prints 8   9
cout << "i= " << i << " j= " << j; //best:prints i= 8 j= 9
```

Two schemes that we have used to properly space output are either to have strings separating output values or to use \n and \t to create newlines and tabbing, respectively. We can also use *manipulators* in the stream output to control output formatting.

A manipulator is a value or function that has a special effect on the stream it operates on. A simple example of a manipulator is endl defined in *iostream.h*. Its effect is to output a newline and then flush the ostream.

```
x = 1;
cout << "x = " << x << endl;
```

This immediately prints the line

```
x = 1
```

Another manipulator flush flushes the ostream, as in

```
cout << "x = " << x << flush;
```

This has almost the same effect as the previous example but would not advance to a newline.

The manipulators dec, hex, and oct can be used to change integer bases. The default base is base ten.

```
//Using different bases in integer I/O.
#include <iostream.h>

main()
{
    int i = 10, j = 16, k = 24;
    cout << i << '\t' << j << '\t' << k << endl;
    cout << oct << i << '\t' << j << '\t' << k << endl;
    cout << hex << i << '\t' << j << '\t' << k << endl;
    cout << "Enter 3 integers, e.g. 11 11 12a" << endl;
    cin >> i >> hex >> j >> k;
    cout << dec << i << '\t' << j << '\t' << k << endl;
}
```

The resulting output is

```
10        16        24
12        20        30
a         10        18
Enter 3 integers, e.g. 11 11 12a
11        17        298
```

The final line of output is 11 followed by 17 because the second 11 in the input was interpreted as hexadecimal, which is 16 + 1.

The above manipulators are found in *iostream.h*. Other manipulators are found in *iomanip.h*. For example, setw(int width) is a manipulator that changes the default field width to the value of its argument. This value returns back to the default after a next argument. The following table briefly lists the standard manipulators, their function, and where they are defined:

Manipulator	*Function*	*File*
endl	output newline and flush	*iostream.h*
ends	output null in string	*iostream.h*
flush	flush the output	*iostream.h*
dec	use decimal	*iostream.h*
hex	use hexadecimal	*iostream.h*
oct	use octal	*iostream.h*
ws	skip white space on input	*iostream.h*
setw (*int*)	set field width	*iomanip.h*
setfill (*int*)	set fill character	*iomanip.h*
setbase (*int*)	set base format	*iomanip.h*
setprecision (*int*)	set floating point precision	*iomanip.h*
setiosflags (*long*)	set format bits	*iomanip.h*
resetiosflags (*long*)	reset format bits	*iomanip.h*

D.3   USER-DEFINED TYPES: OUTPUT

User-defined types have been printed typically by creating a member function print. Let us use the types card and deck of Section 5.6 as an example of a simple user-defined type. We write out a set of output routines for displaying cards.

```
//card output

#include  <iostream.h>

char pips_symbol[14] = { '?', 'A', '2', '3', '4', '5', '6',
                         '7', '8', '9', 'T', 'J', 'Q', 'K'};
char suit_symbol[4] = { 'c', 'd', 'h', 's'};

enum suit {clubs, diamonds, hearts, spades};

class pips {
private:
   int  p;
public:
   void assign(int n) { p = n % 13 + 1; }
   void print() { cout << pips_symbol[p]; }
};
```

```
class card {
private:
   int  cd;          //a cd is from 0 to 51
public:
   suit s;
   pips p;
   void assign(int n) { cd = n; s = suit(n / 13); p.assign(n); }
   void pr_card() { p.print(); cout << suit_symbol[s] << "  "; }
};

class deck {
private:
   card d[52];
public:
   void init_deck();
   void shuffle();
   void deal(int, int, card*);
   void pr_deck();
};

void deck::pr_deck()
{
   for (int i = 0; i < 52; ++i) {
      if (i % 13 == 0)          //13 cards to a line
         cout << endl;
      d[i].pr_card();
   }
}
```

Each card is printed out in two characters. If d is a variable of type deck, then d.pr_deck() prints out the entire deck, 13 cards to a line.

In keeping with the spirit of OOP, it also would be nice to overload << to accomplish the same aims. The operator << has two arguments, an ostream& and the ADT, and it must produce an ostream&. Whenever overloading << or >>, you should use a reference to a stream and return a reference to a stream because you do not want to copy a stream object.

Let us write these functions for the types `card` and `deck`.

```
ostream& operator<<(ostream& out, pips x)
{
    return (out << pips_symbol[x.p]);
}

ostream& operator<<(ostream& out, card cd)
{
    return (out << cd.p << suit_symbol[cd.s] << "  " );
}

ostream& operator<<(ostream& out, deck x)
{
    for (int i = 0; i < 52; ++i) {
        if (i % 13 == 0)          //13 cards to a line
            out << endl;
        out << x.d[i];
    }
    return (out);
}
```

The functions that operate on `pips` and `deck` need to be friends of the corresponding class because they access private members.

D.4   THE INPUT CLASS *istream*

An operator `>>` is overloaded in `istream` to perform input conversions to standard types. The standard input `istream` corresponding to `stdin` is `cin`.

The effect of executing a simple input statement such as

```
cin >> x >> i;
```

is to read from standard input, normally the keyboard, a value for `x` and then a value for `i`. White space is ignored.

The class `istream` contains public members such as

```
istream& operator>>(int& i);
istream& operator>>(long& i);
istream& operator>>(double& x);
istream& operator>>(char& c);
istream& operator>>(char* s);
istream& get(char& c);
istream& get(char* s, int n, char c = '\n');
istream& getline(char* s, int n, char c = '\n');
istream& read(char* s, int n);
```

The member function `get(char& c)` inputs the character representation to c, white-space characters included. The member function `get(char* s, int n, int c = '\n')` inputs at most n characters into the string pointed at by s, up to the specified delimiter character c or an end-of-file. A terminating `'\0'` is placed in the output string. The optionally specified default character acts as a terminator but is not placed in the output string. If not specified, the input is read up to the next newline. The member function `getline()` works like `get(char*, int, char = '\n')` except it discards rather than keeps the delimiter character in the designated `istream`. The member function `read(char* s, int n)` inputs at most n characters into the string pointed at by s. It sets the failbit if an end-of-file is encountered before n characters are read.

```
cin.get(c);            //one character
cin.get(s, 40);        //length 40 or terminated by '\n'
cin.get(s, 10, '*');   //length 10 or terminated by *
cin.getline(s, 40);    //same as get but '\n' is discarded
```

Other useful member functions include

```
int gcount();          //number of recently extracted characters
istream& ignore(int n = 1, int delimeter = EOF); //skips
int peek();            //get next character without extraction
istream& putback(char c);   //puts back character
```

When overloading the operator `>>` to produce input to a user-defined type, the typical form of such a function prototype is

```
istream& operator>>(istream& p, user-defined type& x)
```

If the function needs access to private members of x, it must be made a friend of its class. A key point is to make x a reference parameter so its value can be modified.

D.5   FILES USING *fstream.h*

C systems have stdin, stdout, and stderr as standard files. In addition, systems may define other standard files, such as stdprn and stdaux. Abstractly a file may be thought of as a stream of characters that are processed sequentially.

Written in C	Name	Remark
stdin	standard input file	connected to the keyboard
stdout	standard output file	connected to the screen
stderr	standard error file	connected to the screen
stdprn	standard printer file	connected to the printer
stdaux	standard auxiliary file	connected to an auxiliary port

The C++ stream input/output ties the first three of these standard files to cin, cout, and cerr, respectively. Typically C++ ties cprn and caux to their corresponding standard files stdprn and stdaux. There is also clog, which is a buffered version of cerr. Other files can be opened or created by the programmer. We show how to do this in the context of writing a program to double-space an existing file into an existing or new file. The file names will be specified on the command line and passed in to argv.

File I/O is handled by including *fstream.h*. This contains classes ofstream and ifstream for output file stream and input file stream creation and manipulation. To properly open and manage an ifstream or ofstream related to a system file, you first declare it with an appropriate constructor. First we study the ifstream behavior

```
ifstream();
ifstream(const char*, int = ios::in, int prot = filebuf::openprot);
```

The constructor of no arguments creates a variable that later will be associated with an input file. The constructor of three arguments takes as its first argument the named file. The second argument specifies the file mode. The third argument is for file protection.

The file mode arguments are defined as enumerators in class `ios` as follows:

```
ios::in          //input mode
ios::app         //append mode
ios::out         //output mode
ios::ate         //open and seek to end of file
ios::nocreate    //open but do not create mode
ios::trunc       //discard contents and open
ios::noreplace   //if file exists open fails
```

Thus the default for an `ifstream` is input mode and for an `ofstream` is output mode. If file opening fails, the stream is put into a bad state. It can be tested with `operator!`.

Let us use this scheme to write a simple file handling program.

```
//dbl_sp: a program to double space a file
//Usage: executable  f1 f2
//f1 must be present and readable
//f2 must be writable if it exists

#include <fstream.h>      //includes iostream.h
#include <stdlib.h>

void double_space(ifstream& f, ofstream& t)
{
   char  c;

   while (f.get(c)) {
      t.put(c);
      if (c == '\n')
         t.put(c);
   }
}

main(int argc, char** argv)
{
   if (argc != 3) {
      cout << "\nUsage: " << argv[0]
           << " infile  outfile\n";
      exit(1);
   }

   ifstream  f_in(argv[1]);
   ofstream  f_out(argv[2]);

   if (!f_in) {
      cerr << "cannot open " << argv[1];
      exit(1);
   }
   if (!f_out) {
      cerr << "cannot open " << argv[2];
      exit(1);
   }
   double_space(f_in, f_out);
}
```

DISSECTION OF THE *dbl_sp* PROGRAM

■
```
void double_space(ifstream& f, ofstream& t)
{
   char  c;

   while (f.get(c)) {
      t.put(c);
      if (c == '\n')
         t.put(c);
   }
}
```

The get member function gets a character from an ifstream. The put member function puts a character to an ofstream. These functions do not ignore white-space characters. The newline character is output twice, creating the desired double spacing in the output file.

■
```
ifstream  f_in(argv[1]);
ofstream  f_out(argv[2]);
```

The variable f_in is used for input, and the variable f_out is used for output. They are used to create corresponding ifstream and ofstream variables. The corresponding constructors are invoked on the names found in argv[] passed through the command line. If opening of the input file succeeds, the ifstream f_in is constructed connected to the file named in argv[1]. If opening of the output file succeeds, the ofstream f_out is constructed connected to the file named in argv[2].

■
```
if (!f_in) {
   cerr << "cannot open " << argv[1];
   exit(1);
}
if (!f_out) {
   cerr << "cannot open " << argv[2];
   exit(1);
}
```

If the constructors for either `f_in` or `f_out` fail, they return a bad state tested by `operator!`, and then an error exit is executed. At this point `f_in` can be used analogously to `cin`, and `f_out` can be used analogously to `cout`.

■ `double_space(f_in, f_out);`

The actual double spacing from the input file to the output file occurs here.

Other important member functions that are found in *fstream.h* include

```
//opens ifstream file
void open(const char*, int = ios::in, int prot = filebuf::
    openprot);

//opens ofstream file
void open(const char*, int = ios::out, int prot = filebuf::
    openprot);

void close();
```

These functions can be used to open and close appropriate files. Additional member functions in other I/O classes allow for a full range of file manipulation.

D.6   THE FUNCTIONS AND MACROS IN *ctype.h*

The system provides a standard header file *ctype.h*, which contains a set of functions used to test characters and a set of functions used to convert characters. They may be implemented as macros or inline functions. This is mentioned here because of its usefulness in C++ input/output. Those functions that test only a character return an `int` value that is nonzero (true) or zero (false). The argument is type `int`.

Function	Nonzero (true) is returned if
isalpha(c)	c is a letter
isupper(c)	c is an uppercase letter
islower(c)	c is a lowercase letter
isdigit(c)	c is a digit
isxdigit(c)	c is a hexadecimal digit
isspace(c)	c is a white-space character
isalnum(c)	c is a letter or digit
ispunct(c)	c is a punctuation character
isgraph(c)	c is a printing character, except space
isprint(c)	c is a printable character
iscntrl(c)	c is a control character
isascii(c)	c is an ASCII code

Other functions provide for the appropriate conversion of a character value. Note carefully that these functions do not change the value of c stored in memory.

Function	Effect
toupper(c)	changes c from lowercase to uppercase
tolower(c)	changes c from uppercase to lowercase
toascii(c)	changes c to ASCII code

The ASCII code functions are usual on ASCII systems.

D.7 USING STREAM STATES

Each stream has an associated state that can be tested. The states are as follows:

```
enum io_state {goodbit, eofbit, failbit, badbit, hardfail};
```

The values for a particular stream can be tested using the following public member functions:

```
int good();   //non-zero if not eof or other error bit set
int eof();    //non-zero if istream eofbit set
int fail();   //non-zero if failbit, badbit, or hardfail set
int bad();    //non-zero if badbit, or hardfail set
int rdstate();  //returns error state
void clear(int i = 0);   //resets error state
int operator!();   //return true if failbit or badbit set
operator void*     //return false if failbit or badbit set
```

Testing for a stream being in a non-good state can protect a program from hanging up. A stream state of *good* means the previous input/output operation worked and the next operation should succeed. A stream state of *eof* means the previous input operation returned an end-of-file condition. A stream state of *fail* means the previous input/output operation failed, but the stream is usable once the error bit is cleared. A stream state of *bad* means the previous input/output operation is invalid, but the stream may be usable once the error condition is corrected. And a stream state of *hardfail* means the previous input/output operation failed irreparably. It is also possible to directly test a stream. It is nonzero if it is either in a *good* or *eof* state.

```
if (cout << x )  //output succeeded
   . . .
else
   . . .            //output failed
```

The following program counts the number of words coming from the standard input. Normally this would be redirected to use an existing file. It illustrates ideas discussed in this and the previous two sections.

```
//A word count program
//Usage: executable < file
#include    <iostream.h>
#include    <ctype.h>

main()
{
   int    word_cnt = 0;
   int    found_next_word();

   while (found_next_word())
      ++word_cnt;
   cout << "word count is " << word_cnt << endl;
}

int found_next_word()
{
   char    c;
   int     word_sz = 0;

   cin >> c;
   while ( !cin.eof() && !isspace(c)) {
      ++word_sz;
      cin.get(c);
   }
   return (word_sz);
}
```

DISSECTION OF THE *word_cnt* PROGRAM

■ while (found_next_word())
  ++word_cnt;

The function found_next_word attempts to read the next word. It returns a positive word length for each word it finds. If it reads only the
end-of-file character, it returns a word length of zero.

```
■ int found_next_word()
  {
      char   c;
      int    word_sz = 0;

      cin >> c;
      while ( !cin.eof() && !isspace(c)) {
          ++word_sz;
          cin.get(c);
      }
      return (word_sz);
  }
```

A non-white-space character is gotten from the input stream and assigned to c. The while loop tests that adjacent characters are not white space. The loop terminates when either an end-of-file character or a white-space character is found. The word size is returned as zero when the only non-white-space character found is the end-of-file. One last point: The loop cannot be rewritten as

```
while ( !cin.eof() && !isspace(c)) {
    ++word_sz;
    cin >> c;
}
```

because this would skip white space.

D.8   MIXING I/O LIBRARIES

We have used *iostream.h* throughout this text. It is perfectly reasonable to want to continue using *stdio.h*—it is the standard in the C community and is well understood. Its disadvantage is that it is not type-safe. Functions like *printf* use unchecked variable-length argument lists. Stream I/O requires assignment-compatible types as arguments to its functions and overloaded operators. It is also possible that you would want to mix both forms of I/O.

Such mixing causes synchronization problems because the two libraries use different buffering strategies. This can be avoided by calling

```
ios::sync_with_stdio();
```

This is illustrated in the following:

```
//Mix C and C++ I/O.

#include <stdio.h>
#include <iostream.h>

unsigned long fact(int n)
{
    unsigned long f = 1;
    for (int i = 2; i <= n; ++i)
        f *= i;
    return (f);
}

main()
{
    int n;

    ios::sync_with_stdio();
    do {
        cout << "\nEnter n positive or 0 to halt: ";
        scanf("%d", &n);
        printf("\n fact(%d) = %ld", n, fact(n));
    } while (n > 0);
    cout << "\nend of session" << endl;
}
```

Note that, for integer values greater than 12, the results will overflow.

INDEX